DECODING LATIN MASTERCLASS

Read Latin in 47 Days

ALEXANDER WESTENBERG

Decoding Latin Masterclass: Read Latin in 47 Days by Alexander Westenberg. Published by Decoding Latin Sydney, New South Wales, Australia

www.decodinglatin.org

© 2021 Alexander Westenberg

All rights reserved. No portion of this book may be reproduced in any form without permission from the publisher, except as permitted by Australian copyright law. For permissions contact:

alexander@decodinglatin.org

GET MY FREE LATIN TIPS

I honestly think you've made a great investment in learning Latin by buying this book, and I want to give you the chance to build on this momentum. If you want to learn more about the Decoding Latin method, and stay up to date on everything I release, you can [sign up for my email list]().

On the mailing list I share my favourite tips on learning Latin, resource recommendations, and more, all for free! I'll be publishing more books in this series in the future, so my list is the best place to stay up to date on those! Here's the link to sign up and get the masterclass and a weekly Latin fable for free:

[decodinglatin.org]()

I really hope you enjoy this book, and if you do – or if you have any questions or comments at all – please shoot me an email at [alexander@decodinglatin.org](). I'd love ato hear from you!

Contents

Introduction 7
How to use this book 10
The Decoding Latin Way 11
Part I: Decoding Latin in 7 Lessons 17
    Lesson One 18
    Lesson Two 24
    Lesson Three 35
    Lesson Four 44
    Lesson Five 54
    Lesson Six 65
    Lesson Seven 71
Part II: Aesop's Fables 75
    Decoding Latin– Day 1 76
    Decoding Latin – Day 2 87
    Decoding Latin – Day 3 94
    Decoding Latin – Day 4 101
    Decoding Latin – Day 5 106
    Decoding Latin – Day 6 112
    Decoding Latin – Day 7 118
    Decoding Latin – Day 8 124
    Decoding Latin – Day 9 131
    Decoding Latin – Day 10 139
    Decoding Latin – Day 11 144
    Decoding Latin – Day 12 152

Decoding Latin – Day 13...163
Decoding Latin – Day 14...172
Decoding Latin – Day 15...181
Decoding Latin – Day 16...190
Decoding Latin – Day 17...199
Decoding Latin – Day 18...213
Decoding Latin – Day 19...223
Decoding Latin – Day 20...230
Decoding Latin – Day 21...237
Decoding Latin – Day 22...248
Decoding Latin – Day 23...259
Decoding Latin – Day 24...270
Decoding Latin – Day 25...281
Decoding Latin – Day 26...298
Decoding Latin – Day 27...305
Decoding Latin – Day 28...315
Decoding Latin – Day 29...327
Decoding Latin – Day 30...340
Decoding Latin – Day 31...352
Decoding Latin – Day 32...363
Decoding Latin – Day 33...375
Decoding Latin – Day 34...387
Decoding Latin – Day 35...397
Decoding Latin – Day 36...406
Decoding Latin – Day 37...418

Decoding Latin – Day 38 434
Decoding Latin – Day 39 443
Decoding Latin – Day 40 457
Congratulations! 470

Introduction

Congratulations on picking up this book! I'm so excited for you to be here, I really believe this will make a huge difference to your reading and relationship with the language, and hopefully give you the confidence you need to keep going.

Over the next 47 days you'll make huge leaps and bounds in your Latin fluency. Excited? I am!

I know you're probably itching to get started (like me), but before we do I want to talk a bit about how this course will work.

The course is divided into 2 parts.

Part 1 consists of 7 lessons which 'decode' the structure of the Latin language, helping you understand the way Latin works and moves.

These lessons are NOT for memorisation or repetition, but instead are designed to be gone through in an easy and relaxed way to help give your mind the foundational paradigm for approaching the language.

This will make reading the language much more efficient.

There are 2 rules for part one:

Rule 1: DON'T MEMORISE ANYTHING.

That's right, I shouted it – you needed to hear it.

Your brain will learn better if you just let go, and this is only designed to give you a framework, not for memorising.

Rule 2: cover up all words in red and try to come up with the answer yourself, before you look.

Again, don't worry if you get it wrong, the purpose is just to get your brain working actively.

Part 2 consists of 142 Latin fables translated from the Greek fables of Aesop.

Now, the fables are laid out in my special 'decoded' format. This involves the untranslated text in one column, and a special kind of translation with both the Latin and English in the other column.

Your job is simply to read a certain number of fables each day. That's it.

You read the left-hand column and then immediately read the same block of text in the right-hand column.

As you become accustomed to this, the number of fables you read each day changes:

The first 10 days you'll read 2 fables each day
On days 11-20, 3 fables
On days 21-30, 4 fables
On days 31-38, 5 fables

On days 39 & 40, 6 fables

This book is very light on me talking, since I prefer the Latin to do the bulk, but I just wanted to give you a quick overview of what to expect!

One last thing that **you MUST do before beginning, is read the next chapter called 'using this book' and the chapter on 'the Decoding Latin Way'.**

- Alexander

How to use this book

The most natural way for many people would be to go through part 1 first, and then consolidate their learning with the readings from part 2.

This is certainly an effective method, but I want to encourage you to be flexible.

Another way you could do it is in the reverse; part 2 first to give you a 'feel' for the language, and then part 1 to explain what you've already grasped intuitively.

Yet another possibility is alternating, doing one lesson from part 1, then a few days of reading, then another lesson, and so on (again, this can be done in a different order, reading first then a lesson).

Or you could do half the readings, then the lessons of part 1, then the other half of the readings.

The point is, it's up to you, be flexible.

But remember this: if you're feeling bored, stop and switch it up.

You'll learn better, so don't be rigid about following a set pattern or curriculum.

The Decoding Latin Way

The Decoding Latin approach to learning and teaching Latin is based on a theory known today as Comprehensible Input.

Basically this is the theory that the real key to learning a language is large amounts of exposure to the language, in a context that you can understand.

Now, I've used this method to learn languages on my own, AND to teach my students to read Latin, and let me tell you, it's very effective.

For many this might seem hard to swallow, because we're all so used to associating learning with exercises, marks, right and wrong, and rules and memorising.

But this is NOT learning.

It's especially not the way to learn a language, which is a form of communication before anything else.

So the weird paradox is that the best way to learn Latin is to not try to remember anything.

I know it sounds crazy because we're so used to hearing about memory techniques, the importance of grammar, and all that kind of thing; but while that can be useful, I'm going to share three secrets with you today that are going to revolutionize the way you learn Latin.

But the fact is - and it's a fact I've proven over and over again with my students - the secret to learning Latin is Input.

It's *comprehensible*, *enjoyable*, input.

So, I'm going to share with you three secrets about input and how you can use it to learn more Latin, more effectively, and more quickly, than with any other method.

And I know what you're probably thinking: this just isn't possible, because you can't learn a language without learning the grammar rules and remembering the vocabulary.

But again, I'm going to show you a great way you can create your own immersion on demand and get amazing results.

So the first secret is that learning grammar is learning *about* Latin, not *actually learning Latin*.

The big idea here is that the best – and only – way to learn something is to practice it directly.

This is important because learning grammar doesn't give you practice in Latin, it only gives you practice in rules about Latin! Not so helpful…

The second secret is your brain remembers what it's used to.

The main thing to understand here is that your brain can't absorb something straight away, it needs to get comfortable in it, so you need to give it lots of Latin so it starts to recognise Latin as a friend.

This means it will start assimilating it internally and you'll start remembering and understanding the grammar and vocabulary effortlessly.

The third secret is you only learn within a context.

The main thing to understand here is that every memory you have is connected in some way to a context; that's why it's so easy to remember things from your favourite movie or TV show, but not things you tried to memorise for a test – there's no context.

This is key because Latin is a language, and like every language, it's all about communication ideas and experiences. So the best way to remember and learn it is in the context of stories, in the context of real communication.

Now, I know what you're thinking.

It's that you need to get the foundations right or else you'll pick up bad habits and never really understand properly.

Well the tricky thing is that hanging around the 'foundations' level is a never-ending task, because real language isn't graded in levels! That means that there is no 'beginner' Latin, and no way to 'get it right' before jumping in – you just have to get going and keep going!

And so I've created this Decoding Latin Masterclass Membership so you can get enough input easily to learn to read and understand Latin fluently, no matter what level you're at.

The material here is uniquely designed to allow you to read real Latin – and understand it – from day one.

And so what this is going to do is really motivate you because you're reading real Latin, and it's also going to take your comprehension forward in leaps and bounds as your brain immerses itself in the language!

And I, as your guide, who has spent the last twenty years searching for the best way to learn a language, will help you read it, and just enjoy the story – that's the secret!

SO...

To help you get the most out of this book, here are my 'rules' of Decoding Latin:

1. Don't try to memorise anything
2. Focus on the story, not the language – don't try to analyse!
3. Read one section from the left column and then the same from the right.

4. *Always read for speed and general gist, not for accuracy and perfection.*

Prioritise quantity over quality. I know this flies in the face of what we're used to, but in the case of language, quantity is everything.

Enjoy yourself! If that means you only read one fable at a time and read the other fable later in the day, do it!

Part I
Decoding Latin in 7 Lessons

Lesson One

"He's a soldier of Troy, and an active one"

The odds are, even if you've been learning Latin for a while, you probably won't be able to say that sentence out loud, *in Latin*, all that easily (or maybe not at all!).

But by the end of this lesson – in just a few minutes' time, actually – you'll be able to say this and more!

Pretty cool, right?

So let's get started!

The word for 'is' in Latin, is:

    est

Now, the Romans didn't tend to use words like 'he', she', or 'it, unless they absolutely had to – they would only use them if it would be confusing if they *didn't*, or if they wanted to emphasise it.

This means that the word **est** can mean simply 'is', but it can also mean *he* is, or *she* is, or *it* is.

So, how would you say 'he is'?

    est

The word for 'soldier' is:

    miles

And again, the Romans didn't say 'they or 'a', so **miles** can also mean 'a solider or 'the soldier'. So how would you say 'he is a soldier'?

Est miles

'of Troy' in Latin is:

Trojae

Given this, how do you think you'd say 'he is a soldier of Troy'?

Est miles Trojae

Well done!

Now, if I wanted to say 'you are' in Latin, I would say:

es

So what would 'you are a soldier of Troy' be?

Es miles Trojae

That's a good start, but before we go any further, I want to stop and talk a bit about how you can 'decode' Latin vocabulary, using what you already know about English.

Because English is one of a group of languages influenced by Latin (those we would normally call 'Romance' languages, which is just another way of saying 'Roman' languages), a lot of the words we use every day actually come from Latin originally.

Studying the history of words is called etymology, and it can be pretty interesting, but what's important for us here is that we can *use* this history to help us 'decode' Latin words from normal English words. So we can learn Latin words without memorising them, because we already know them!

Now *that* is a nice thought.

One example of this is English words that end in **–ive**, like 'native', 'creative', 'motive', and so on. These words generally come from Latin, and we can 'decode' their Latin origin by changing the **–ive** at the ending to **–ivus**.

So, changing these endings, 'native' becomes **nativus**, 'creative' becomes **creativus**, and so on.

How you think you would say 'motive'?

> **motivus**

What about 'captive'

> **captivus**

Putting this together with what we've already learnt, how would you say 'he is an active soldier of Troy'?

> **Est activus miles Trojae**

Now, saying it this way *is* correct Latin. But there's something interesting about Latin which means that this isn't the *only* way to say it.

The first thing we need to understand about Latin is that it's very 'thing-focused'.

What I mean by this is that Latin likes to focus on and emphasise words for things, ideas, objects, and so on (called 'nouns' and 'adjectives'), rather than words for what's happening (called 'verbs'). For the Romans, the *things* being talked about are much more important and much more interesting than *what they're doing*.

Now, the way that the Romans usually emphasise things is by putting them first in the sentence. This means that very often they put the doing or being words at the end.

So a good rule of thumb is to put words like **est** at the end of the sentence, unless you want to emphasise them.

Let's try that with our sentence now. How would you say 'he is an active soldier of Troy', if you don't want to emphasise the word 'is'?

> **Activus miles Trojae est.**

Remember, this *still* means 'he is an active soldier of Troy', but its emphasis is a bit different. In this order, it's like saying' he's an *active* soldier of Troy.' But if you wanted to say he *is* an active soldier of Troy' – perhaps some said he wasn't, and you're disagreeing, for example – then you'd say it the way he had it before.

So let's try that, just to make sure we have it under control. How would you say 'he is an active soldier of Troy', emphasising the 'is'?

> **Est activus miles Trojae**

And if you wanted to emphasise 'active'?

> **Activus miles Trojae est**

Of course, we can keep going with this, changing the order around more. If we wanted to emphasise that he's a *soldier* of Troy (as opposed to a gardener, or shopkeeper, for example), how might we say it? Remember, we're still saying the same sentence – 'he's an active soldier of Troy' – we're just changing the emphasis.

Let's work it out together: we're going to put the **est** at the end, because we're not emphasising it, and we're going to put **miles** at the start. How would that look?

21

Miles activus Trojae est.

Good. Now let's try emphasising the 'of Troy' bit, as if we were saying he's a soldier *of Troy*, rather than of Rome, or some other city.

Because the Romans are very 'thing-focused', we're going to keep the **miles** as close to the **Trojae** as possible, because the two things are so closely related. And, because we're emphasising 'of Troy', that's going to go first.

So what would 'he is a soldier of Troy' be, emphasising 'of Troy'?

Trojae miles activus est

Well done! Remember, all these mean the same thing, they're just changing the emphasis!

The word for 'and' in Latin is:

> **et**

So how would you say 'he is a soldier and he is active'? Remember that if we're not emphasising 'is', we don't put it first.

Miles est et activus est.

Of course, this is a little bit clumsy, isn't it? We wouldn't usually say this in English or Latin. Instead, we'd say something like 'he's a soldier, and an active one'.

Now, the easy thing about Latin is that it doesn't usually worry about words like 'person', or 'one', or 'man' or 'woman'. So the word **activus** can not only mean 'active', but also 'an active man', or 'an active person', or just simply, 'an active one'.

Let's try this out. How would you say 'an active man'?

> **activus**

And 'he's an active man'? Remember, this will look exactly the same as 'he is active'.

> **Activus est**

If you said **est activus**, this would have been right as well, but just remember that the Romans naturally try to emphasise the things or the ideas, so that's why **activus** would probably be first.

Going back to our sentence 'he's a soldier and an active one', we would say it exactly the same as as we said 'he is a soldier and he is active', but we wouldn't use the word **est** a second time, we'd just use it once, and leave it at that.

So how would we say 'he's a soldier and an active one'?

> **Miles est et activus**

Excellent! Now let's try putting this all together to say 'he is a soldier of Troy, and an active one', emphasising that he's a soldier. How would we say that?

> **Miles Trojae est et activus**

Well done! That's a great start, and you've already started to get a feel for the Latin word order.

You can now say the sentence at the start of the lesson, and much more!

Lesson Two

"Caesar attacked the city of Rome with his army and his enemies fled".

Alright, let's get into it with a very action-packed sentence today! Last time we learnt a lot about how the Romans changed their word order to show emphasis, and today we're going to be expanding that to see how they did something similar with the words themselves.

The word for Rome in Latin is:

Roma

And do you remember the word for 'is'?

> est

Now, last time we talked about how **est** in Latin can mean just 'is', but it can also me 'he is', 'she is', or 'it is'. So how would 'he is' be?

> est

And 'she is'?

> est

And what about 'it is'?

> est

Don't worry, we're not going to spend the whole lesson saying 'est'! Let's put this together with the word for Rome. So how would you say 'it's Rome'?

Roma est

Remember, unless specified otherwise, the Romans prefer to emphasise the *thing*, so we've put the word for 'Rome' first.

So again, what would 'it's Rome' be, without any emphasis, or emphasising that it's *rome*?

Roma est

Good. How about if we wanted to emphasise that it *is* Rome (maybe someone thinks it's Paris!)?

Est Roma

Now, when we use the word **est**, if we take away the 'es' bit (I call it the 'is' bit), we're just left with the last letter, the **-t**.

Just as the Romans changed their sentences around to show different meanings or emphases, they also changed the *words themselves*, to show a bit more about what was happening. So the **–t** ending on the word **est**, is actually what tells us the it's *he* is, or *she* is, or *it* is.

Using this, we can start to recognise other verbs (doing words) in Latin that are talking about 'he', 'she', or 'it', because they'll have that same **–t** ending.

So if 'to attack' in Latin is

oppugnare

Then, remembering that the **–t** ending tells us it's he, she, or it that's doing something, what do you think this means?

> **oppugnat**

If you answered 'he attacks', or 'she attacks', or 'it attacks', you're 100% correct!

Let's try this again. The word 'to love' in Latin is:

> **amare**

So if **amare** means 'to love', then what do you think this means?

> **amat**

That's right, it means 'he loves', or 'she loves', or 'it loves'.

Now, if I want to say *Caesar* loves, then I use the exact same word, and just put the word 'Caesar' next to it. So how would that look?

> **Caesar amat**

What about 'Caesar attacks'?

> **Caesar oppugnat**

Well done!

26

If we want to say 'Caesar loves *Rome*,' we have to change the word **Roma** before we can use it. The reason for this is that, because we know we can change the words around depending on what we want to emphasise, it might get confusing about whether we meant to say 'Caesar loves Rome' or 'Rome loves Caesar'. So, the Romans want to make things clear by changing the word's ending to tell us, just like they do with the **–t** ending.

To indicate that it's 'Caesar loves *Rome*, we use an **–m** ending. So 'Rome' (meaning you've done or you're doing something to Rome) is:

Romam

We actually do this in English when we change 'he' to 'him'. You would say 'he hit the ball', but you wouldn't say 'the ball hit he', would you? Instead, we change it to 'the ball hit *him*'. The only difference is that, while English only does it in very special cases, Latin *always* does it.

So again, what's the word for 'Rome' with nothing happening to it?

Roma

And what about if something *is* happening to it?

Romam

Okay, now let's put this together. How would you say 'Caesar loves Rome'?

27

Caesar Romam amat

If you put the words in a different order, that's still correct, as long as you remembered to say **Romam** instead of **Roma** (you'd just be using a different emphasis).

What about 'Caesar attacks Rome'?

Caesar Romam oppugnat

The word for 'city' in Latin is:

urbs

This is where we get our word 'urban' from. If we want to say that something's happening to the city, it's:

urbem

Notice again we're using the **–m** ending to make it clear that something's happening here.

Now, when you want to use two words together, like 'the city of Rome', they *both* need to 'match', because, of course, they're talking about the same thing. So 'the city of Rome', *without* anything happening, is:

Urbs Roma

What do you think 'the city of Rome' would be *with* something happening to it?

Urbem Romam

So what would 'Caesar loves the city of Rome' be?

Caesar urbem Romam amat

If we wanted to emphasise that it was the city of Rome that Caesar loved, of course, we'd put that first. So how would that look; how would you say 'Caesar loves the city of Rome', emphasising that it's the city of Rome he loves?

Urbem Romam Caesar amat

Excellent!

If we wanted to say he *attacked* instead of 'attack', we would say:

oppugnavit

Notice that we still have that **–t** ending, but the bit before it is a bit different, to show that it's in the past (just like we add **–ed** to the word 'attack' in English to show it's the past).

So how would we say 'he attacked the city'?

Urbem oppugnavit

What about 'he attacked the city of Rome'?

Urbem Romam oppugnavit

The word for 'army' in Latin is:

exercitus

So to say 'the army attacked', we would just put the word for 'army' next to the word for 'attacked'. How would that look?

Exercitus oppugnavit

How would we say 'the army attacked Rome', emphasising that it was *Rome* that the army attacked?

Romam exercitus oppugnavit

The word for 'with' in Latin is:

cum

If we wanted to say 'with the army', the word for 'army' changes a bit, to show this. This kind of change is something I call an 'adverbial' change, and it just means that the word is showing something is happening 'with', or 'to,' or 'in', or 'for' the army, and so on. It doesn't tell us which, which is why we still need the word 'with'.

So the word for 'army', when we're saying something is happening *with, by, to, for, in* it (and so on), is:

exercitu

Notice that here the ending is a vowel. A good rule of thumb in Latin is that 'adverbial' endings like this usually end in a vowel!

So how would we say 'with the army'?

Cum exercitu

What about 'he's with the army'?

Cum exercitu est

'Caesar is with the army'?

Caesar cum exercitu est

Remember, you can put the words in different orders, depending on what you're emphasising (but you have to keep **cum** and **exercitu** together!).

How would you say 'Caesar attacks with his army'?

Caesar cum exercitu oppugnavit

Good.

If we want to keep emphasising the 'Caesar', but still emphasise 'attacked' more than 'with the army', we would keep **Caesar** at the front, and put 'attacked' in front of 'with the army'. So how would that look; what would 'Caesar attacked with his army' be, emphasising Caesar, and *then* emphasising that he attacked?

Caesar oppugnavit cum exercitu

Perfect, well done!!

Now, if we want to talk about more than one person doing something, we change our **–t** ending to an **–nt** ending.

So if 'they attack' is

> **oppugnat**

Then, changing the **–t** at the end into **–nt**, what do you think 'they attack' would be?

> **oppugnant**

Excellent. And the word for they *attacked*, instead of they attack, is:

> **oppugnaverunt**

Again, notice the ending is the same, but the bit before it is different, just to help us see it's in the past.

So how would you say 'they attacked the city of Rome', remembering that 'city' and 'Rome' need to be the same?

> **Urbem Romam oppugnaverunt**

Good.

The word for 'enemies' in Latin is

> **hostes**

(As you can probably guess, this is where our word 'hostile' comes from).

So how would we say 'the enemies attacked Rome', emphasising that it's the *enemies* who attacked?

Hostes Romam oppugnaverunt

Now, if someone attacks you and you're not able to fight them, you're going to need to run away, right? So the word for 'they ran away' in Latin is

fugerunt

See how we still have that **–nt** ending to remind us that *they* ran away?

So how would we say 'the enemies ran away'?

Hostes fugerunt

How about 'Caesar attacked and the enemies ran away'?

Caesar oppugnavit et hostes fugerunt

In Latin, if we want to say *his* enemies, we actually don't need to say the 'his' part at all, if it's clear from what we're saying. In this case, because we've just said that Caesar attacked, it's pretty clear that the enemies are *his* enemies, so we don't need to say anything different.

So, if **hostes fugerunt** can mean '*the* enemies ran away' as well as '*his* enemies ran away', how would we say 'Caesar attacked and his enemies ran away'?

Caesar oppugnavit et hostes fugerunt.

We're now ready to say the sentence we started with! Just to recap, how would you say 'Caesar attacked the city of Rome', emphasising 'the city of Rome'?

> **Urbem Romam Caesar oppugnavit**

How about 'with his army'?

> **Cum exercitu**

And how would you say 'and his enemies ran away'?

> **Et hostes fugerunt**

Putting this together, how would you say 'Caesar attacked the city of Rome with his army, and his enemies ran away'? Take your time!

> **Urbem Romam Casear oppugnavit cum exercitu et hostes fugerunt**

Great work!!

Lesson Three

"Romulus founded a tiny city on the Platine hill after the death of his brother."

If you're going to learn Latin, you should at least be able to say *something* about the history of Rome, right?

Right.

So let's learn how to tell someone that Romulus founded the city after his brother's death.

Let's get started!

So far we've talked about how to show someone is doing something, and how to show that a thing is having something happen to it.

Let's review that quickly now.

What's the word for 'Rome'?

Roma

And the word for 'Rome' when something is happening to it?

Romam

Good!

What about the word for 'city'?

Urbs

And if something were happening to it, what would it be?

Urbem

Okay, and can you remember the word for 'he attacked'? Remember, it's the same word whether it's he, she, or it.

Oppugnavit

What about 'he attacked the city of Rome? Let's emphasise that it's the city of *Rome* that he's attacking, so we'll put that first.

Romam urbem oppougnavit

The word for 'built' or 'founded' in Latin is:

Constituit

So how would we say 'he founded the city of Rome, emphasising that he founded it?

Constituit urbem Romam

What about 'he built the city of Rome'?

Constituit urbem Romam

Can you remember how to say 'Troy' in Latin?

Troja

What do you think it would be if something's happening to it?

Trojam

Good! If you didn't guess that, don't worry – it becomes easier the more we go through it.

So, if

Trojam

36

Means 'Troy' when something's happened to it, how would we say 'he built Troy'? Let's emphasise that it's *Troy* he built. What would that be?

> **Trojam constituit**

Let's suppose someone wanted to know where Troy was, though.

The word for 'where' in Latin is:

> **Ubi**

And can you remember how to say 'is'?

> **Est**

So how would someone ask 'where is Troy?'

> **Ubi Troja est?**

Since the 'where' makes the question pretty obvious, a Roman would probably not bother to say **est**, since it would be pretty clear what they were asking. So they could just ask 'where Troy?'.

How would that look?

> **Ubi Troja?**

Let's figure out how to answer that now.

The place where Troy was is called Asia Minor, which in Latin is:

> **Asia Minor**

Pretty easy to remember!

Of course, when someone askes you

Ubi Troja est?

Or simply

Ubi Troja?

One way of answering is just to say 'Asia Minor'

But what if your wanted to say *in* Asia Minor?

The word for 'in' in Latin is:

In

Another easy one!

Last lesson I mentioned that phrases like '*in* the house', '*on* the table', '*with* the dog', and so on, are called 'adverbial' phrases, and the 'thing' words show they're part of an adverbial phrase by ending with a vowel.

So, since 'in' is part of an adverbial phrase, the words **Asia** and **Minor** need to end in a vowel.

Asia already does, so no need to change anything there, but **Minor** doesn't. So to show that **Minor** goes with **in** we would change it to:

Minore

So what would the full sentence 'in Asia Minor' be?

In Asia Minore

Well done!

The word for 'Italy' in Latin is:

Italia

Since it already ends with a vowel, it doesn't change when we want to say 'in Italy'. So what would 'in Italy' look like in Latin?

In Italia

The word for 'mountain' in Latin is:

Mons

So if I wanted to say 'the mountain is in Italy', what would that be? Remember, they don't say 'the' in Latin.

Mons in Italia est

Good!

Now the word for 'on' in Latin is the same as the word for 'in':

in

Can mean 'in' OR 'on'.

That might *sound* confusing, but of course in English it's always pretty clear which you mean.

So let's say 'he is on the mountain'. 'on the mountain' is another adverbial phrase, so

Mons

Will have to change to:

Monte

What would 'on the mountain' be in Latin, then, remembering that the word for 'on' is the same as the word for 'in'?

In monte

And 'he is on the mountain', emphasising that he's *on the mountain*?

In monte est

If you wanted to say on the *Palatine* mountain, you would say:

In monte Palatino

Or:

In Palatino monte

Can you remember how to say 'founded' or 'built'?

Constituit

And how would you say 'city', showing that something is happening to it?

urbem

So how would you say 'Romulus founded a city on the Palatine hill'? Remembr that 'hill' and 'mountain' are the same word in Latin.

So what would 'Romulus founded a city on the Palatine hill' be?

Romulus urbem in monte Palatino constituit

If you put the words in a different order, that's fine, as long as **in** was together with **monte** and **Palatino**.

'A tiny city' in Latin is:

Urbs exigua

And if you want to show something has happened to it, you would say:

Urbem exiguam

To say 'after' or 'behind' in Latin is:

Post

We see this in English in words like 'postpone', literally meaning to 'to put after or later', and words like post-work drinks, meaning 'after-work drinks'.

For the Romans, 'after' or 'behind' means something is kind of happening to the thing we're talking about, because you're metaphorically 'placing' it after or behind something else.

That means that when you use the word **post** in Latin, the word or words it's going with have to show that something is happening to it.

So 'behind the city' wouldn't be **post urbs**, but instead:

Post urbem

Likewise, even though the word for 'death' in Latin is:

Mors

'after death' is:

Post mortem

That should be pretty familiar if you're a fan of detective shows!

The word for 'brother' in Latin is:

41

Frater

Which gives us words like 'fraternity'.

To say something is 'of' my brother, or belonging to my brother, you would say:

Fratris

You can see that it's the same word, but it's changed so we know that we're talking about something related to thmy brother.

So 'my brother's death' would be:

Fratris mors

What would '*after* my brother's death' be? Remember, when you're saying something is 'after' or 'behind', the Romans think that means something is happening to it, so you'd need to make that clear.

How would it look?

Post fratris mortem

Well done if you got it!

We're now ready to try the whole sentence, 'Romulus founded a tiny city on the Palatine hill after his brother's death'.

Take your time, see how you go!

Romulus urbem exiguam in monte Palatino constituit, post fratris mortem.

That's a lot of material! Did you get it right?

Lesson Four

Now let's look at a real sentence from the Roman historian, Eutropius:

"Then at Rome the senators ruled for periods of five days, and, with them in charge, a year passed."

Why this sentence? Because it's a very easy sentence for an English-speaker, and yet, if you ask someone to say it in Latin, even if they've been studying for a long time, they'll struggle.

But Latin is FULL of sentences like this, and they're really not that difficult, as you'll see… so let's jump in!

What's the Latin word for 'Rome'?

Roma

Now, when the Romans wanted to say they were *at* a place – *at* Rom, *at* home, and so on – they didn't add a word like we do in English; instead they changed the ending of the name for thing you're at.

This might seem a bit strange to us, but if you remember that Latin is a very 'thing-focussed' language, then it makes a little more sense; they don't want to put a whole lot of extra words in, because that will take the focus away from the 'thing'.

This means that the word for '*at* Rome' is:

44

Romae

You might remember that this is the same as the word for 'of Rome'. That's because the Romans didn't see much of a difference between these two ideas, whereas English-speakers do.

Anyway, using this, then, how would you say 'Caesar is at (or in) Rome?

Caesar Romae est

Again, remember that the word order can be different, so if you put the words another way around, that's okay. But if no special emphasis is being given, it's best to put the 'things' up the front, and the 'happening' (in this case 'is') at the back.

Okay, so that's how you could say 'at Rome', or 'in Rome'; can you remember how to say 'Rome', meaning something has happened to it?

Romam

What about 'he attacked', or 'she attacked'?

Oppugnavit

So what would 'Caesar attacked Rome' be? Let's emphasise it's *Rome* he attacked.

Romam Caesar oppugnavit

Good!

Now what was the word for 'at Rome' again?

Romae

And what about the word for 'enemies'?

Hostes

Now, because **hostes** is plural (meaning there's more than one enemy), it doesn't have that **-m** ending to show something is happening to it; it either has an **-s** ending or an **–a** ending.

Since **hostes** already has an **–s** ending, we don't need to change it!

So the word for 'enemies' when something is happening to it, would be:

Hostes

Okay, so putting all this together, how would you say 'Caesar attached his enemies at Rome'? Again, let's emphasise that he attacked them *at Rome*.

Take your time!

Romae Caesar hostes oppugnavit

To say how long something is going on for in Latin, the Romans would actually say it happened *through* that time.

For example, if you want to say 'I travelled for five months' in Latin, you'd actually say 'I travelled *through* five months'.

We kind of have this in English, when we say someone 'went through that for five years', or something like that.

Now the word for 'through' in this sense is:

Per

And, since when something is going through, it means something is happening, the word (or words) after **per** needs to show that something is happening to it.

Keeping that in mind, what do you think 'through Troy' would be?

Remember, 'Troy' needs to show that something is happening to it.

> **Per trojam**

Good! Going back to our earlier sentence, let's work out how to say 'Caesar attacked Rome for five days'.

'day' in Latin is:

> **Dies**

And take a moment to guess what 'day' might be if we want to show something is happening to it!

> **Diem**

Now, if you didn't get that, don't worry!

Just make sure you <u>recognise</u> the **–m** ending (like 'I hit *him*') showing something happening.

So what would 'for a day' (literally '*through*' a day) in Latin would be?

> **Per diem**

Good!

'days' in Latin looks the same:

> **Dies**

The great thing is, since there's already an **–s** ending here, we don't need to change it when we want to say something is happening to it when there's more than one day.

Let's make sure we understand that. How would you say 'days' in Latin, when you don't need to show something is happening?

> **Dies**

And what about 'days' when something *is* happening to it?

> **Dies**

Good!

One more: how would you say 'day', when something isn't happening to it?

> **Dies**

This is a pretty easy word right?

Okay, now if you wanted to say 'for *five* days', you'd say:

> **Per quinos dies**

So how would you say 'at Rome, Caesar attacked for five days'? Let's emphasise that it's for five days, then that it's at Rome.

> **Per quinos dies Romae Caesar oppugnavit**

Well done!!

The word for 'senators' in Latin is:

> **Senatores**

Not very different, is it?

And the word for 'they ruled' is:

Imperaverunt

So how would you say 'the senators ruled'?

Senatores imperaverunt

What about 'the senators ruled at Rome, emphasising they ruled *at Rome*?

Romae senatores imperaverunt

Nicely done!

When you want to say 'passed', as in 'three days passed', in Latin you would actually say 'three days were completed'.

The word for 'completed' is:

Completus

To was 'was completed', in Latin you don't say 'was', you say 'is' – because if it *was* completed in the past, then it *is* completed now, right?

So if 'was' completed' is actually 'is completed', how would that look?

Completus est

Correct!

The word for 'a year' in Latin is:

Annus

This is where we get our words like 'annual', 'anniversay', and so on.

So how would you say 'a year pass'ed? Remember, in Latin you would say 'a year is complted'.

Annus completus est

Not so hard, is it?

If we wanted to say 'a year was completed with the poets', we need to change the word for 'poets' to show that it's an adverbial – something is happening *with* them.

But first, can you remember the word for 'poet'?

Poeta

Now when you want to show that a thing is part of an adverbial in Latin, it normally ends in a vowel, remember?

But what about when there's more than one of them?

Then the ending is usually one of two endings. I'll show you the other one later, but in the case of **poeta**, we would use an **–is** ending, like this:

Poetis

This would mean 'with the poets', by the poets', 'from the poets', and so on.

So how would we say 'a year passed with the poets'?

Annus poetis completus est

Good!

Now if we use the word for 'soldiers' instead of 'poets', we'll see the other ending for an adverbial when there's more than one thing.

Can you remember the word for 'soldier'?

> **Miles**

Good! now if you wanted to say 'with the soldiers', you'd say:

> **Militibus**

Which gives us our second ending for when we have an adverbial of several things: **ibus** (sometimes it's **–ebus**).

So how would you say 'a year passed with the soldiers'?

> **Annus militibus completus est**

If we just want to talk about 'them' instead of poets, or soldiers, or anything in particular, we would say:

> **His**

Notice again that **–is** ending!

Let's give that a try now. How would we say 'a year passed with them'?

> **Annus his completes est**

What if we wanted to emphasise that it was with *them*?

> **His annus completes est**

Good!

We're almost able to say the sentence with which we started; all we need now is to say 'in charge', or 'ruling'. In Latin this is:

Regnantibus

Notice that **–ibus** ending?

This is also where we get our word for 'reigning' from – as in 'the queen reigned for many years'.

Which, of course, is just another way of saying 'the queen *ruled'* (or *was in charge*) for many years'.

And the word for 'then', or 'next', or 'afterwards' in Latin is:

Deinde

Now we're ready for the sentence at the start of the lesson! So how would you say 'then at Rome the senators ruled for five days, and, with them in charge, a year passed'?

Let's take it in two parts.

How would we say 'then at Rome the senators ruled for five days'? Let's emphasise the 'for five days' bit more than 'senators'.

> **Deinde romae per quinos dies senatores imperaverunt**

Good. And how would you say 'and with them in charge'?

> **Et his regnantibus**

And 'a year passed'? Literally, 'a year is filled'.

Annus completus est

Now let's put the whole thing together. How would you say 'then at Rome the senators rule for five days, and, with them in charge, a year passed'?

Deinde Romae per quinos dies senatores imperaverunt et his regnantibus annus unus completus est.

Perfect!!

Lesson Five

"He again prepared for the wars; he conquered the Albans, who are twelve miles from Rome."

Another very Roman sentence!

The word for 'war' in Latin is:

> **Bellum**

This is where words like 'belligerent' and 'bellicose' come from.

So how would you say 'there is a war'?

> **Bellum est**

Good.

To say 'he prepared', or 'he prepared for' is:

> **Paravit**

So what would 'he prepared for war' be?

> **Bellum paravit**

Remember again, Latin is very 'thing-focussed', so it likes to put the 'things' first.

Now, as we've discussed before, in Latin when you say 'he' did something, the same word could also be 'she' did it, or even 'it' did it.

So what would 'she prepared for war' be?

> **Bellum paravit**

Most of the time it's pretty easy to tell who you mean.

But sometimes you do want to make it clear – even if you're talking about a group of men, so you know it's a he, you still might not be clear on **which** 'he' it is, right?

So in Latin they emphasise 'he' by saying 'this man' or 'that man', which helps differentiate.

So let's learn that now.

To say 'he' when you want to emphasise or be extra clear, you say:

Hic

This literally means 'this man'.

So how would you say '*he* prepared for war', emphasising that *he* did it? Literally, we'll say 'this man prepared for war'.

Hic bellum paravit

Well done! Remember we put the **hic** first, because we're emphasising it the most.

In English, when we want to say that we're doing something again, we put 're' in front of it, so we're *re*-doing it, don't we?

The easy thing is, the Romans would often do exactly the same thing!

So if

Paravit

Means 'he prepared', and the Romans used 're' at the start to show it was happening again, how would you say 'he prepared *again*'?

Reparavit

Good!

What about 'he prepared again for war', still emphasising 'he'?

Hic bellum reparavit

Not so hard, was it?

Of course, if you wanted to emphasise that **she** prepared again for war, instead of 'this man' you'd say 'this woman,' which in Latin is:

Haec

So how would you say '*she* prepared again for war', emphasising that *she* did it? Remember, you're literally going to say 'this woman prepared again for war'.

Haec bellum reparavit

Can you remember the word for 'soldier'?

Miles

Great! Then how would you say 'she is not a soldier'?[1] Again, we want to emphasise 'she'

Haec miles non est

Well done!

---

[1] Women couldn't be soldiers in Ancient Rome.

Since we've already learnt 'this man' and 'this woman', let's learn 'this' for when we're talking about something which is neither feminine nor masculine:

Hoc

In Latin, EVERY word is either masculine, feminine, or neuter (which just means 'neither'), so we use all three of these words a lot..

'war' in Latin is neuter, so how do you think we would say 'this war'?

Hoc bellum

Spot on!

Do you remember how to say 'enemies'?

Hostes

Now, if you remember, we spoke a few lessons ago about how when a word is plural (meaning there's more than one of the 'things'), and you want to show that something is happening to it, the Romans put an **–s** (normally **–os,-as**, or **–es**, but sometimes **–us** as well) or an **–a** ending on it.

We also said that, since **hostes** is already both plural and ends in **–s**, we don't need to change it, right?

So what's 'enemies' in Latin, meaning something has happened to it?

Hostes

Okay, now let's take the name for the Alban people, who lived near Rome. The word for 'the Albans' is:

Albani

The word for 'they are' is:

Sunt

So how would you say 'they're Albans'?

Albani sunt

Good! What about 'the Albans are enemies'?

Albani hostes sunt

Don't forget, if you put the words in a different order, that's still correct – but this order is because the Romans like to emphasise the 'things', so they put them earlier.

Now, **Albani** is obviously plural, because we're talking about more than one Alban person, right?

So to show that something's happened to them, we need to have an **–s** or an **–a** ending.

In this case 'the Albans', when we want to show something's happened to it, is:

Albanos

Can you remember how to say 'he attacked'?

Oppugnavit

So how would you say 'he attacked the Albans'?

Albanos oppugnavit

The word for 'conquered' or 'won' in Latin is:

Vicit

Hence 'victory'.

How would you say 'he conquered the Albans?

> **Albanos vicit**

And can you remember the word for 'Trojans'?

> **Trojani**

Since this looks a lot like **Albani**, when we want to show something happened to the Trojans, the end will look the same as **Albanos** as well.

So how do you think that will look, if we want to say 'Trojans', meaning something has happened to them?

> **Trojanos**

And 'he conquered the Trojans'?

> **Trojanos vicit**

Good!

But what about that **–a** ending I said sometimes is used?

Well, if a word is *neuter*, meaning it's not masculine or feminine, then when it's plural it ends in **–a**, whether something is happening to it or not.

Can you remember what the word for 'war' is?

> **Bellum**

Now 'war' in Latin is neuter, so 'wars' ends in **–a**, like this:

> **Bella**

And if we wanted to say 'wars', when something was happening, it would still be:

> **Bella**

Remembering that

> **Vicit**

Can also mean 'won', as well as 'conquered', how do you think you'd say 'he won the wars'?

> **Bella vicit**

Perfect!

The word for 'who' or 'those who' in Latin is:

> **Qui**

Putting this together with what we've learnt so far, how would we say 'he conquered the enemy, who are Albans'?

Take your time!

> **Hostes vicit, qui Albani sunt**

Good!

And if we want to say 'from', 'by', or 'away from', we say:

> **Ab**

Can you remember the word for 'city'?

> **Urbs**

Good.

But if we want to say 'away from the city' we have to show that 'city' is an adverbial, which would look like this:

Urbe

So what would 'from the city' be?

Ab urbe

And 'from the city of Rome'? Remember the Romans would just say 'from the city Rome':

Ab urbe Roma

Good! And 'they are from the city'?

Ab urbe sunt

And 'they're from the city of Rome'?

Ab urbe Roma sunt

Now, we have the word **ab** in English with the word 'absent', meaning 'away *from* here'.

In fact, our word 'absent' comes straight from the Latin word for 'away' or 'away from', or even just 'absent':

Absunt

As you can see, it's just

Sunt

Meaning 'they are', and

Ab

Meaning 'from' or 'away from'.

So

Absunt

Means 'they are from' or 'away from'.

Since 'from' is an Adverbial phrase, when we're saying what it is they're away from, we need to show that it's being used as an adverbial, which means it needs to end in a vowel.

So what was 'they are from the city' again?

Ab urbe sunt

But if we wanted to say 'they are *away* from the city' (as in 'they're 10 miles from the city'), we need to use **absunt** instead of **sunt**.

So how would that look?

What would 'they are away from the city' be?

Ab urbe absunt

And 'they're away from the city of Rome'?

Ab urbe Roma absunt

Good!

If you want to say how far away something is in Latin, you don't say twelve miles', you say 'on the twelfth mile'.

'on the twelfth mile' in Latin is:

Duodecimo milario

So how would you say 'they're 12 miles away', literally, 'they're on the twelfth mile away'?

Duodecimo milario absunt

And 'they're 12 miles from the city of Rome? Let's emphasise that it's from the city of Rome they're 12 miles from, so we'll put that bit first:

Ab urbe Roma duodecimo milario absunt

Brilliant!

Now let's try the whole sentence from the start of this lesson.

Let's say 'he prepared again for the wars; he conquered the Albans, who are 12 miles fom the city of Rome'.

Let's take it in parts.

What is 'he prepared again for the wars'?

Hic bella reparavit

And 'he conquered the Albans'?

Albanos vicit

And can you remember the word for 'who' or 'those who'?

Qui

And 'they're 12 miles from the city of Rome'?

Ab urbe Roma duodecimo milario absunt

Let's put it all together. How would you say 'he prepared again for the wars; he conquered the Albans, who are 12 miles from the city of Rome'?

Hic bellum reparavit; Albanos vicit, qui ab urbe Roma duodecimo milario absunt.

Amazing progress!!

Lesson Six

'He said that Apollo couldn't be deceived, nor could anything hide from him.'

You've come a long way!

One thing we haven't discussed yet is how to say what someone else has said.

To say this, Latin uses an old construction that we still *understand* in English, but we don't use it very much.

In English if you want to say you think someone's an idiot, you would normally say 'I think he is an idiot', right?

But if someone said to you

>   I think him to be an idiot

You'd completely and easily understand them, right?

Right.

This way of putting it is old-fashioned in English, but we still understand it… which is good, because that's exactly how the Romans say it!

So 'he said Apollo can't be deceived' would, in Latin, actually be 'he said Apoolo not to be able to be deceived'.

Bit of a mouthful in English!

The word for 'he said' or 'she said' in Latin is:

Dixit

And the word for 'Apollo' is:

Apollo

Now, if we wanted to change this to show something has happened to it – to make it like 'him' instead of 'he', we say:

Apollinem

'to be deceived' or 'to be tricked' is:

Decipi

So if I want to say 'he said Apollo was tricked', in Latin I'd literally say 'he said Apollo to be tricked'.

How would that look?

Because we're reporting what someone else say, the 'he said' part should go first, but after that we still want to emphasise Apollo, because he's a 'thing', right?

So how would 'he said Apollo was tricked' look?

Dixit Apollinem decipi

Good! Remember, we need to say

Apollinem

Not

Apollo

Because they're using the 'I think *him* to be an idiot' construction.

'to be able' in Latin is:

Posse

So how do you think you might say 'he said Apollo *can be* (or *is able to*) be deceived'?

Dixit Apollinem decipi posse

Not so hard, is it?

The word for 'anything' is:

Quicquam

This word looks the same whether something is happening to it or not, so it doesn't need to change.

So how would you say 'he said anything can be deceived'?

Dixit quicquam decipi posse

The word for 'him' is:

Eum

Now if we want to say 'he said anything can trick him', how do we show which is which, since they would both look like something is happening to them?

The answer is, in this case they follow the same order as they do in English.

So, if 'anything' is before 'him' in English, it goes first in Latin; and if **eum** is after **quicquam** in Latin, then it is in English too.

So how would you say 'he said anything can trick him'?

Dixit quicquam eum decipi posse

What about 'he said Appollo can deceive him'?

Dixit Apollinem eum decipi posse

And 'Appollo said he could be tricked? For this one, we only need **eum**. How would it look?

Apollo dixit eum decipi osse

Well done!!

Can you remember the word for 'he loves' or 'she loves'/

Amat

Good. now if we see this word with a **–re** ending instead of a **–t** ending, it tells us it means 'to love'. So 'to love' is:

Amare

And can you remember how to say 'he attacks' or 'she attacks'?

Oppugnat

Okay, so if

Amat

Means 'he loves or 'she loves', and

Amare

Means 'to love, and

Oppugnat

Means 'he attacks' or 'she attacks', then what do you think 'to attack' would be

Oppugnare

Well done!

So how would we say 'he said Apollo attacked him?

> **Dixit Apollinem eum oppugnare**

And 'he said Apollo loved him'?

> **Dixit Apollinem eum amre**

Easy, right?

Now, if the word

> **Latet**

Means 'he hides', 'he hides from', 'she hides' or 'she hide froms'[2], what do you think 'to hide' would be?

> **Latere**

Did you get it right?

Okay, so how would you say 'he said anything can hide from him'

> **Dixit quicquam eum latere**

Good!

If we want to say 'neither' and 'nor' in Latin, we use the same word, which is:

> **Neque**

Putting this altogether, how would we say 'he said that Apollo can neither be tricked, nor can anything hide from him'?

---

[2] Hence our word 'latent'

Take your time! And remember you use **neque** just like 'neither' and 'nor' in English.

> **Dixit Apollinem eum decipi posse, neque quicquam eum latere**

Get it?

Well done!!

Lesson Seven

'O Apollo, what I'm carrying, is it alive or dead?'

We're up to our last sentence!

To say 'what' in Latin, when you don't know if it's masculine, feminine, or neuter, is:

Quod

So how would you ask 'what is it'?

Quod est?

Good.

What about 'he loves' or 'she loves'?

Amat

And 'what does he love'? Remember, the Romans don't bother to say 'does'

Quod amat?

Good!

Now, in Latin, if you want to say *I* am doing something, instead of *he* or *she* is doing something, the verb (the 'doing word') ends in **–o**.

So 'I love' or 'I am loving' is:

Amo

And 'I say' or 'I am saying' is:

Dico

So how would you say 'what I am saying'?

Quod dico

Good! and what about 'what I am loving'?

Quod amo

'I am carrying' in Latin is:

Fero

Hence our word 'ferry', something which *carries* you across the river or bay!

So how would you say 'what I'm carrying'?

Quod fero

'alive' is:

Vivum

So how would you say 'it's alive'?

Vivum est

And 'what is alive'?

Quod vivum est?

'dead' is:

Mortuum

So how would you say 'it's dead'?

Mortuum est

Well done!

Now, to ask in Latin 'whether', as in 'whether or not' you use two words.

Before the first option you say

> **Utrum**

And before the second, you say:

> **An**

So how would you say 'whether alive or dead'?

> **Utrum vivum an mortuum**

And 'whether *it's* alive or dead'? In this case you'll need to put the 'is' with the first option.

So how would that look?

> **Utrum vivum est an morutuum**

Good!

Now we're almost ready to say the whole sentence from the start of the chapter.

All we need is to say 'O Apollo', which, in Latin, is:

> **O Apollo**

Not hard, right?

So how would you say 'O Apollo, what I'm carrying, is it alive or dead?'

> **O Apollo, quod fero, utrum vivum est an mortuum?**

Perfect!!

Congratulations!

You've now gone over all the basic constructions that you'll see again and again in reading Latin.

Of course, that doesn't mean you're fluent in Latin, but what these 7 lessons have given you is a **framework** of the language, so that as you get more and more exposure to Latin, you're not floundering, because you have some idea of how to make sense of it all.

The next step now is to read, *read, READ!*

That's what Decoding Latin is all about, so jump right into Part II and start being amazed at your progress!

Part II
Aesop's Fables

Aesop's Fables, are credited to a Greek freedman (i.e. a former slave) called Aesop, a storyteller believed to have lived in ancient Greece between 620 and 564 BC. The stories were used for education and language learning all the way through to the Renaissance. The stories are diverse, some funny, some strange, but all memorable, and a great way to start building up fluency in Latin!

Decoding Latin– Day 1

Don't forget the rules:

5. Don't try to memorise anything
6. Focus on the story, not the language – don't try to analyse!
7. Read one section from the left column and then the same from the right.
8. *Always read for speed and general gist, not for accuracy and perfection.*

PHILOMELA THE NIGHTINGALE ET AND ACCIPTER THE HAWK	**PHILOMELA ET ACCIPTER**
Philomela a nightingale super over arbore a tree sedens sitting (i.e. sitting in a tree) de from more custom (i.e. as is its custom) canebat sang (i.e. a nightingale was singing, sitting in a tree) .	Philomela super arbore sedens de more canebat.
Accipter a hawk autem but (i.e. but a hawk) eam her conspicatus having caught sight (i.e. having caught sight of her), ac	Accipter autem eam conspicatus, ac cibi indigens, cum advolasset, corripuit.

and cibi of food indigens needing (i.e. and needing food), cum when advolasset he might have flown to (i.e. when he'd flown to her), corripuit he snatched her.

Quae who (i.e. the nightingale), quum when peritura about to perish esset she might be (i.e. when the nightingale was about to perish), orabat she prayed accipitrem (to) the hawk (i.e. she begged the hawk), ne that not devoraretur she be devoured (i.e. she begged him that she should not be eaten/not to eat her); neque not enim for (i.e. for not) satis enough esse to be dixit she said ad for accipitris the hawk's ventrem stomach implendum to be filled (i.e. she said she wasn't

Quae, quum peritura esset, orabat accipitrem, ne devoraretur; neque enim satis esse dixit ad accipitris ventrem implendum, sed oportere ipsum, cibo egentem, ad majores aves converti.

enough to fill the hawk's stomach), sed but oportere to behove ipsum himself (the hawk, i.e. the hawk should), cibo for egentem wanting (i.e. but the hawk should, wanting food), ad to majores larger aves birds converti be turned (i.e. she said that she wasn't enough to fill his stomach, and that it'd be better for him, if he wanted food, to turn to larger birds).

Accipiter the hawk autem but (i.e. but the hawk), cum when respondisset it might have answered, ait said (i.e. but the hawk, having answered, said this), Sed but ego I certe certainly, amens mindless (i.e. stupid) sim I would be (i.e. I would be stupid), si if, qui (those things)

Accipiter autem, cum respondisset, ait, Sed ego certe amens sim, si, qui in manibus paratus est, cibo dimisso , quae non uspiam videntur , persequar.

78

which in in manibus (my) hands paratus prepared est is (i.e. I'd be stupid if, those things which are ready in my hands), cibo with the food dimisso being sent away, quae (those things) which non not uspiam anywhere videntur are seen, persequar I pursue (I'd be stupid if, having thrown away the food which is already prepared in my hands, I pursued what couldn't be seen).

Fabula significat (the) fable signifies, ut that ex out of hominibus people etiam also ii those sint might be inconsulti rash (i.e. that those people are rash), qui who, spe in hope majorum of (i.e. for) greater (things), quae (those things) which incerta uncertain sunt are (i.e. those things which are uncertain), quae (those

Fabula significat, ut ex hominibus etiam ii sint inconsulti, qui spe majorum, quae incerta sunt, quae in manibus habentur, ammittant.

things) which *in* in *manibus* hands *habentur* are held, *ammittant* lose *(i.e. the fable signifies that those people are stupid who lose what's in their hands in the hope of something greater).*

AQUILA THE EAGLE ET AND VULPES THE FOX

Aquila an eagle et and vulpes a fox inita having entered into amicitia friendship prope near se themselves (i.e. having entered into an agreement with each other) invicem mutually habitare to live decreverunt they decided (i.e. they decided to live together), confirmationem (as) a confirmation amicitiae of (their) friendship facientes making familiaritatem familiarity

AQUILA ET VULPES

Aquila et vulpes inita amicitia prope se invicem habitare decreverunt, confirmationem amicitiae facientes familiaritatem.

80

(i.e. making familiarity a sign of their friendship).

Itaque and so Aquila the eagle super above alta a on a high arbore tree nidum (her) nest fixit fixed (i.e. she set her nest above on a high tree).

Vulpes the fox vero but (i.e. but the fox) in in proximis the nearest (i.e. nearby) arbustis shrubs filios (her) children peperit brought forth (i.e. gave birth to).

Ad for pabulum food, igitur therefore, aliquando sometime vulpe with the fox profecta having left (with the fox having left once to get food), Aquila the eagle cibi of food inopia with a lack laborans labouring (i.e. struggling

| Itaque Aquila super alta arbore nidum fixit.

Vulpes vero in proximis arbustis filios peperit.

Ad pabulum igitur aliquando vulpe profecta, Aquila cibi inopia laborans, cum devolasset in arbusta et filios huius sustulisset, una cum suis pullis eos devoravit.

with a lack of food), **cum when** devolasset **she might have flown down (i.e. having flown down)** in arbusta **into the shrubs** et **and** filios **the children** huius **of this (i.e. of the fox)** sustulisset **she might have taken up,** una **one (i.e. together)** cum suis **with her own** pullis **young ones** eos **them** devoravit **she devoured them.**

Vulpes **the fox** vero **but (i.e. but the fox)** reversa **having returned,** et **and** re **with the matter (i.e. what had happened)** cognita **being known,** non **not** tam **so much** filiorum **of her children** tristata **saddened** est **she is (i.e. was)** morte **by the death (i.e. she was not so much saddened by the death of her children),** quam **as** vindicatae **of revenge**

Vulpes vero reversa, et re cognita, non tam filiorum tristata est morte, quam vindicatae inopia: quia enim terrestris esset, alatam persequi haud poterat.

82

inopia by the lack (i.e. as by the lack of revenge): quia because enim for (i.e. for, because) terrestris earthly esset she might be (i.e. because she was land-based), alatam the winged (one, i.e. the eagle) persequi to pursue haud scarcely poterat she was able (i.e. because, being land-based, she was scarcely able to pursue the eagle).

Quae wherefore (i.e. for which reason) procul at a distance stans standing (i.e. standing at a distance), quod which etiam even impotentibus for the weak est is facile easy, inimicae to (her) enemy maledicebat she cursed.

Non not multo must autem but post after (i.e. not much later), capram

Quae procul stans, quod etiam impotentibus est facile, inimicae maledicebat.

Non multo autem post, capram quibusdam in agro sacrificientibus, cum

83

a she-goat quibusdam in a certain in agro in a field (i.e. in a certain field) sacrificientibus from those sacrificing, cum when devolasset she might have flown down Aquila the eagle (i.e. when the eagle was away), partem part victimae of the victim (i.e. part of the sacrificed she-goat) cum ignitis with the ignited carbonibus coals rapuit she (i.e. the fox) grabbed, et and in nidum into the nest tulit she brought (i.e. she threw the burning goat it into the nest).

Vento with the wind autem but (i.e. but with the wind) vehementer vehemently tunc then flante blowing (i.e. and with the wind then blowing vehemently), et and flamma with the

devolasset Aquila, partem victimae cum ignitis carbonibus rapuit, et in nidum tulit.

Vento autem vehementer tunc flante, et flamma excitata, aquilae pulli, implumes adhuc cum essent, assati in terram deciderunt.

flame **excitata** having been excited (i.e. fanned up), **aquilae** the eagle's **pulli** chicks, **implumes** featherless **adhuc** as yet (i.e. as yet without feathers to fly) **cum** when **essent** they might be (i.e. since they were still featherless), **assati** roasted in into **terram** the earth **deciderunt** they fell down (i.e. they fell to the earth).

Vulpes the fox **vero** but (i.e. but the fox), **cum** when **accurrisset** she might have run up, in **conspectus** into the sight **Aquilae** of the eagle **omnes** all (the chicks) **devoravit** she ate up (i.e. the fox ate all the chicks in sight of the eagle).

Fabula significat the fable signifies, *eos* (that) those, *qui* who *amicitiam*

Vulpes vero, cum accurrisset, in conspectus Aquilae omnes devoravit.

Fabula significat, eos, qui amicitiam violant, licet ab affectis injuria fugiant

friendship **violant** *violate*, **licet** *although* **ab** *from* **affectis** *(those) affected* **injuria** *by the injury* **fugiant** *they may avoid* **ultionem** *the revenge (i.e. that those who vioilate friendship, even though they may avoid revenge)* **ob** *on account of* **impotenetiam** *the weakness (of th person injured)* **divinum** *divine* **tamen** *however* **supplicium** *punishment* **non depulsuros** *(they are) not about to repel (avoid, i.e. they won't avoid divine punishment)*.

ultionem ob impotenetiam divinum tamen supplicium non depulsuros.

Decoding Latin – Day 2

Don't forget the rules:

1. Don't try to memorise anything
2. Focus on the story, not the language – don't try to analyse!
3. Read one section from the left column and then the same from the right.
4. *Always read for speed and general gist, not for accuracy and perfection.*

VULPES THE FOX ET AND HIRCUS THE HE-GOAT

VULPES ET HIRCUS

Vulpes a fox et and hircus a he-goat sitientes thirsting (i.e. a fox and a goat, being thirsty), in into puteum a well descenderunt they went down (i.e. they went down into a well), sed but postquam after bibissent they had drunk, hirco with the he-goat indagante looking for ascensum an ascent (i.e. a way back up), vulpes the fox ait said,

Vulpes et hircus sitientes in puteum descenderunt, sed postquam bibissent, hirco indagante ascensum, vulpes ait,

'Confide trust (me), utile useful quid something (i.e. something useful), et and in into utriusque of each (i.e. of both of us) etiam also salutem the safety excogitavi I have thought up (i.e. I've thought up something useful for the safety of us both); si if enim for (i.e. fo if) rectus straight steteris you will have stood (i.e. for if you stand straight), et and anteriores (your) front pedes feet parieti to the wall applicueris you will have applied (i.e. put your feet against the wall) , et and cornua (your) horns partier likewise in into anteriorem the front partem part inclinaveris you have inclined (i.e. if you incline your horns forward), quum when percurrero I will have run ipsa I myself per

'Confide, utile quid, et in utriusque etiam salutem excogitavi; si enim rectus steteris, et anteriores pedes parieti applicueris, et cornua partier in anteriorem partem inclinaveris, quum percurrero ipsa per tuos humeros et cornua, ey extra puteum illinc exiluero, et te postea extraham hinc'

through (i.e. across) **tuos** your **humeros** shoulders **et** and **cornua** (your) horns, **et** and **extra** outside **puteum** the well **illinc** from there **exiluero** I shall have leaped, **et** and **te** you, **postea** afterwards, **extraham** I will draw out (i.e. pull out) **hinc** from here'

Ab by **hirco** the he-goat, **autem** however, **ad hoc** to this (i.e. for this purpose) **prompte** promptly **officio** with the duty **praestito** presented (i.e. but, with this job being readily done by the he-goat), **illa** she (i.e. the fox), **quum** when **ex** out of **puteo** the well **sic** thus **exiluisset** she had leaped out, **exultabat** she jumped about **circum** around **os** the mouth (of the well) **laeta** happily.

An hirco autem ad hoc prompte officio praestito, illa, quum ex puteo sic exiluisset, exultabat circum os laeta.

Hircus the he-goat autem but (i.e. but the he-goat), ipsam her accusabat accused, quod because transgressa transgressed fuisset she might have been (i.e. because she'd broken) conventiones the agreements (i.e. she'd broken the deal): Illa she autem but (i.e. but she/the fox), 'Sed but si if tot so many,' inquit she said, 'mentes minds possideres you possessed, quot as many as in in barba (your) beard pilos hairs (i.e. if you had as much brains as hair in your beard), non not ante before descendisses you would have gone done quam than[3] de about ascensu the ascent considerasses you had considered (i.e.

Hircus autem, ipsam accusabat, quod transgressa fuisset conventiones: Illa autem, 'Sed si tot,' inquit, 'mentes possideres, quot in barba pilos, non ante descendisses quam de ascensu considerasses.

---

[3] **Ante** (before) followed later by **quam** (which) is a way of expressing in Latin that what happens between the two words happened before what comes *after* **quam**. In this case, the fox is saying the goat shouldn't have gone down before he'd considered a way of getting out.

you shouldn't have gone done before thinking of a way up).

Fabula significat the fable signifies, *sic* (that) thus *prudentem* a prudent *virum* man *oportere* to behove (i.e. that a prudent man ought), *prius* before *fines* the ends *altius* more highly (i.e. more deeply/carefully) *considerare* to consider *rerum* of things (i.e. that a prudent man should first consider more carefully the consequences of things), *deinde* then (after) *sic* thus *ipsas* the same (things) *aggredi* to attempt.

VULPES THE FOX ET AND LEO THE LION

Vulpes a fox, **quum** when (i.e. since) **nunquam** never **vidisset** had she seen **Leonem** a lion (i.e.

Fabula significat, sic prudentem virum oportere, prius fines altius considerare rerum, deinde sic ipsas aggredi.

VULPES ET LEO

Vulpes, quum nunquam vidisset Leonem, quum casu quodam ei occurrisset, primum sic

91

since she'd never seen a lion), **quum** when **casu** by a fall (i.e. by chance[4]) **quodam** a certain (i.e. when, by a certain chance), **ei** to it (i.e. a lion) **occurrisset** she might have run against (i.e. when she had run into/met one), **primum** (at) first **sic** thus **timuit** she feared (i.e. she was so afraid), **ut** that **ferme** almost **moreretur** she would have died (i.e. she was so afraid she nearly died).

Deinde then, **quum** when **secondo** secondly (i.e. a second time) **vidisset** she might have seen (him), **timuit** she feared (i.e. was afraid), **certe** certainly, **non** not **tamen** yet (i.e. not, however) **ut** as **prius** before: **tertio** thirdly (i.e. the third time) **autem** but

timuit, ut ferme moreretur.

Deinde, quum secondo vidisset, timuit certe, non tamen ut prius: tertio autem quum ipum vidisset, sic contra eum ausa est, ut accideret, et colloqueretur.

---

[4] A Latin idiom

(i.e. but for the third time) **quum** when **ipsum** him **vidisset** she had seen, **sic** thus **contra** against **eum** him **ausa** dared **est** she is (i.e. she dared so against him/she was so bold), **ut** that **accideret** she should approach (i.e. she was so bold she approached him), **et** and **colloqueretur** conversed (with him).

Fabula significat the fable signifies, *familiaritatem* (that) familiarity *vel* or (i.e. even) *terribilia* terrible (things) *accessu* in the approach *faciilia* easy (things) *facere* to make/do (i.e. familiarity makes even terrible things easy in the approach/to be approached).

Fabula significat, familiaritatem vel terribilia accessu faciilia facere.

Decoding Latin – Day 3

Don't forget the rules:

1. Don't try to memorise anything
2. Focus on the story, not the language – don't try to analyse!
3. Read one section from the left column and then the same from the right.
4. *Always read for speed and general gist, not for accuracy and perfection.*

VULPES THE FOXES | VULPES

Vulpes *a fox* laqueo *in a snare* capta *being caught* (i.e. being caught in a snare), quum *when,* abscissa *with being cut off* cauda *her tail* (i.e. having cut off her tail), evasisset *she might have escaped* (i.e. when she'd escaped with her tail cut off), non *not* vitalem *liveable* prae *for* (i.e. for the reason of) pudore *shame* existimabat *she thought* vitam *(her) life* (i.e. she was so ashamed

Vulpes laqueo capta, quum, abscissa cauda, evasisset, non vitalem prae pudore existimabat vitam:

94

she thought her life unliveable):

decrevit she decided itaque and so (i.e. and so she decided) et and (i.e. also) aliis to the other vulpibus foxes hoc this itidem the same persuadere to persuade (i.e. she decided to persuade the other foxes to do the same thing); ut so that, communi with a common malo evil suum her own celaret she could conceal dedecus disgrace (i.e. so she could conceal her own disgrace with a common problem).

decrevit itaque et aliis vulpibus hoc itidem persuadere; ut communi malo suum celaret dedecus.

Et and jam already, omnibus to all (the foxes) collectis gathered together, suadebat she persuaded (i.e. she tried to persuade them all, gathered together)

Et jam, omnibus collectis, suadebat caudas abscindere quod non indecens soluum hoc membrum sit, sed et supervacuum onus appensum.

caudas (their) tails abscindere to cut off (i.e. to cut off their tails) quod because non not indecens indecent soluum only (i.e. not only indecent) hoc this membrum member sit is (i.e. was), sed but et also supervacuum empty (i.e. unnecessary) onus burden appensum appended (i.e. she persuaded them to cut off their tales, saying it was not only an indecent thing to have, but an unnecessary burden to have attached to them).

Respondens answering autem but (i.e. but in answer) ex out of ipsis them quadam a certain one, ait said (i.e. but one of them said in answer):

Respondens autem ex ipsis quadam, ait:

Heus *ha!* tu *you*, nisi *unless* tibi *to you* hoc *this* conduceret *would profit*, nobis *to us* non consuleres *you wouldn't advise (i.e. you wouldn't tell us to do it if it didn't benefit you)*.

Fabula significat the fable signifies, pravos *(that) depraved* homines *people* non *not* prae *for (i.e. for reason of)* benevolentia *goodwill* propinquis *to their neighbours* consullere *advise (i.e. that depraved people don't give advice to their neighbours out of kindness)*, sed *but* propter *on account of* suam *their own* ipsorum *of (i.e. for) themselves* utilitatem *the use (i.e. but for their own use)*.

VULPES THE FOX ET AND RUBUS THE BRAMBLE

Heus tu, nisi tibi hoc conduceret, nobis non consuleres.

Fabula significat, pravos homines non prae benevolentia propinquis consullere, sed propter suam ipsorum utilitatem.

VULPES ET RUBUS

Vulpes a fox, **sepe** with a hedge **conscensa** being mounted (i.e. having mounted a hedge), **quum** when, **lapsa** having slipped, **casura** about to fall **foret** she would be (i.e. having slipped, she was about to fall), **apprehendit** she grabbed, **in** into (i.e. for) **adjutorium** assistance, **rubum** a bramble.

Quamobrem for which reason, **quum** when **pedes** feet **suos** her own **illius** of it **aculeis** with the prickles **cruentasset** she might have made bloody (i.e. when she'd made her paws bloody with its thorns), **et** and **doleret** she might (i.e. did) suffer, **ei** to it **dixit** she said;

Hei alas **mihi** to me! **cum** when **enim** for (i.e. for when) **confugissem** I

Vulpes, sepe conscensa, quum lapsa casura foret, apprehendit, in adjutorium, rubum.

Quamobrem, quum pedes suos illius aculeis cruentasset, et doleret, ei dixit;

Hei mihi! cum enim confugissem ad te,

98

might have fled (i.e. for when I fled) **ad** to **te** you, **tanquam** as if **ad** to **auxiliatorem** a helper, **tu** you **pejus** worse **me** me **tractasti** had (i.e. have) treated.

Sed but **errasti** you have erred (i.e. you're wrong), **heus** ho! **tu** you, **inquit** said **rubus** the bramble, **quae** who **me** me **apprehendere** to grab **voluisti** you wanted (i.e. but you, the bramble said, were wrong, you who wanted to grab me), **qui** (I) who **omnes** all (i.e. everyone) **apprehendere** to grab **soleo** I tend (i.e. I who am accustomed to grab all).

Fabula significat the fable signifies, *sic* (that) thus *et* and (i.e. also) *homines* people *esse* to be *stultos* stupid (i.e. that people are

tanquam ad auxiliatorem, tu pejus me tractasti.

Sed errasti, heus tu, inquit rubus, quae me apprehendere voluisti, qui omnes apprehendere soleo.

Fabula significat, sic et homines esse stultos, qui ad eos auxilii gratia accurrunt, quibus magis

99

also stupid), **qui** *who* **ad** *to* **eos** *those* **auxilii** *of help* **gratia** *for the sake (i.e. for the sake of help)* **accurrunt** *run to (i.e. people are stupid who run to those for help)*, **quibus** *to whom* **magis** *more* **injuria** *with injury* **afficere** *to affect* **a** *by* **natura** *nature* **insitum** *implanted* **est** *it is (i.e. they're stupid who run for help from those in whose nature it is more to injure).*

injuria afficere a natura insitum est.

Decoding Latin – Day 4

Don't forget the rules:

1. Don't try to memorise anything
2. Focus on the story, not the language – don't try to analyse!
3. Read one section from the left column and then the same from the right.
4. *Always read for speed and general gist, not for accuracy and perfection.*

GALLI THE COCKS ET AND PERDIX THE PARTRIDGE	**GALLI ET PERDIX**
Gallos cocks quidam a certain (man) habens having domi at home (i.e. a certain man, having roosters at home), emptam a bought quoque also perdicem partridge, cum with illis them dimisit he sent down pasci to be fed (i.e. also sent down a bought partridge to be fed with them):	Gallos quidam habens domi, emptam quoque perdicem, cum illis dimisit pasci:

101

illis with them vero but (i.e. but with them) verberantibus beating ipsam her (i.e. the partridge), et and expellentibus driving (her) out, illa she tristabatur was saddened valde very much, existmans thinking, ut as alienigenam an alien, haec these (things) se herself pati to suffer a gallis from the cocks (i.e. thinking she suffered these things from the roosters as an alien/because she was different).

Quum when vero but (i.e. but when) paulo a little post after (i.e. a little later) et and (i.e. also) illos them (i.e. the roosters) videret she might see pugnare to fight (i.e. but when a little later she saw them fight), et and seipsos

illis vero verberantibus ipsam, et expellentibus, illa tristabatur valde, existmans, ut alienigenam, haec se pati a gallis.

Quum vero paulo post et illos videret pugnare, et seipsos caedere, moerore soluta, ait;

102

themselves **caedere** to beat, **moerore** from grief **soluta** frees (i.e. freed from grief), **ait** she said;

Sed but, **quidem** indeed, **posthac** after this **non tristabor** I will not be saddened, **videns** seeing **et** and (i.e. also) **ipsos** themselves **pugnare** to fight **inter** among **se** themselves (i.e. I won't be sad, seeing them fighting amongst themselves).

Fabula significat the fable signifies, **quod** that **prudentes** the prudent **facile** easily **ferant** may bear **ab** from **alienis** strangers **injurias** injuries (i.e. that prudent people can easily bear injuries from strangers), **quum** when **ipsos** themselves **videant** they (i.e. the prudent) may see **neque**

Sed quidem posthac non tristabor, videns et ipsos pugnare inter se.

Fabula significat, quod prudentes facile ferant ab alienis injurias, quum ipsos videant neque a suis abstinere.

103

noeither a *from* **suis** *their own* **abstinere** *to abstain (i.e. when they see that they don't refrain from doing the same to their own).*

VULPES THE FOX

Vulpes a fox in into **domum** the house **profecta** having proceeded **mimi** of a mime (i.e. having entered a mime's house), **et** and **singula** the each (i.e. the several) **ipsius** of him (i.e. of the mime) **vasa** the vessels **perscrutans** searching thoroughly (i.e. and searching through the different vessels of the mime), **invenit** found **et** and (i.e. also) **caput** a head **larvae** of a mask **ingeniose** ingeniously **fabricatum** wrought (i.e. ingeniously made), **quo** which, **et** and (i.e. and

VULPES

Vulpes in domum profecta mimi, et singula ipsius vasa perscrutans, invenit et caput larvae ingeniose fabricatum, quo et accepto manibus, ait, O quale caput, et cerebrum non habet.

104

which), **accepto** being taken up, **manibus** in (the fox's) hands, **ait** (the fox) says, **O quale** O what **caput** a head, **et** and **cerebrum** a brain **non habet** it doesn't have.

Fabula the fable (is written) **in** *into (i.e. for)* **viros** *men,* **magnificos** *magnificent* **quidem** *indeed* **corpore** *in body,* **sed** *but* **animo** *in mind* **inconsultos** *thoughtless.*

Fabula in viros, magnificos quidem corpore, sed animo inconsultos.

105

Decoding Latin – Day 5

Don't forget the rules:

1. Don't try to memorise anything
2. Focus on the story, not the language – don't try to analyse!
3. Read one section from the left column and then the same from the right.
4. *Always read for speed and general gist, not for accuracy and perfection.*

CARBONARIUS A COLLIER (I.E. A CHARCOAL BURNER) **ET FULLO** AND A FULLER (I.E. ONE WHO CLEANS CLOTH)

CARBONARIUS ET FULLO

Carbonarius a collier (i.e. someone who burns charcoal) in in quadam a certain habitans living domo house (i.e. living in a certain house), rogabat asked fullonem a fuller etiam also advenientem coming to (him) secum with himself cohabitare to live together (i.e. coming

Carbonarius in quadam habitans domo, rogabat fullonem etiam advenientem secum cohabitare.

106

to a fuller, he asked him to live with himself).

Fullo *the fuller* autem *but (i.e. but the fuller)* respondens *answering,* ait *said:*

Fullo autem respondens, ait:

Sed *but* non *not* hoc *this* possem *would be able* ego *I (i.e. I wouldn't be able)* facere *to do (it);*

Sed non hoc possem ego facere;

timeo *I fear* enim *for (i.e. for I am afraid),* ne *lest (i.e. I'm afraid that),* quae *(those things) which* ego *I* delavo *wash out* tu *you* fuligine *with soot* repleas *may refill.*

timeo enim, ne, quae ego delavo tu fuligine repleas.

Fabula significat the fable signifies, omne *(that) every (thing)* dissimile *dissimilar* esse *to be (i.e. is)* insociabile *unsociable.*

Fabula significat, omne dissimile esse insociabile.

PISCATORES THE FISHERMEN

PISCATORES

107

Piscatores fishermen trahebant drew verriculum a drag-net, quod which, quum when grave heavy foret it might be (i.e. when it was heavy), gaudebant they rejoiced, et exultabant and exalted, multum much inesse to be in (there) praedae of prey existimanes thinking (i.e. thinking it was heavy because there was a lot of their prey, the fish, inside the net);

Sed but quum when in into litus the shore ipsum it (i.e. the net) traxissent they had drawn, piscesque and fish[5] paucos few (i.e. and few fish) quidem indeed, sed but lapidem a stone in in eo it permagnum very large (i.e. a very large stone in the net) invenissent they had

Piscatores trahebant verriculum, quod quum grave foret, gaudebant, et exultabant, multum inesse praedae existimanes;

Sed quum in litus ipsum traxissent, piscesque paucos quidem, sed lapidem in eo permagnum invenissent, tristari ceperunt, et moerere, non tam ob piscium paucitatem, quam quod et contraria ante animo presumpserant.

---

[5] **Que** on the end of a word indicates 'and' before it: **piscesque (pisces que)** → and fish

108

found (i.e. when they'd found few fish but a very large stone in it), **tristari** to be saddened **ceperunt** they began (i.e. they became saddened), **et** and **moerere** to mourn, **non** not **tam** so much **ob** on account of **piscium** of the fishes **paucitatem** the paucity (i.e. not so much because of the very small amount) of fish, **quam** as **quod** because **et** and (i.e. also) **contraria** contrary things (i.e. the complete opposite) **ante** before **animo** in their mind **presumpserant** they had anticipated (i.e. they were sadder because they had anticipated something else in their minds).

Quidam a certain one **autem** but (i.e. but a certain one) **inter** among **eos** them **natu** in birth **grandior** greater (i.e. older) **dixit** siad;

Quidam autem inter eos natu grandior dixit;

Ne not **tristemur** we should be sad (i.e,. we shouldn't be sad), **o socii** O companions!

Nam for **voluptati** to pleasure, **ut** as **videtur** it is seen (i.e. as it seems), **soror** the sister **est** is **tristitia** sadness (i.e. sadness is a sister to pleasure);

Et and **nos** us **igitur** therefore **oportebat** it did behove us (i.e. we ought) **tantum** so much **ante** before **laetatos** having rejoiced (i.e. having rejoiced so much earlier), **omnino** altogether **aliqua** in some **in** in **re** matter (i.e. in some matter/manner) **etiam** also **tristari** to be saddened (i.e. it's fitting/we ought to be saddened, having already been so happy earlier).

Ne tristemur, o socii!

Nam voluptati, ut videtur, soror est tristitia;

Et nos igitur oportebat, tantum ante laetatos, omnino aliqua in re etiam tristari.

Fabula significat the fable signifies, **non oportere** *(that) not to behove (i.e. that one ought not)* **tristari** *to be saddened* **frustrate** *by a frustrated* **spe** *hope*.

Fabula significat, non oportere tristari frustrate spe.

Decoding Latin – Day 6

Don't forget the rules:

1. Don't try to memorise anything
2. Focus on the story, not the language – don't try to analyse!
3. Read one section from the left column and then the same from the right.
4. *Always read for speed and general gist, not for accuracy and perfection.*

JACTATOR THE BOASTER

Vir *a man* quidam *a certain (i.e. a certain man)*, peregrinatus *having travelled abroad*, deinde *afterwards* in *into* suam *his own* patriam *country* reversus *having returned*, aliaque *and other things* multa *many (i.e. many and varied things)* in *in* diversis *different* viriliter *manfully* gessisse *to have carried on* locis *in places (i.e. to have done many things in different places very manfully)* jactabant *he boasted (i.e. he boasted*

JACTATOR

Vir quidam peregrinatus, deinde in suam patriam reversus, aliaque multa in diversis viriliter gessisse locis jactabant atque etiam Rhodi saltasse saltum, quem nullus eius loci potuerit saltare:

112

about having performed many and varied things manfully in different places) **atque** and **etiam** even **Rhodi** at Rhodes **saltasse** to have jumped **saltum** a jump, **quem** which **nullus** no one **eius** of that **loci** place **potuerit** had been able **saltare** to jump:

Ad to **hoc** this (feat) **et** and (i.e. also) **testes** witnesses, **qui** who **ibi** there **interfuerant** had been present, **dicebat** he said **se** himself **habere** to have (i.e. he said he had witnesses to this feat who had been there).

Quidam a certain one **autem** but (i.e. but a certain man) **ex** out of **iis** those (i.e. but one of those), **qui** who **aderant** were present, **respondens** answering **ait** said:

Ad hoc et testes, qui ibi interfuerant, dicebat se habere.

Quidam autem ex iis, qui aderant, respondens ait:

113

Heus *ho!* tu *you,* si *if* verum *true* hoc *this* est *is (i.e. if this is true),* non est *there isn't* tibi *to you* opus *a need (i.e. you have no need)* testibus *for (i.e. of) witnesses:*	Heus tu, si verum hoc est, non est tibi opus testibus:
En *behold* Rhodus *Rhodes;*	En Rhodus;
En *behold* et *and (i.e. also: behold also)* salvus *the jump.*	En et salvus.
Fabula significat the fable signifies, nisi *(that) unless* prompta *a ready* rei *of the matter* demonstratio *demonstration* sit *there might be (i.e. unless there's a ready demonstration of a thing),* omnem *all* sermonem *speech* supervacuum *superfluous* esse *to be (i.e. all speech is empty)*	*Fabula significat, nisi prompta rei demonstratio sit, omnem sermonem supervacuum esse*
IMPOSSIBILIA IMPOSSIBLE (THINGS)	**IMPOSSIBILIA PROMITTENS**

PROMITTENS
PROMISING

Vir *a man* pauper *poor (i.e. a poor man)* aegrotans *being sick*, et *and* male *badly* affectus *affected (i.e. in bad shape)*, quum *when* a *by* medicis *the doctors* desperatus *despaired of* esset *he might have been (i.e. when he was despaired of by the doctors)*, deos *the gods* rogabat *he asked*;

Si *if* sanitatem *health* sibi *to himself* rursus *again* fecissent *they made (i.e. if they restored his health)*, centum *a hundred* boves *oxen* ipsis *to themselves* se *himself* oblaturum *about to offer* esse *to be* pollicens *promising* in sacrificium *in sacrifice (i.e. promising that he would offer a hundred oxen in sacrifice if they restored his health).*

Vir pauper aegrotans, et male affectus, quum a medicis desperatus esset, Deos rogabat;

Si sanitatem sibi rursus fecissent, centum boves ipsis se oblaturum esse pollicens in sacrificium.

115

Uxore with wife **autem** but **ejus** of him (i.e. but with his wife) **sciscitata** having enquired,	Uxore autem ejus sciscitata,
Et and **ubi** where **tibi** to you **haec** these things **erunt** there will be (i.e. where will you get these things) **si** if **convalueris** you will have recovered (i.e. if you recover)?	Et ubi tibi haec erunt si convalueris?
Ille he **ait** says, **Putas** do you think **enim** for (i.e. for do you think) **surgere** to rise **me** me to rise (i.e. that [if] I rise) **hinc** from here, **ut** that **dii** the gods **haec** these things **a** from **me** me **repentant** would seek back?	Ille ait, Putas enim surgere me hinc, ut Dii haec a me repentant?
Fabula significat the fable signifies, *multos* (that) many (people) *facile* easily *polliceri* promise, *quae* (things) which *re* in fact *perfinere* to perform (i.e. actually to do) *non sperent* they hope not	*Fabula significat, multos facile polliceri, quae re perfinere non sperent.*

(i.e. people promise things they hope they won't have to do).

Decoding Latin – Day 7

Don't forget the rules:

1. Don't try to memorise anything
2. Focus on the story, not the language – don't try to analyse!
3. Read one section from the left column and then the same from the right.
4. *Always read for speed and general gist, not for accuracy and perfection.*

MALIGNUS THE MALIGNANT

Vir a man malignus malignant (i.e. a malignant man) ad to eum him, qui who in in Delphis Delphi est is (i.e. who is in Delphi), ivit went Apollinem Apollo (i.e. a malignant man went to that Apollo, which is in Delphi), tentare to test eum him volens wanting (i.e. wanting to test him).

Atque and ideo for that reason, comprehenso with a seized (i.e. having

MALIGNUS

Vir malignus ad eum, qui in Delphis est, ivit Apollinem, tentare eum volens.

Atque ideo, comprehenso passerculo manu, et eo veste contecto, stetitque

118

seized) **passerculo** a little sparrow **manu** in his hand, **et** and **eo** with it **veste** in (his) garment(s) **contecto** covered, **stetitque** and he stood **proxime** very near **tripodem** the tripod (of burning incense), **ac** and **rogavit** asked **deum** the god, **dicens** saying,

O Apollo O Apollo, **quod** what **manibus** in my hands **fero** I'm carrying **utrum** whether **vivum** alive **est** it is, **an** or **mortuum** dead (i.e. what I'm carrying in my hands, is it alive or dead)?

Statuens determining (i.e. intending), **si** (that) if **mortuum** dead **diceret** he (i.e. Apollo) would say, **vivum** alive **ostendere** to show **passerculum** the little sparrow (i.e. that if Apollo said it was dead, he would show the little sparrow alive);

proxime tripodem, ac rogavit Deum, dicens,

O Apollo, quod manibus fero utrum vivum est, an mortuum?

Statuens, si mortuum diceret, vivum ostendere passerculum;

Sin but if **vivum** alive (i.e. but if Apollo said it was alive), **statim** immediately **suffocatum** having been suffocated **mortuum** dead **illum** him (i.e. the little sparrow) **proferre** to produce (i.e. if Apollo said alive, he would immediately suffocate him and produce him dead).	Sin vivum, statim suffocatum mortuum illum proferre.
Sed but **deus** the god, **maligna** with malignant **ipsius** of this (man) **cognita** being known **mente** mind (i.e. knowing what he was planning), **ait** said	Sed Deus, maligna ipsius cognita mente, ait
Utrum whether, **heus** ho! **tu** you (heus was the Latin equivalent of Ha! In English), **vis** you want **facere** to make/do, **facite** do (i.e. whichever you want to do, do):	Utrum, heus tu, vis facere, facite:
Penes in the power of **te** you **enim** for **est** it is (i.e. for it's in your power)	Penes te enim est illud facere, sive vivum, quod

120

illud that facere to make/do, sive either vivum alive, quod what contines you're holding, sive or mortuum dead ostendere to show (i.e. it's in your power to show what you're holding as alive or dead).

Fabula significat the fable signifies, deum (that) god neque neither decipi to be deceived posse to be able (i.e. that god can neither be deceived), neque nor quicquam (can) anything eum him latere hide from (i.e. nor can anything hide from him).

PISCATORES THE FISHERMEN

Piscatores fishermen egressi (having) gone out ad for venationem hunting (i.e. to hunt), quum when multo with much tempore time defatigati wearied

contines, sive mortuum ostendere.

Fabula significat, deum neque decipi posse, neque quicquam eum latere.

PISCATORES

Piscatores egressi ad venationem, quum multo tempore defatigati nihil cepissent, et admodum

121

(i.e. when they were wearied after a long time) nihil nothing cepissent they had taken (i.e. they'd caught nothing), et and admodum very much tristabantur they were saddened, et and discedere to leave apparabant they prepared (i.e. they prepared to leave).

Sed but statim immediately thunnus a tunny[6], a by maximis greater (i.e. larger) petitus being sought (i.e. chased) piscibus fishes (i.e. a tuna, being chased by larger fishes), in into navigium the vessel ipsorum of the same (fishermen) insiluit leaped (i.e. a tuna leapt into the fishermen's vessel):

tristabantur, et discedere apparabant.

Sed statim Thunnus, a maximis petitus piscibus, in navigium ipsorum insiluit:

---

[6] A kind of tuna, usually a bluefin

122

Illi they vero but (i.e. but they), hoc with this (tunny) capto being taken (i.e. having grabbed the fish), cum voluptate with pleasure abiere they departed. *Fabula significat the fable signifies,* saepe *(that) often* quae *(those things) which* ars *art (i.e. skill)* non praebuit *doesn't afford (i.e. those things which one can't get through skill),* ea *those things* donasse *to have given* fortunam *fortune (.e. fortune gives).*	Illi vero, hoc capto, cum voluptate abiere. *Fabula significat, saepe (quae ars non praebuit, ea donasse fortunam.*

123

Decoding Latin – Day 8

Don't forget the rules:

1. Don't try to memorise anything
2. Focus on the story, not the language – don't try to analyse!
3. Read one section from the left column and then the same from the right.
4. *Always read for speed and general gist, not for accuracy and perfection.*

DECEPTOR THE DECEIVER	**DECEPTOR**
Vir a man pauper poor (i.e. a poor man) aegrotans being sick, vovebat vowed diis to the gods, si (that) if evaderet he would escape (the disease), boves oxen centum a hundred (i.e. a hundred oxen) in into (i.e. for) sacrificium a sacrifice se himself oblaturum about to offer (i.e. he vowed he would offer 100 oxen in sacrifice if he could escape death);	Vir pauper aegrotans vovebat Diis, si evaderet, boves centum in sacrificium se oblaturum;

124

Sed but dii the gods, tentare to test eum him volentes wanting (i.e. wanting to test him), a from morbo the disease liberarunt freed (him, i.e. they freed him from the disease).	Sed Dii, tentare eum volentes, a morbo liberarunt.
At but ille he, refectus being restored (i.e. being restored to good health), quoniam since bobus the oxen carebat he lacked, ex from pasta a paste boves oxen centum a hundred (i.e. a hundred oxen) a by se himself formatos moulded in ara on the altar positos placed sacrificavit he sacrificed (i.e. he sacrificed a hundred oxen made by himself out of paste, and placed on the altar):	At ille refectus , quoniam bobus carebat, ex pasta boves centum a se formatos in ara positos sacrificavit :
Sed but dii the gods statuentes determining eum him punire to punish (i.e. deciding to punish	Sed Dii statuentes eum punire, in somniis adstantes ei, dixerunt:

125

him), in in somniis his dreams adstantes standing near ei to him (i.e. coming to him in his dreams), dixerunt they said:

Abi go away ad to litus the shore ad to eum that locum place (i.e. to a particular place):

Illic there enim for (i.e. for there) Atticas Attic mille a thousand drachmas drachmas (i.e. a thousand Attic drachmas) invenies you will find (i.e. for you will find there a thousand Aattic drachmas).

Ille he autem but (i.e. but he) excitatus being roused (i.e. awoken), cum voluptate with pleasure et and alacritate alacrity ad to demonsratum the pointed-out locum place perrexit proceeded, aurum the gold disquirens diligently seeking (i.e.

Abi ad litus ad eum locum:

Illic enim Atticas mille drachmas invenies.

Ille autem excitatus, cum voluptate et alacritate ad demonsratum locum perrexit, aurum disquirens.

126

diligently seeking the gold).

Sed but **illic** there **in** into **piratas** pirates **incidit** he fell into (i.e. he ran into pirates), **ab** by **ipsisque** and these same (i.e. and by these same pirates) **comprehensus** seized **est** he is (i.e. was; he was captured by these same pirates).

Captus being taken, **ergo** therefore, **ut** that **dimitteretur** he might be dismissed (i.e. let go) **piratas** the pirates **orabat** he prayed (i.e. he begged the pirates that he might be let go), **mille** a thousand **auri** of gold **talenta** talents (i.e. a thousand talents of gold) **se** himself **daturum** about to give (i.e. he would give) **ipsis** to them **promittens** promising (i.e. he begged them to let him go,

Sed illic in piratas incidit, ab ipsisque comprehensus est.

Captus ergo, ut dimitteretur piratas orabat, mille auri talenta se daturum ipsis promittens.

127

promising to give them a thousand gold talents).

Sed but quum when non crederetur he was not believed, abactus (he was) driven away ab ipsis by them, divenditus sold est he is (i.e. was) mille (for) a thousand drachmis drachma.

Fabula significat the fable signifies, mendacibus (that) to lying hominibus people inimicum hostile esse to be (i.e. is) deum god (i.e., that god is hostile to people who lie).

RANAE THE FROGS

Ranae frogs duae two (i.e. two frogs) in in palude a marsh pascebantur were fed (i.e. were fed in a marsh), aestate in summer autem but (i.e. but in summer), sicata having dried up palude the marsh

---

Sed quum non crederetur, abactus ab ipsis, divenditus est mille drachmis.

Fabula significat, mendacibus hominibus inimicum esse Deum.

RANAE

Ranae duae in palude pascebantur, aestate autem sicata palude, illa derelicta, querebant aliam:

128

(i.e. with the marsh dried up), **illa** it **derelicta** (was) abandoned, **querebant** they sought (i.e. looked for) **aliam** another:

Et and, **quidem** indeed, **profundum** a deep **invenerunt** they found **puteum** well (i.e. they found a deep well).

Quo which **viso** being seen, **altera** the one **alteri** to the other **inquit** said (i.e. one said to the other),

Descendamus let's go down, **heus tu** hey you, **in** into **hunc** this **puteum** well.

Illa she **vero** but (i.e. but she/the other) **respondens** answering, **ait** said:

Et quidem profundum invenerunt puteum.

Quo viso, altera alteri inquit,

Descendamus, heus tu, in hunc puteum.

Illa vero respondens ait:

129

Si if *igitur* therefore, *et* and (i.e. also) *hic* here *acqua* the water *aruerit* will have dried up (i.e. if the water also dries up here), *quomodo* in what way (i.e. how) *ascendemus* will we come (back) up?

Fabula declarat the fable declares, *non opportere* (that) not to behove (i.e. that one ought not) *inconsiderate* inconsiderately *res* things *aggredi* to attempt (i.e. that one oughtn't attempt things without thought).

Si igitur et hic acqua aruerit, quomodo ascendemus?

Fabula declarat, non opportere inconsiderate res aggredi.

Decoding Latin – Day 9

Don't forget the rules:

1. Don't try to memorise anything
2. Focus on the story, not the language – don't try to analyse!
3. Read one section from the left column and then the same from the right.
4. *Always read for speed and general gist, not for accuracy and perfection.*

SENEX THE OLD MAN **ET** AND **MORS** DEATH

SENEX ET MORS

Senex an old man, quondam formerly (i.e. once, an old man), sectis being cut e from monte a mountain lignis logs (i.e. having cut logs from a mountain), ac and in into (i.e. onto) humeros his shoulders elevatis having lifted (them), ubi when multam much viam way (i.e. a long way) oneratus burdened ivisset he might have gone (i.e. when, burdened, he'd gone a long way), defessus (he

Senex, quondam, sectis e monte lignis, ac in humeros elevatis, ubi multam viam oneratus ivisset, defessus, et deposuit ligna, et Mortem ut veniret, invocabat.

was) tired, et and deposuit put down ligna the logs, et and Mortem Death ut that veniret he (i.e. Death) should come, invocabat he invoked (i.e. he invoked Death to come).

At but, Morte with Death illico immediately adstante standing near, et and causam the reason rogante asking (i.e. asking the reason), qua for which se himself vocasset he (i.e. the old man) had called (i.e. Death asked for what reason the old man had called him);

Senex the old man ait said, ut so that onus burden hoc this (i.e. this burden) super over (i.e. upon) humeros (my) shoulders imponeres you might place mihi for me.

At, Morte illico adstante, et causam rogante, qua se vocasset;

Senex ait, ut onus hoc super humeros imponeres mihi.

Fabula significat the fable signifies, *omnem* (that) every *hominem* person *vitae* of life *studiosum* zealous *esse* to be (i.e. that everyone is fond of life), *et* and *licet* although, *infinitis* in infinite *periculis* dangers *immersus* immersed (i.e. and, although, covered in infinite dangers), *videatur* he may seem *mortem* death *appetere* to seek (i.e. he may seem to seek death), *tamen* yet *vivere* to live *multo* much *magis* more *quam* than *mori* to die *eligere* to choose (i.e. yet they choose to live much more than to die).

ANUS THE OLD WOMAN ET AND MEDICUS THE DOCTOR

Mulier a woman *anus* an old woman *dolens* grieving (i.e. suffering in) *oculos* the eyes, *conduxit* hired *medicum* a physician

Fabula significat, omnem hominem vitae studiosum esse, et licet, infinitis periculis immersus, videatur mortem appetere, tamen vivere multo magius quam mori eligere.

ANUS ET MEDICUS

Mulier anus dolens oculos, conduxit medicum quendam mercede, conventione facta, si se

133

quendam a certain (i.e. a certain physician) mercede with the reward, conventione by agreement facta being made (i.e. with the agreed reward/payment) , si (that) if se herself curaret he cured (i.e. if he cured her), pactam the agreed mercedem reward ei to him se herself daturam about to give (i.e. that she would pay him if he cured her);	curaret, pactam mercedem ei se daturam;
Sin but if, autem however, minime not at all (was she cured), nihil nothing daturam she was about to give (i.e. she would give nothing).	Sin autem minime, nihil daturam.
Aggressus attempted est he is (i.e. he attempted) igitur therefore, medicus the doctor curam a cure (i.e. the doctor attempted, therefore, a cure):	Aggressus est igitur medicus curam:

134

Quotidie *daily* vero *but (i.e. but every day)* recedens *going back* ad *to* vetulam *the old woman*, et *and* oculos *the eyes* ei *for her* ungens *anointing (i.e. anointing her eyes for her)*, quum *when* illa *she* nequaquam *by no means* videre *to see* posset *was able (i.e. when she couldn't see at all)* ea *in that* hora *hour* ob *on account of* unctionem *the anointing*, ipse *he himself* vas *vessel* aliquod *some (i.e. some vessel)* ex *out of* domo *the house* auferens *carrying away* quotidie *daily* discedebat *departed (i.e. he left each day stealing something from her house)*.

Anus *the old woman*, igitur *therefore*, suam *her own* supellectilem *furniture* videbat *saw* singulis *in each* diebus *days (i.e. each day)* minui *diminished* adeo *thus (i.e.*

Quotidie vero recedens ad vetulam, et oculos ei ungens, quum illa nequaquam videre posset ea hora ob unctionem, ipse vas aliquod ex domo auferens quotidie discedebat.

Anus igitur suam supellectilem videbat singulis diebus minui adeo, ut tandem omnino illi senatae nihil relinqueretur.

135

in this way), **ut** so that **tandem** at last **omnino** wholly **illi** to her, **senatae** (now) healed, **nihil** nothing **relinqueretur** was left (i.e. wholly nothing/nothing at all was left to her when she was healed).

At but **medicus** the doctor, **quum** when **iam** now (i.e. at that time) **pactam** the agreed **pecuniam** money **ab** from **ea** her **efflagitaret** might have demanded (i.e. when he demanded the payment), **ut** as **quae** who (i.e. as she) **pure** clearly **iam** now **videret** would see (i.e. since she could clearly now see), **et** and **testes** witnesses **adduceret** brought up;

Magis rather, **certe** surely, **ait** says **illa** she, **nunc** now **nihil** nothing **video** I see (i.e. I see nothing now):

At medicus quum iam pactam pecuniam ab ea efflagitaret, ut quae pure iam videret, et testes adduceret;

Magis certe, ait illa, nunc nihil video:

136

Nam *for* quum *when* oculis *with my eyes* laborabam *I laboured* (i.e. when my eyes worked), multa *many things* mea *mine* (i.e. my many things) in *in* mea *my* videbam *I saw* domo *house* (i.e. I saw many things in my house);

Nunc *now* autem *but* (i.e. but now), quum *when* me *me* tu *you* videre *to see* inquis *you declare* (i.e. when you say I see), nihil *nothing* omnino *at all* ex *out of* illis *these* video *do I see* (i.e. I see none of these things).

Fabula significat the fable signifies, pravos (that) corrupt homines people, ex out of iis those things, quae which agant they may do, ignaros unknowing contra against seipsos themselves argumentum a charge afferre bring (i.e. that

Nam quum oculis laborabam, multa mea in mea videbam domo;

Nunc autem, quum me tu videre inquis, nihil omnino ex illis video.

Fabula significat, pravos homines, ex iis, quae agant, ignaros contra seipsos argumentum afferre.

depraved people unwittingly bring a charge against themselves in the things they do).

Decoding Latin – Day 10

Don't forget the rules:

1. Don't try to memorise anything
2. Focus on the story, not the language – don't try to analyse!
3. Read one section from the left column and then the same from the right.
4. *Always read for speed and general gist, not for accuracy and perfection.*

AGRICOLA THE FARMER ET AND FILII THE SONS IPSIUS OF HIM (I.E. AND HIS SONS)	**AGRICOLA ET FILII IPSIUS**
Agricola a farmer quidam a certain (i.e. a certain farmer) vita from life excessurus about to depart (i.e. about to depart from life), ac and volens wanting suos his own filios sons periculum a trial facere to make (i.e. to make a trial) a trial de from (i.e. concering/about) agricultura agriculture (i.e. wanting his sons to make	Agricola quidam vita excessurus, ac volens suos filios periculum facere de agricultura, vocatis ipsis, ait, Filii mei, ego jam e vita discedo, vos autem, si quae in vinea a me occultata sum, quaesieritis, invenietis omnia.

139

a try of agriculture), vocatis with called to himself ipsis them (i.e. having called them to himself), ait he said, Filii sons mei mine (i.e. my sons), ego I jam now e from vita life discedo I depart (i.e. I'm now leaving life), vos you autem but (i.e. but you), si if quae those things which in in vinea the vineyard a by me me occultata hidden sum I am (i.e. which I've hidden in the vineyard), quaesieritis (if) you should seek, invenietis you will find omnia all (those things which I've hidden).

Illi they igitur therefore, rati having thought thesaurum (that) a treasure illic there defossum buried esse to be (i.e. thinking that a treasure was buried there), omnem all vineae of the vineyard terram the

Illi igitur, rati thesaurum illic defossum esse, omnem vineae terram post interitum patris suffoderunt, et thesaurum quidem non invenerunt, sed vinea pulchre fossa

140

earth (i.e. all the earth of the vineyard) post after interitum the death patris of their father suffoderunt they dug up, et and thesaurum a treasure, quidem indeed, non invenerunt they didn't find, sed but vinea the vineyard pulchre beautifully fossa dug up multiplicem many-fold fructum fruit reddidit gave back (i.e. the vineyard gave back plenty of fruit).

multiplicem fructum reddidit.

Fabula significat the fable signifies, laborem (that) labour thesaurum a treasure esse be (i.e. is) hominibus for people (i.e. that labour is a treasure for people).

Fabula significat, laborem thesaurum esse hominibus.

HERUS THE MASTER ET AND CANES HIS DOGS

HERUS ET CANES

Vir a man quidam a certain (i.e. a certain man) a tempestate by a tempest

Vir quidam a tempestate in suo suburbio deprehensus, primum

in in suo his own suburbio suburb deprehensus being caught (i.e. being caught by a tempest in his own suburb), primum first oves the sheep comedit ate up (i.e. he first ate the sheep), dehinc next capras the goats.

Tempestate with the tempest, autem but (i.e. but with the tempest) invalescente growing stronger, et and (i.e. also) operarios the working boves oxen, jugulatos being strangled, comedit he ate (them) up.

Canes the dogs vero but (i.e. but the dogs), his with these (things) visis seen (i.e. having seen these things happen) dixerunt said inter se amongst themselves, 'Sed but fugiamus let us flee nos us (i.e. we should flee) hinc from here.'

oves comedit, dehinc capras.

Tempestate autem invalescente, et operarios boves jugulatos comedit.

Canes vero, his visis dixerunt inter se, 'Sed fugiamus nos hinc.'

Si *if* enim *for (i.e. for if)* operariis *from the working* bobus *oxen* herus *master* noster *our (i.e. our master)* non abstinent *doesn't refrain*, quomodo *how* nobis *from us* abstinebit *will he refrain (i.e. how will he refrain from us)*?

Fabula significat *the fable signifies*, eos *(that) those* maxime *mostly* fugere *to flee* et cavere *and to beware* opportere *to behove (i.e. that one ought to flee and be wary of chiefly those)*, qui *who* ne *not* suis *from their own* quidem *indeed (i.e. not even from their own)* abstinent *refrain*.

Si enim operariis bobus herus noster non abstinent, quomodo nobis abstinebit?

Fabula significat, eos maxime fugere et cavere opportere, qui ne suis quidem abstinent.

143

Decoding Latin – Day 11

Don't forget the rules:

1. Don't try to memorise anything
2. Focus on the story, not the language – don't try to analyse!
3. Read one section from the left column and then the same from the right.
4. *Always read for speed and general gist, not for accuracy and perfection.*

MULIER THE WOMAN ET AND GALLINA (HER) HEN

MULIER ET GALLINA

Mulier a woman quadam a certain (i.e. a certain woman) vidua widow (i.e. a certain widow woman) gallinem a hen habebat had (i.e. had a hen), singulis in each diebus days (i.e. every day) ovum an egg sibi for her parientem producing (i.e. she had a hen producing an egg for her every day):

Mulier quadam vidua gallinem habebat, singulis diebus ovum sibi parientem:

Rata *having thought* vero *but (i.e. but having thought)*, si *(that) if* plus *more* gallinae *to the hen* hordei *of barley* projiceret *she would cast (i.e. if she threw more barley to the hen)*, eam *it* bis *twice* parituram *would produce* die *in (one) day*, hoc *this* fecit *she did*.

Sed *but* gallina *the hen* pinguefacta *being fattened*, ne *not* semel *once* quidem *indeed (i.e. not even once)* die *(each) day* parere *to produce* potuit *was able*.

Fabula significat the fable signifies, eos *(that) those*, qui *who* ob *on account of* avaritiam *(their) avarice* plurimum *more* sunt *are* appetentes *seeking*, et *and* ea *those (things)* quae *which* adsunt *are present (i.e. which they have)*, amittere *(they) lose (i.e. the fable*

Rata vero, si plus gallinae hordei projiceret, eam bis parituram die, hoc fecit.

Sed gallina pinguefacta, ne semel quidem die parere potuit.

Fabula significat, eos, qui ob avaritiam plurimum sunt appetentes, et ea quae adsunt, amittere.

signifies that those seeking more on account of their greed, lose the things they have).

MORSUS BITTEN A BY CANE A DOG

Morsus *bitten* a cane *by a dog* quidam *a certain (person, i.e. a certain person, bitten by a dog)* medicaturum *(someone) about to heal* circuibat *he went around* quaerens *seeking (i.e. he went around looking for someone to heal him).*

Quum *when* autem *but (i.e. but when)* occurrisset *might have run up* quidam *a certain (person)* ei *to him (i.e. but when a certain person had met him),* et *and* cognosceret *would know* quod *what* quaerebat *he sought (i.e. what was looking for),* Heus tu *hark you,* ait *he*

MORSUS A CANE

Morsus a cane quidam medicaturum circuibat quaerens.

Quum autem occurrisset quidam ei, et cognosceret quod quaerebat, Heus tu, ait, si sanari vis, accipe panem, atque eo sanguinem vulneris sicca, et ei, qui momordit, cani ad edendum da:

146

said, si if sanari to be healed vis you want (i.e. if you want to be healed), accipe receive panem bread, atque and eo with it sanguinem the blood vulneris of the wound sicca dry up, et and ei to that, qui who momordit has bitten (you), cani dog (i.e. to that dog who has bitten you) ad for edendum eating da give (it) (i.e. give it to the dog that bit you to eat):

At but is he, ridendo laughing, ait said, Sed but si if hoc this fecero I did (i.e. but if I did this), oportebit it will behove me me (i.e. I must) ab by omnibus all, qui who in in urbe the city sunt are (i.e. who are in the city), canibus dogs morderi to be bitten (i.e. I must be bitten by all the dogs in the city).

At is ridendo ait, Sed si hoc fecero, oportebit me ab omnibus, qui in urbe sunt, canibus morderi.

147

Fabula significat the fable signifies, *pravos (that corrupt)* etiam even homines people (i.e. that even corrupt people) *beneficio* by kindness *affectos* affected (i.e. affected by kindness), *magis* more *ad* for *inferendam* bringing on *injuriam* an injury *exacti* be (i.e. are) sharpened (i.e. more attuned to) (i.e. the fable signifies that corrupt people, even affected by kindness, are sharpened more to an injury to be brought on by the kindness).

ADOLUSCENTULI THE YOUNG LADS ET AND COCUS THE COOK

Duo two *adoluscentuli* young men *Coco* to a cook *assidebant* sat near (i.e. sat near a cook), *et* and *Coco* with the cook *in* in *aliquo* some *domestico* domestic

Fabula significat, pravos etiam homines beneficio affectos, magis ad inferendam injuriam exacti.

ADOLUSCENTULI ET COCUS

Duo adoluscentuli Coco assidebant, et Coco in aliquo domestico opere occupato, alter horum partem quandam carnium subreptam in alterius demisit sinum.

148

opere work occupato engaged (i.e. with the cook being busy with some domestic work), alter the other (i.e. one) horum of these (young lads) partem a part quandam a certain (i.e. a certain part) carnium of the fleshes (i.e. a certain bit of meat) subreptam stolen in into alterius the other's demisit he sent down sinum bosom (i.e. having stolen a bit of meat, he placed it in the other's lap).

Converso being turned autem but Coco with the cook (i.e. but with the cook having turned), et and carnem the flesh (i.e. the meat) quaerente seeking (i.e. looking for the meat), qui he who abstulerat had carried (it) away, jurabat swore se (that) he himself non

Converso autem Coco, et carnem quaerente, qui abstulerat, jurabat se non habere:

habere not to have (i.e. he swore he didn't have it):

Qui he who autem but (i.e. but he who) habebat had (it), se (swore that) he himself non abstulisse not to have carried (it) away (i.e. he swore he hadn't stolen it).

Cocus the cook vero but (i.e. but the cook), cognita being known malitia the malice ipsorum of them (i.e. realising their malice/trick), ait said, 'Sed but, etsi although me me latueritis you may have escaped (i.e. though you may have escaped me), pejeratum a perjured deum god non igitur not, therefore, latebitis will you escape.

Fabula significat the fable signifies, quod that licet although homines people pejerantes perjuring (i.e. by

Qui autem habebat, se non abstulisse.

Cocus vero, cognita malitia ipsorum, ait, 'Sed, etsi me latueritis, pejeratum deum non igitur latebitis.

Fabula significat, quod licet homines pejerantes

150

swearing falsely/telling lies) **lateamus** *we may escape (i.e. though we, swearing falsely, may escape people),* **deum** *god,* **tamen** *however,* **non latebimus** *we will not escape.*

lateamus, deum tamen non latebimus.

Decoding Latin – Day 12

Don't forget the rules:

1. Don't try to memorise anything
2. Focus on the story, not the language – don't try to analyse!
3. Read one section from the left column and then the same from the right.
4. *Always read for speed and general gist, not for accuracy and perfection.*

INIMICI THE ENEMIES	**INIMICI**
Duo two quidem certain (i.e. a certain two, two people) inter between se themselves inimici enemies (i.e. who were mutual enemies) in in eadem the same navi ship navigabant were sailing;	Duo quidem inter se inimici in eadem navi navigabant;
Quorum of whom alter one in puppi in the stern, alter the other in prora in the prow sedebat sat.	Quorum alter in puppi, alter in prora sedebat.
Tempestate with a storm autem but (i.e. but with a	Tempestate autem superveniente, et nave jam

152

storm) **superveniente** coming up, **et** and **nave** with the ship **jam** now **submergenda** about to be sunk, **qui** he who **erat** was in **puppi** in the stern **gubernatorem** the pilot **rogabat** asked (i.e. asked the pilot), **utra** whether (or not) **pars** part **navigii** of the vessel **prius** before (i.e. first) **obruenda** to be overwhelmed **esset** would be (i.e. he asked whether any part of the ship would be destroyed first).

Quumque and when **ille** he **proram** the prow **dixisset** had said (i.e. and when he'd said the prow would be destroyed first), '**Sed** but **mihi** to me **non est** it's not **grave** a heavy (thing),' **ait** he said, '**mors** death (i.e. death isn't a heavy thing to me), **si** if **visurus** about to see **sum** I am **ante me** before me **inimicum** (my) enemy **morientem** dying (i.e.

submergenda, qui erat in puppi gubernatorem rogabat, utra pars navigii prius obruenda esset.

Quumque ille proram dixisset, 'Sed mihi non est grave,' ait, 'mors, si visurus sum ante me inimicum morientem.

153

death's not so bad if I get to see my enemy die first).

Fabula significat the fable signifies, *multos* (that) many *homines* people *nihil* nothing *suum* their own *damnum* loss *curare* to care (i..e that many people care nothing for their own loss), *si modo* if only *inimicus* enemies *suos* their own (i.e. their enemies) *videant* they may see *ante* before *se* themselves *male* badly *affectos* affected/injured.

FELIS THE CAT ET AND MURES THE MICE

In in *domo* a house *quadam* a certain (i.e. in a certain house) *quum* when *multi* many *esset* there might be *mures* mice (i.e. in a certain house, when there were many mice), *felis* a cat, *eo*

Fabula significat, multos homines nihil suum damnum curare, si modo inimicus suos videant ante se male affectos.

FELIS ET MURES

In domo quadam quum multi esset mures, felis, eo cognito, ivit eo, ac eorum singulos captos devorabat.

154

with this (fact) **cognito** being known, **ivit** he went **eo** to there (i.e. to the house), **ac** and **eorum** of them **singulos** each **captos** taken **devorabat** he devoured (i.e. he devoured them, capturing and eating them one by one).

At but **illi** they, **quotidie** every day **quum** when (i.e. when every day) **se** themselves **absumi** to be taken away **viderent** they saw (i.e. when they saw themselves being taken every day), **dixerunt** they said **inter** between (i.e. among) **se** themselves,

Ne that not **posthac** after this (i.e. henceforth) **infra** below **descendamus** we should descend (i.e. we shouldn't go down into the house anymore), **ne** lest **penitus** utterly

At illi, quotidie quum se absumi viderent, dixerunt inter se,

Ne posthac infra descendamus, ne penitus intereamus.

155

intereamus *we should perish*.

Nam *for* si *if* felis *the cat* non potest *isn't able* huc *to here* venire *to come* (i.e. if the cat can't get here), nos *we* salvi *safe* erimus *will be* (i.e. we'll be safe).

Sed *but* felis *the cat*, non *not* amplius *more* muribus *with the mice* descendentibus *descending* (i.e. but the cat, with the mice coming down no more), statuit *resolved* per astutiam *through* (i.e. by means of) cunning eos *them* decipiens *deceiving* evocare *to call out* (i.e. he resolved to call them out by cunning, deceiving them), et *and* jam *now* quum *when* pestulum *a bolt* quondam *certain* conscendisset *he had mounted* (i.e. when he'd

Nam si felis non potest huc venire, nos salvi erimus.

Sed felis, non amplius muribus descendentibus, statuit per astutiam eos decipiens evocare, et jam quum pestulum quondam conscendisset, de eo se suspendit, et mortuum se esse simulabat.

156

climbed on top of a certain bolt), de *from* eo *it* se *himself* suspendit *he suspended* (i.e. he hung himself from a bolt), et *and* mortuum *dead* se *himself* esse *to be* simulabat *he pretended* (i.e. and he pretended to be dead).

Ex *out of* muribus *the mice* autem *but* quidam *a certain* (one, i.e. but a certain on of the mice) acclinatus *being bent* (i.e. looking down), visoque *and having seen* eo *it*, ait *said*, Heus *ha!* tu *you*, etsi *although* saccus *a bag* fias *you become* (i.e. even if you become a bag), non *not* te *you* adibo *I will approach* (i.e. even if you become a bag I won't approach you).

Fabula significat the fable signifies, prudentes *(that) prudent* homines *people,*

Ex muribus autem quidam acclinatus, visoque eo, ait, Heus tu, etsi saccus fias, non te adibo.

Fabula significat, prudentes homines, quum aliquorum pravitatem experti fuerint,

157

quum when *aliquorum* of some people *pravitatem* the depravity *experti* being experienced *fuerint* they might have been (i.e. when they'd experienced the depravity of some people), *non amplius* no more *eorum* of them *falli* to be deceived *simulationibus* by pretences (i.e. prudent people, when they've experienced the depravity of some people, no more are they deceived by their pretences).

VULPES THE FOX ET AND SIMIUS THE APE

In *in* concilio *an assembly* quodam *once* irrationabilium *of irrational* animalium *animals* saltavit *danced* simius *an ape* (i.e. an ape once danced in an assembly of irrational animals), et *and*, approbatus *being*

non amplius eorum falli simulationibus.

VULPES ET SIMIUS

In concilio quodam irrationabilium animalium saltavit simius, et approbatus, Rex ab ipsis electus est.

approved (of by them), Rex *king* ab ipsis *by them* electus *elected* est *he is* (i.e. being approved of by them, he was elected as king).

Vulpes *a fox* autem *but* (i.e. but a fox) quum *when* ei *to him* invideret *he might envy* (i.e. but a fox, since he envied him), quum *when* in casse *in a net* quodam *a certain* (i.e. in a certain net) carnem *flesh* vidisset *he'd seen* (i.e. when he'd seen some meat in a particular net), simium *the ape* secum *with himself* sumptum *taken* illuc *there* duxit *he led* (i.e. he led the ape, taken up, with him), quod *that* invenisset *he'd found* ipse *he himself* thesaurum *treasure* illum *that*, dicens *saying* (i.e. saying that he himself had found that treasure), non tamen *not, however*, et *and* se *himself* uti *to use* eo *that*

Vulpes autem quum ei invideret, quum in casse quodam carnem vidisset, simium secum sumptum illuc duxit, quod invenisset ipse thesaurum illum, dicens, non tamen et se uti teo;

159

(i.e. that he himself, however, had not made use of it);

Quippe because, quum when lex the law regi to the king tribuerit had attributed (it, i.e. the fox said she hadn't used it because the law attributed it to the king):

Atque and hortata exhorted est she is (i.e. and she exhorted/encouraged) ipsum him, ut as regem the king, thesaurum the treasure accipere to receive.

At but ille he inconsiderate inconsiderately profectus having set out, et and captus captured a casse by the net, ut as quae she who decepisset had

Quippe quum lex regi tribuerit:

Atque hortata est ipsum, ut regem, thesaurum accipere.

At ille inconsiderate profectus, et captus a casse, ut quae decepisset, accusabat vulpem.

160

deceived (him), accusabat did accuse vulpem the fox.

Illa she autem but (i.e. but she) ei (said) to him, O simie O Ape, quum when talem such tu you habeas you may have stultitiam stupidity (i.e. O ape, when you have such stupidity), imperium the power in bruta in (i.e. over) the brute tenebis will you hold (i.e. shall you hold power over the animals when you have such stupidity)?

Illa autem ei, O simie, quum talem tu habeas stultitiam, imperium in bruta tenebis?

Fabula significat the fable signifies, *eos* (that) those, *qui* who *actiones* actions *aliquas* some (i.e. any actions) *inconsulte* unthinkingly *aggrediuntur* attempt, *in* into *infortunia* misfortunes *incidere* to fall (i.e. the fable signifies that those who do things unthinkingly fall into misfortune).

Fabula significat, eos, qui actiones aliquas inconsulte aggrediuntur, in infortunia incidere.

161

Decoding Latin – Day 13

Don't forget the rules:

1. Don't try to memorise anything
2. Focus on the story, not the language – don't try to analyse!
3. Read one section from the left column and then the same from the right.
4. *Always read for speed and general gist, not for accuracy and perfection.*

THUNNUS THE TUNNY FISH ET AND DELPHIN THE DOLPHIN

Thunnus a tunny fish[7] a delphino by a dolphin cursu in (his) course pressus being pressed, magnoque and with great impetu violence latus being born (i.e. and enduring great violence), quum when capiendus to be caught esset he might be (i.e. when he was about to be caught), inscius unknowing (i.e.

THUNNUS ET DELPHIN

Thunnus a delphino cursu pressus, magnoque impetu latus, quum capiendus esset, inscius ob vehementem impetum decidit in insulam quandam, ab eodem vero impetu et delphin cum eo ejectus est.

---

[7] A kind of tuna, usually a bluefin

unintentionally) **ob** on account of **vehementem** vehement (i.e. excessive) **impetum** force **decidit** he fell **in insulam** into (i.e. onto) an island **quandam** certain (i.e. he fell/landed on a certain island), **ab** from **eodem** the same **vero** in truth, **impetu** force **et delphin** the dolphin also **cum eo** with him **ejectus** cast out **est** is (i.e. was: the dolphin was thrown out of the sea by the same force).

Thunnus the tunny **autem** but (i.e. but the tunny) **conversus** having turned, **et agentem** and the acting **animam** life (i.e. the dying) **delphinum** dolphin **conspicatus** having seen (i.e. and having seen the dolphin dying), **ait** says,

"**Non amplius** not more **mihi** to me **mors** death **molesta** troublesome **est**

	Thunnus autem conversus, et agentem animam delphinum conspicatus, ait,
	"Non amplius mihi mors molesta est, quum eum

164

is (i.e. death is no longer a problem for me), **quum** when **eum** him **videam** I might see (i.e. when I can see him), **qui** who **mihi** to me **causa** the cause **fuit** was **ipsius** of the same (thing, i.e. death), **una** in one (i.e. together) **mecum** with me **perire** to perish (i.e. death is no longer troublesome for me when I see him who was the cause of it dying with me)."

Fabula significat the fable signifies, *facile* (that) easily *miserias* miseries *ferre* to be *homines* people (i.e. that people bear miseries easily), *eos* those, *qui* who *illarum* of them (i.e. of the miseries) *auctores* the authors *fuerunt* were (i.e. those who were the authors of the trouble), *infeliciter* unfortunately *agere* to act *videntes* seeing (i.e. the fable signifies that people bear miseries easily, seeing those who were the

videam, qui mihi causa fuit ipsius, una mecum perire."

Fabula significat, facile miserias ferre homines, eos, qui illarum auctores fuerunt, infeliciter agere videntes

cause of it doing badly themselves)

MEDICUS THE PHYSICIAN ET AND AEGROTANS THE BEING SICK (I.E. AND THE SICK PERSON)

Medicus the physician **aegrotum** a sickened (person, i.e. a sick person) **curabat** attended to (i.e. a physician attended to a sick person):

Aegroto with the sickened **autem** but (i.e. but with the sick person) **mortuo** being dead, **ille** he (i.e. the doctor) **efferentibus** to (those) carrying out (i.e. to those burying him) **dicebat** said;

Homo man **hic** this (i.e. this man), **si** if **vino** from wine **abstinuisset** he might have abstained (i.e. if he'd

MEDICUS ET AEGROTANS

Medicus aegrotum curabat:

Aegroto autem mortuo, ille efferentibus dicebat;

Homo hic, si vino abstinuisset, et clysteribus

abstained from wine), **et** and **clysteribus** with clysters (i.e. enemas) **usus** used **fuisset** he might have been (i.e. and if he'd used clysters), **non interisset** he wouldn't have perished.

Quidam a certain (person) **autem** but (i.e. but a certain person) **ex iis** out of those **qui** who **aderant** were present, **respondens** answering, **ait** said, **Optime** excellent, **non oportebat** it didn't behove **te** you **haec** these things **nunc** now **dicere** to say (i.e. you didn't need to say these things now), **quum** when **nulla** no **utilitas** usefulness **est** there is; **sed** but **tunc** then **admonere** to admonish (i.e. warn), **quum** when **his** with them **uti** to use **poterat** he was able (i.e. it's no use saying these things now, you should have said them

usus fuisset, non interisset.

Quidam autem ex iis qui aderant, respondens, ait, Optime, non oportebat te haec nunc dicere, quum nulla utilitas est; sed tunc admonere, quum his uti poterat.

167

then when he could have used them).

Fabula siugnificat the fable signifies, *oportere* to behove *amicos* friends (i.e. that friends ought) *tempore* in time *necessitatis* of necessity *praebere* to afford *auxilia* helps (i.e. that friends ought to offer help in time of necessity); *et non* and not, *cum* when *jam* already *de rebus* about things *desperatur* it is despaired (i.e. and not when it's already despaired about things), *cavillari* to find fault.

AUCEPS THE BIRD-CATCHER ET AND VIPERA THE VIPER

Auceps a bird-catcher, visco with bird-lime accepto being taken, et arundinibus and reeds (i.e. having taken reeds and bird-lime), aucupatum to catch birds exiit he went

Fabula siugnificat, oportere amicos tempore necessitatis praebere auxilia; et non, cum jam de rebus desperatur, cavillari.

AUCEPS ET VIPERA

Auceps, visco accepto, et arundinibus, aucupatum exiit.

out (i.e. he went out to catch birds).

Viso being seen autem but turdo a thrush super upon alta a high arbore tree sedente sitting (i.e. but with a thrush being seen sitting in a high tree), et arundinibus and with the reeds inter between se themselves in longitudinem into (i.e. in) length conjunctis being joined (i.e. and having joined the reeds together in length), sursum upwards ad to eum him (i.e. the thrush) capere to take volens wanting (i.e. wanting to take him), suspiciebat he (i.e. the bird-catcher) looked up.

Viso autem turdo super alta arbore sedente, et arundinibus inter se in longitudinem conjunctis, sursum ad eum capere volens, suspiciebat.

Ceterum but ignarus ignorant, viperam a viper dormientem sleeping sub under pedibus his feet conculcavit he trampled (i.e. he unwittingly

Ceterum ignarus viperam dormientem sub pedibus conculcavit.

169

trampled under his feet a sleeping viper).

Quum when vero but (i.e. but when) irata being enraged, momordisset she (i.e. the viper) might have bitten ipsum him (i.e. but when the viper had bitten him), ille he jam now agens acting animam spirit (i.e. breathing out his life) dicebat he said;

Quum vero irata momordisset ipsum, ille jam agens animam dicebat;

Me me miserum wretched (i.e. poor me)! alium another enim for (i.e. for another) capere to take volens wanting (i.e. for, wanting to take another), ipse myself ab by alio another captus taken sum I am (i.e. I myself am taken by another) ad mortem to death.

Me miserum! alium enim capere volens, ipse ab alio captus sum ad mortem.

Fabula significat the fable siginfies, *eos* (that) those, *qui* who *proximis* for the nearest (i.e. about those

Fabula significat, eos, qui proximis insiduantur, ignarus saepe ab aliis id ipsun pati

170

near them) **insidiantur** *plot,* **ignarus** *ignorant (i.e. unexpectedly)* **saepe** *often* **ab aliis** *from others* **id** *that* **ipsun** *self (i.e. the very same thing)* **pati** *to suffer (i.e. the fable signifies that those who plot against those nearest to them, very often suffer the same from others)*

Decoding Latin – Day 14

Don't forget the rules:

1. Don't try to memorise anything
2. Focus on the story, not the language – don't try to analyse!
3. Read one section from the left column and then the same from the right.
4. *Always read for speed and general gist, not for accuracy and perfection.*

CANIS THE DOG ET COCUS AND THE COOK	**CANIS ET COCUS**
Canis a dog cum when (i.e. when a dog) irrupisset might have broken in (i.e. when a dog had broken in) in culinam into a kitchen, coco wth the cook occupato being engaged, corde (and) with a heart arrepto being snatched up, fugit fled.	Canis cum irrupisset in culinam, coco occupato, corde arrepto, fugit.
At but cocus the cook, conversus having turned, ut when vidit he saw	At cocus conversus, ut vidit ipsum fugientem, inquit;

172

ipsum him fugientem fleeing, inquit he said;

Heus tu hey you, scito know, ubi where fueris you will have been, me me te you observaturum about to watch (i.e. know that I will watch where you've been from now on): non enim for not mihi to (i.e. from) me cor a heart abstulisti have you taken away, sed but mihi to me cor a heart dedisti you have given potius rather (i.e. but, rather, you have given me heart).

Fabula significat the fable signifies, saepe often nocumenta injuries hominibus to men documenta instructions fieri to become (i.e. the fable signifies that injuries often become instructions to people).

Heus tu, scito, tibi fueris, me te observaturum: non enim mihi cor abstulisti, sed mihi cor dedisti potius.

Fabula significat, saepe nocumenta hominibus documenta fieri.

173

CANIS **THE DOG** ET LUPUS **AND THE WOLF**

Canis *a dog* ante *before* stabulum *a stable* quoddam *certain* dormiebat *slept (i.e. a dog slept in front of a certain stable)*; quumque *and when* lupus *a wolf* irripuisset *might have broken in (i.e. and when a wolf had broken in)*, et *and* cibum *food* facturus *about to make* eum *him* esset *he might be (i.e. and he/the wolf was about to make him/the dog into food)*, rogabat *he asked*, ne *that not* tunc *then (i.e. at that time)* se *himself* mactaret *he should sacrifice (i.e. he asked the wolf not to sacrifice him at that time)*.

Nunc *now (i.e. at that time)* enim *for (i.e. for, now)*, inquit *he said*,

CANIS ET LUPUS

Canis ante stabulum quoddam dormiebat; quumque lupus irripuisset, et cibum facturus eum esset, rogabat, ne tunc se mactaret.

Nunc enim, inquit, tenuis sum et macilentus: si autem parumper

174

tenuis thin sum I am (i.e. for now I'm slim) et and macilentus lean: si if autem but (i.e. but if) parumper a little (while) expectaveris you wait (i.e. but if you wait a while), mei my domini masters/owners facturi about to make sunt are nuptias nuptials (i.e. my owners are about to make nuptials/celebrate a wedding), et and ego I tunc then (i.e. at that time), multa many (things) depastus having fed (i.e. having fed on many things), pinguior fatter ero I will be (i.e. I'll be fatter), et and tibi to you suavior sweeter cibus food fiam I will become (i.e. and I'll become sweeter food for you).

Lupus the wolf, igitur therefore, persuasus being persuaded, abiit went away.

expectaveris, mei domini facturi sunt nuptias, et ego tunc, multa depastus, pinguior ero, et tibi suavior cibus fiam.

Lupus igitur persuasus abiit.

175

Post after aliquot some vero but (i.e. but, after some) dies days reversus having returned (i.e. but, having returned after some days), invenit he found superius higher super upon domus of the house tectum the room (i.e. upon the roof of the house) canem the dog dormientm sleeping (i.e. he found the dog sleeping higher upon the roof), et and, stans standing inferius lower (i.e. below) ad to se himself (i.e. to the dog) vocabat he called, admonens reminding eum him foederis of the agreement.

Et canis and the dog (said), At and, O Lupe O wolf, si if posthac after this (i.e. hereafter) ante before (i.e. in front of) stabulum the stable me me videris you see dormientem sleeping (i.e. and if, hereafter, you see

Post aliquot vero dies reversus, invenit superius super domus tectum canem dormientm, et stans inferius ad se vocabat, admonens eum foederis.

Et canis, At, O Lupe, si posthac ante stabulum me videris dormientem, non amplius espectes nuptias.

176

me sleeping in front of the stable), **non amplius** no more **espectes** should you wait for **nuptias** nuptials (i.e. if you catch me down there again, don't wait for nuptials).

Fabula significat the fable signifies, *prudentes* (that) prudent *homines* people, *quum* when *aliqua* in some *in* in *re* matter (i.e. in some matter) *periculitati* having been endangered (i.e. prudent people, having been endangered in some matter), *salvi* safe *facti* made *fuerint* they will have been (i.e. when they're made safe), *ab eo* from (i.e. regarding) it, *quamdiu* as long as *vixerint* they live, *cavere* to beware (i.e. the fable signifies that prudent people are wary of something for as long as they live, having once been endangered and safe from it).

Fabula significat, prudentes homines, quum aliqua in re periculitati, salvi facti fuerint, ab eo, quamdiu vixerint, cavere.

177

CANIS **THE DOG** ET GALLUS **AND THE ROOSTER**

Canis **a dog** et gallus **and a rooster**, inita **with entered into** societate **alliance (i.e. having entered into an alliance)**, iter **a journey** faciebant **they made (i.e. they made a journey)**.

Vespera **with evening** autem **but (i.e. but with the evening)** superveniente **coming on**, gallus **the rooster**, conscensa **with mounted** arbore **a tree (i.e. having mounted a tree)**, dormiebat **slept**, at **but** canis **the dog** ad **to (i.e. at)** radicem **the root** arboris **of the tree** cavitatem **a cavity** habentis **having (i.e. but the dog had a cavity at the base of the tree)**.

Quum **when** vero **but (i.e. but when)** gallus **the**

CANIS ET GALLUS

Canis et gallus, inita societate, iter faciebant.

Vespera autem superveniente, gallus, conscensa arbore, dormiebat, at canis ad radicem arboris cavitatem habentis.

Quum vero gallus, secundam consuetudinem,

rooster, secundam according to consuetudinem his custom, noctu at night cantasset sang, vulpes a fox, ut as (i.e. when) audivit it heard (the singing), accurrit ran to (i.e. ran up), et and, stans standing inferius lower (i.e. below), ut that ad to se herself descenderet he (i.e. the rooster) would descend, rogabat she (i.e. the fox) did ask (i.e. the fox asked the rooster to come down to her):	noctu cantasset, vulpes, ut audivit, accurrit, et stans inferius, ut ad se descenderet, rogabat:
dixit she said enim for (i.e. for, she said), se herself cupere to desire animal an animal bonam good ita so vocem voice (i.e. a voice so good) habens having complecti to embrace (i.e. for she said she herself desired to embrace an animal having such a good voice).	dixit enim, se cupere animal bonam ita vocem habens complecti.

Quum when autem but (i.e. but when) is he (i.e. the rooster) dixisset said, ut that janitorem the gatekeeper prius before (i.e. first) excitaret she (i.e. the fox) should rouse, ad to (i.e. at) radicem the root dormientem sleeping (i.e. sleeping at the root), ut that, quum when ille he (i.e. the gatekeeper) aperuisset had opened, descenderet he (i.e. the rooster) would come down, et and illa with her (i.e. the fox) quaerente seeking, ut that ipsum him (i.e. the gatekeeper) vocaret she could call (i.e. the fox, seeking to call the gatekeeper), canis the dog statim immediately prosiliens leaping forth eam her (i.e. the fox) dilaceravit tore to pieces.

Fabula significat the fable signifies, prudentes (that) prudent homines people inimicos (their) enemies

Quum autem is dixisset, ut janitorem prius excitaret, ad radicem dormientem, ut, quum ille aperuisset, descenderet, et illa quaerente, ut ipsum vocaret, canis statim prosiliens eam dilaceravit.

Fabula significat, prudentes homines inimicos insultantes ad fortiores astu mittere.

180

insultantes insulting (i.e. insulting their enemies) *ad fortiores* to stronger (people) *astu* by craft *mittere* to send (i.e. the fable signifies that prudent people, insulting their enemies, send them to stronger people by craft).

Decoding Latin – Day 15

Don't forget the rules:

1. Don't try to memorise anything
2. Focus on the story, not the language – don't try to analyse!
3. Read one section from the left column and then the same from the right.
4. *Always read for speed and general gist, not for accuracy and perfection.*

LEO THE LION ET RANA AND THE FROG

Leo a lion, audita having heard aliquando sometime rana a frog valde very strongly clamante crying out, vertit turned se himself ad to vocem the

LEO ET RANA

Leo audita aliquando rana valde clamante, vertit se ad vocem, ratus magnum aliquod animal esse;

voice, ratus having thought magnum great aliquod some animal animal (i.e. some great animal) esse to be (i.e. thinking that it was some great animal);

cum when parumper a little while autem but (i.e. but when, a little while) expectasset he'd waited, vidit he saw ipsam her stagno from the pond egressam coming out, et and, accedens approaching propius nearer, proculcavit he trampled (her).

Fabula significat the fable signifies, non oportere not to behove (i.e. that one ought not), antequam before videas you may see (it), auditu by hearing solo alone perturbari to be disturbed (i.e. the fable signifies that one should be disturbed by

cum parumper autem expectasset, vidit ipsam stagno egressam, et accedens propius proculcavit.

Fabula significat, non oportere, antequam videas, auditu solo perturbari.

hearing alone, before you can see the thing).

LEO THE LION, ET ASINUS AND THE ASS, ET VULPES AND THE FOX

Leo *a lion*, et asinus *and an ass*, et vulpes *and a fox*, societate *with an alliance* inita *being entered into*, agressi *having advanced* sunt *they are (i.e. they went out)* ad *for* venandum *hunting*.

Multa *many* igitur *therefore*, praeda *booty (i.e. a lot of spoils)* capta *being taken*, jussit *ordered* leo *the lion (i.e. the lion ordered)* asino *to the ass* dividere *to divide* sibi *for themselves*.

At *but* ille *he*, tribus *with three* partibus *parts* factis *being made* aequaliter *equally*, ut *that* eligerent

LEO, ET ASINUS, ET VULPES

Leo, et asinus, et vulpes, societate inita, agressi sunt ad venandum.

Multa igitur praeda capta, jussit leo asino dividere sibi.

At illa, tribus partibus factis aequaliter, ut eligerent eos hortabatur.

183

they should choose (their part) **eos** them **hortabatur** he encouraged (i.e. the donkey, having divided them into three equal parts, encouraged the others to choose).

Et and **leo** the lion, **ira** with anger **percitus** roused, **asinum** the ass **devoravit** devoured (i.e. the lion, roused by anger, devoured the ass).

Inde then **vulpi** to the fox, **ut** that **divideret** he should divide (the spoils), **jussit** he ordered.

Illa she **vero** but (i.e. but she), **in** into **unam** one **partem** part **omnibus** with all **congestis** being heaped (i.e. with everything heaped into one part), **sibi** for herself **minimum** very little **quiddam** a certain thing (i.e. a very little something) **reliquit** she

Et leo, ira percitus, asinum devoravit.

Inde vulpi, ut divideret, jussit.

Illa vero, in unam partem omnibus congestis, sibi minimum quiddam reliquit.

184

left (i.e. she left a very little amount for herself).

Tum *then* leo *the lion* ipsi *to her (said)*, Quis *who* te *you*, O optima *O best (creature)*, dividere *to divide* sic *thus* docuit *has taught* (i.e. the lion said to her, who has taught you to divide like this, O best creature)?

Tum leo ipsi, Quistte, O optima, dividere sic docuit?

Ea *she* vero *indeed*, inquit *said*, asini *of the ass* calamaitas *the calamity* (i.e. she said 'the calamity of the ass, indeed).

Ea vero, inquit, asini calamaitas.

Fabula significat the fable signifies, *castigamenta* (that) corrections *hominibus* to people *esse* to be *proximorum* of the nearest (people) *infortunia* the misfortunes (i.e. the fable signifies that the misfortunes of those nearest are

Fabula significat, castigamenta hominibus esse proximorum infortunia.

185

corrections/lessons for people).

LEO **THE LION** ET URSUS **AND THE BEAR**

Leo *a lion* et ursus *and a bear* simul *at the same time* magnum *a great* hinnulum *fawn* nacti *having got*, de *about* eo *it* pugnabant *they fought* (i.e. they both caght the fawn at the same time and were fighting over it).	Leo et ursus simul magnum hinnulum nacti, de eo pugnabant.
Graviter *heavily* (i.e. seriously/severely) igitur *therefore,* a *by* se *themselves* invicem *mutually* affecti *being affected* (i.e. damaged: being seriously wounded each by the other), adeo *so much* ut *that* ex *from* multa *much* pugna *fight* (i.e. from a lot of fighting) etiam *even* vertigine *with daziness* corriperentur	Graviter igitur a se invicem affecti, adeo ut ex multa pugna etiam vertigine corriperentur, defatigati jacebant.

LEO ET URSUS

they were seized (i.e. they were so damaged that they were taken by daziness from so much fighting), **defatigati** worn out **jacebant** they lay down.

Vulpes a fox **autem** but (i.e. but a fox) **circumcirca** round about **eundo** by going (i.e. going round about) **ubi** where **prostratos** prostrated **eos** them **vidit** she saw (i.e. a fox, going about the place, saw where they lay prostrated), **et** and **hinnulum** the fawn **in** in **medio** the middle **jacentem** lying (i.e. and the fox saw the fawn lyin in the middle between the lion and bear), **hunc** (and) this (i.e. the fawn), **per** through **medios** the middles (i.e. through the middle of) **utrosque** each (i.e. both) **percurrens** running through (i.e. and, running through the

Vulpes autem circumcirca eundo ubi prostratos eos vidit, et hinnulum in medio jacentem, hunc, per medios utrosque percurrens, rapuit, fugiensque abiit.

middle of them), **rapuit** she (i.e. the fox) snatched (i.e. she snatched the fawn), **fugiensque** and fleeing **abiit** she went away.

At but **illi** they **videbant** saw **quidem** indeed **ipsam** her (i.e. but, indeed, they saw her), **non** not **valentes** being strong (enough) **vero** but (i.e. but, not being strong enough) **surgere** to rise, **Nos** us **miseros** wretched (i.e. 'poor us'), **dicebant** they said, **quod** because **vulpi** for the fox **laboravimus** we have laboured.

Fabulla significat the fable signifies, *aliis* (that) with others (i.e. with some) *laborantibus* labouring, *alios* others *lucrari* to gain (i.e. the fable signifies that while some labour, others gain).

At illi videbant quidem ipsam, non valentes vero surgere, Nos miseros, dicebant, quod vulpi laboravimus.

Fabulla significat, aliis laborantibus, alios lucrari.

188

Decoding Latin – Day 16

Don't forget the rules:

1. Don't try to memorise anything
2. Focus on the story, not the language – don't try to analyse!
3. Read one section from the left column and then the same from the right.
4. Always read for speed and general gist, not for accuracy and perfection.

VATES THE PROPHET	**VATES**
Vates a prophet in in foro the forum sedens sitting (i.e. sitting in the forum) disserebat discoursed (i.e. spoke/lectured).	Vates in foro sedens disserebat.
Quum when autem but (i.e. but when) supervenisset had come up quidam a certain (i.e. person) derepente suddenly (i.e. but when a certain person had suddenly come up), et and renunciasset had announced, quod that	Quum autem supervenisset quidam derepente, et renunciasset, quod domus ipsius fenestrae apertae omnes essent, et, quae intus erant, ablata omnia, exilivit suspirans, et cursim ibat.

190

domus of the house ipsius of him fenestrae the windows (i.e. the windows of his house) apertae opened omnes all essent might be (i.e. the person announced that all the windows of his house were open), et and, quae (those things) which intus within (i.e. inside) erant were, ablata carried away omnis all (i.e. and the things inside were all carried away), exilivit he leapt forth suspirans sighing, et and cursim quickly ibat he went.

At but currentem running quidam a certain (person) ipsum him conspicatus having caught sight of (i.e. but, a certain person catching sight of him running), Heus tu hey you inquit he said, qui who alienas foreign res things (i.e. the things of others) prescire to know beforehand profiteris you

At currentem quidam ipsum conspicatus, Heus tu inquit, qui alienas res prescire profiteris, tuas ipsius non prevaticinabare!

191

profess (i.e. you who profess to foreknow others' things), **tuas** your own **ipsius** of yourself **non prevaticinabare** you didn't prophecy!

Fabula the fable *in* (is) into (i.e. for) *eos* those, *qui* who *suam* their own *vitam* life *prave* corruptly *gubernantes* piloting (i.e. those who, conducting their own life badly), *quae* (things) which *nihil* nothing *ad* to *se* themselves *attinent* belong *prescire* to know before hand *conantur* they try (i.e. those who conduct their own life badly, try to predict things which don't belong to them at all).

FORMICA THE ANT ET COLUMBA AND THE DOVE

Fabula in eos, qui suam vitam prave gubernantes, quae nihil ad se attinent prescire conantur.

FORMICA ET COLUMBA

192

Formica *an ant* sitiens *thirsting (i.e. being thirsty)* descendit *went down* in into *fontem* a fountain, ac *and* tracta *dragged* a *by* fluxu *the stream* suffocabatur *was (nearly) suffocated*.

Columba *a dove* vero *but (i.e. but a dove)*, hoc *with this* viso *being seen (i.e. having seen this)*, ramum *a branch* arboris *of a tree* decerptum *plucked off* in into *fontem the fountain* projecit *threw (i.e. threw a branch broken off a tree into the fountain)*, super *upon* quo *which* sedens *sitting (i.e. sitting on which)* formica *the ant* evasit *escaped*.

Auceps *a bird-catcher* autem *but* quidam *a certain (i.e. but a certain bird-catcher)* post *after* hoc *this*, calamis *with reeds* compositis *being*

Formica sitiens descendit in fontem, ac tracta a fluxu suffocabatur.

Columba vero, hoc viso, ramum arboris decerptum in fontem projecit, super quo sedens formica evasit.

Auceps autem quidam post hoc, calamis compositis, ad columbam comprehendendam ibat.

193

arranged, **ad** for **columbam** the dove **comprehendendam** to be seized **ibat** went (i.e. a certain bird-catcher went with reeds being arranged to catch the dove).

Hoc this **autem** but **viso** being seen (i.e. but having seen this), **formica** the ant **aucupis** of the bird-catcher **pedem** the foot **momordit** bit (i.e. the ant bit the foot of the bird-catcher); **ille** he **vero** but (i.e. but he), **dolens** grieving (i.e. in pain), **et** and **calamos** the reeds **projecit** threw away, **et** and, **ut** that **Columba** the dove **statim** immediately **fugeret** could flee, **auctor** the author **fuit** was (i.e. he was the author of the dove's escape).

Fabula significat the fable signifies, *oportere* to behove (i.e. that one should)

Hoc autem viso, formica aucupis pedem momordit; ille vero dolens, et calamos projecit, et, ut Columba statim fugeret, auctor fuit.

Fabula significat, oportere benefactoribus gratiam referre.

194

benefactoribus to benefactors *gratiam* thanks *referre* give back (i.e. that one should repay a favour to benefactors).

VESPERTILIO THE BAT ET RUBUS AND THE BRIAR ET MERGUS AND THE CORMORANT

VESPERTILIO ET RUBUS ET MERGUS

Vespertilio a bat, et Rubus and a briar, et Mergus and a comorant, societate with an alliance inita being entered into (i.e. having entered into an agreement), mercatoriam a mercantile decreverunt they determined vitam life agere to act (i.e. they determined to act/live a mercantile life).

Vespertilio, et Rubus, et Mergus, societate inita, mercatoriam decreverunt vitam agere.

Itaque and so vespertilio the bat argentum silver mutuatus having borrowed (i.e. having borrowed silver/money),

Itaque vespertilio argentum mutuatus, deposuit in medium, rubus vestem secum acceit,

deposuit laid (it) down in into medium the middle (i.e. put it in the middle), rubus the briar vestem clothing secum with him accepit took (i.e. the briar took clothing with him), mergus the cormorant tertius the third, aes (took) brass, et and enavigaverunt they sailed away:	mergus tertius aes, et enavigaverunt:
Tempestate with a storm autem but (i.e. but, with a storm) vehementi vehement oborta having arisen (i.e. but with a vehement storm having risen), et and navi with (their) ship eversa overturned, omnibus with all things (i.e. everything) perditis being lost, ipsi they themselves in into (i.e. onto) terram land evaserunt escaped.	Tempestate autem vehementi oborta, et navi eversa, omnibus perditis, ipsi in terram evaserunt.

Ex from illo that (time), igitur therefore, mergus the cormorant litoribus to the shores semper always assidet sits near (i.e. the cormorant always sits near the shore), si if quopiam anywhere aes (his) brass ejiciat may cast out mare the sea (i.e. he sits near the shore, if/in case the sea throws out any of his brass):	Ex illo igitur mergus litoribus semper assidet, si quopiam es ejiciat mare:
Vespertilio the bat vero but (i..e but the bat), creditores his creditors timens fearing (i.e. fearing his creditors), interdiu by day non apparet doesn't appear sed but nocte by night ad for pabulum food exit goes out.	Vespertilio vero creditores timens, interdiu non apparet sed nocte ad pabulum exit.
Rubus the briar vero but (i.e. but the briar) praetereuntium of those passing by vestem the clothing prehendit seizes, sicubi if anywhere suam its	Rubus vero praetereuntium vestem prehendit, sicubi suam cognoscat, quaerens.

197

own **cognoscat** it may recognise, **quaerens** seeking (i.e. seeking to recognize its own clothing anywhere).

Fabula significat the fable signifies, *in* into *ea* those things, *quibus* to which *incumbimus* we lean on, *in* into *posterum* posterity *nos* us *recidere* to fall back (i.e. the fable signifies that we fall back in later life on those things to which we devote ourselves).

Fabula significat, in ea, quibus incumbimus, in posterum nos recidere.

Decoding Latin – Day 17

Don't forget the rules:

1. Don't try to memorise anything
2. Focus on the story, not the language – don't try to analyse!
3. Read one section from the left column and then the same from the right.
4. *Always read for speed and general gist, not for accuracy and perfection.*

AEGROTUS THE SICK (MAN) ET MEDICUS AND THE PHYSICIAN	**AEGROTUS ET MEDICUS**
Aegrotans a being sick (i.e. sick man) quidem a certain (i.e. a certain sick man), et and a by medico a physician rogatus having been asked, quomodo how valuisset he was well (i.e. a certain man, being sick, was asked by his doctor how he was doing)?	Aegrotans quidem, et a medico rogatus, quomodo valuisset?
Plus more, ait he said, quam than oporteretit	Plus, ait, quam oporteret, sudasse.

might behove (i.e. more than he should), **sudasse** to have sweated (i.e. he answered that he had been sqeating more than he should).

Ille he (i.e. the doctor) **autem** but (i.e. but he) **bonum** a good (thing) **ait** said **hoc** this **esse** to be (i.e. he said it was a good thing).

Secundo secondly (i.e. a second time/the next time) **vero** but (i.e. but a second time) **ab** by **ispo** the same man (i.e. the physician) **iterum** again **rogatus** being asked, **quomodo** how **se** himself **habuisset** he had (i.e. how he had been), **Horrore** with shivering **correptum** seized, **ait** he says, **valde** very strongly **concussum** shaken **fuisse** to have been (i.e. he said that, being seized with the shivers, he

Ille autem bonum ait hoc esse.

Secundo vero ab ispo iterum rogatus, quomodo se habuisset, Horrore correptum, ait, valde concussum fuisse.

200

had been very badly shaken).

Ille he (i.e. the doctor) **vero** but (i.e. but he) **et** and (i.e. also) **hoc** this **bonum** a good (thing) **esse** to be **ait** said (i.e. this also the doctor said was a good thing).

Ille vero et hoc bonum esse ait.

Tertio thirdly (i.e. a third time) **rursum** again **rogatus** being asked, **quomodo** how **valuisset** he was in health; **ait** he said, **in** into **hydropem** dropsy **incidisse** to have fallen into (i.e. he said he had fallen into dropsy/edema).

Tertio rursum rogatus, quomodo valuisset; ait, in hydropem incidisse.

Ille he (i.e. the doctor) **et** and (i.e. also) **hoc** this **rursus** again **bonum** a good (thing) **ait** said **esse** to be (i.e. he said this also was a good thing).

Ille et hoc rursus bonum ait esse.

Inde then ex out of domesticis his domestics (i.e. his servants) quodam a certain (i.e. from a certain one of his servants) ipsum he himself ((i.e. the sick man) rogante being asked (i.e. being asked by one of his servants), Ut how habes do you have (yourself: **ut habes** is a Latin idiom for 'how are you doing')?

Ego I, ait he said, heus tu hark you (i.e. 'get this'), prae before (i.e. through) bonis good things pereo I'm perishing (i.e. he said, 'get this; I'm dying through good things').

Fabula significat the fable signifies, maxime (that) greatly ex out of hominibus people nos us odio in hatred eos them habere to have (i.e. that we [ought] to have/hold those people in hatred/contempt), qui who

Inde ex domesticis quodam ipsum rogante, Ut habes?

Ego, ait, heus tu, prae bonis pereo.

Fabula significat, maxime ex hominibus nos odio eos habere, qui ad gratiam semper loqui student.

202

ad to *gratiam* favour *semper always* **loqui** *to speak* **student** *strive (i.e. the fable signifies that we hold in contempt those who always strive to speak to/gain favour).*

LIGNATOR *THE WOOD-CUTTER* ET MERCURIUS *AND MERCURY*

LIGNATOR ET MERCURIUS

Lignator *a wood-cutter* quidam *a certain (i.e. a certain wood-cutter)* juxta *near* fluvium *a river* suam *his own* amisit *lost (i.e. lost his)* securim *axe*.

Lignator quidam juxta fluvium suam amisit securim.

Inops *destitute* igitur *therefore,* consilii *of advice (i.e. devoid of any plan),* juxta *near* ripam *the riverbank* sedens *sitting (i.e. sitting near the riverbank),* plorabat *he lamented*.

Inops igitur consilii, juxta ripam sedens plorabat.

203

Mercurius Mercury autem but (i.e. but Mercury), intellecta with understood causa the cause (i.e. understanding the reason for his lamenting), et and miseratus having pitied (i.e. taken pity on) hominem the man, urinatus having dived in into fluvium the river, auream a golden sustulit brought up securim an axe (i.e. he brought up a golden axe), et and, an whether haec this esset might be, quam (that) which perdiderat he had lost, rogavit he asked (i.e. he brought up a golden axe and asked whether this was the one he had lost).

Illo with him vero but (i.e. but with him/the woodcutter), non not eam it esse to be, dicente saying (i.e. but, when he said it wasn't the one), iterum again urinatus having dived

Mercurius autem, intellecta causa, et miseratus hominem, urinatus in fluvium, auream sustulit securim, et, an haec esset, quam perdiderat, rogavit.

Illo vero, non eam esse, dicente, iterum urinatus argeneam sustulit.

204

argenteam a silver (one) sustulit he brought up (i.e. he brought up a silver axe).

Illo with him vero but (i.e. but, with him), neque neither hanc this esse to be suam his own, dicente saying (i.e. but, with him saying this wasn't his either), tertio thirdly (i.e. a third time) urinates having dived, illam that ipsam itself (i.e. his actual axe) sustulit he brought up.

Illo with him vero but (i.e. but with him), hanc this vere truly esse to be deperditam lost, dicente saying (i.e. but when he said this was truly the one he had lost), Mercurius Mercury, probata having approved ipsius of his aequitare equity (i.e. fairness), omnes all (the

Illo vero, neque hanc esse suam, dicente, tertio urinates, illam ipsam sustulit.

Illo vero, hanc vere esse deperditam, dicente, Mercurius, probata ipsius aequitare, omnes ei donavit.

205

axes) ei to him donavit gifted.

Ille he vero but (i.e. but he,) profectus having set out, omnia all things sociis to his companions, quae which acciderant had happened, narravit he narrated (i.e. he told his friends everything that had happened):

Quorum of whom unus one quidam a certain (i.e. a certain one of whom) eadem the same things facere to do (i.e. to do the same things) decrevit determined (i.e. on of his friends decided to do the same things), et and ad fluvium to the river profectus having set out (i.e. and having set out to the river), et and suam his own securim axe consulto intentionally demisit he sent down (i.e. let fall) in into fluvium the river, et

Ille vero profectus, omnia sociis, quae acciderant, narravit:

Quorum unus quidam cadem facere decrevit, et ad fluvium profectus, et suam securim consulto demisit in fluvium, et plurans sedebat.

206

and **plurans** lamenting **sedebat** he sat (i.e. and, intentionally letting his axe fall into the river he sat lamenting).

Apparuit appeared **igitur** therefore **Mercurius** Mercury (i.e. Mercury appeared, therefore), **et** illi and (i.e. also) to him (i.e. Mercury appeared to him also), **et** and, **causa** with the cause **intellecta** being understood **pluratus** of (his) weeping (i.e. and having understood the reason for his weeping), **urinatus** having dived **similiter** likewise **auream** a golden **securim** axe **extulit** he brought out, **et** and **rogavit** asked, **an** whether **hanc** this **amisisset** he had lost (i.e. he asked whether he had lost this)?

Illo with him **cum** with **gaudio** joy, **et** and, **Vero** indeed **haec** this **est** it is,

Apparuit igitur Mercurius et illi, et, causa intellecta pluratus, urinatus similiter auream securim extulit, et rogavit, an hanc amisisset?

Illo cum gaudio, et, Vero haec est, dicente, perosus deus tantam impudentiam,

207

dicente saying (i.e. but when he said with joy 'this is it indeed'), perosus full of hate deus the god (i.e. the god, full of hate) tantam (at) such impudentiam impudence, non solum not only illam that (i.e. the golden axe) detinuit held back, sed but ne not propriam his own quidem indeed (i.e. but not even his own) reddidit did he give back.

Fabula significat the fable signifies, quantum (that) how much justis to the just deus god auxiliatur aids, tantum so much (i.e. that much) injustis to the unjust eum him esse to be contrarium opposed (i.e. the fable signifies that however much god helps the just, the same amount he opposes the unjust).

ASINUS THE DONKEY ET

non solum illam detinuit, sed ne propriam quidem reddidit.

Fabula significat, quantum justis deus auxiliatur, tantum injustis eum esse contrarium.

ASINUS ET HORTULANUS

208

HORTULANUS AND THE GARDENER

Asinus a donkey, serviens serving olitori to a market-gardener[8], quoniam since parum a little comedebat he ate (i.e. since he ate only a little), plurimum (and) very much vero indeed laborabat he worked, precatus prayed est he is (i.e. he prayed) Jovem (to) Jove/Jupiter, ut that, ab from olitore the market-gardener liberatus (he would be) freed, alteri to another venderetur he would be sold domino to an owner (i.e. that he would be sold to another owner)

Quum when vero but (i.e. but when) Jupiter Jupiter exoratus having been entreated (i.e. being

Asinus serviens olitori, quoniam parum comedebat, plurimum vero laborabat, precatus est Jovem, ut, ab olitore liberatus, alteri venderetur domino.

Quum vero Jupiter exoratus, jussisset ipsum figulovendi, iterum iniquo animo ferebat, plura,

---

[8] The Romans would say 'serving *to* a market-gardener', but in English we would just say 'serving a market-gardener'.

209

prevailed upon), jussisset he might have ordered (i.e. he ordered) ipsum him figulo to a potter vendi to be sold (i.e. he ordered him to be sold to a potter), iterum again iniquo with an uneven (i.e. unhappy/impatient) animo mind ferebat he (i.e. the donkey) bore (i.e. he bore/endured the new situation unhappily), plura more, quam than prius before, onera burdens portans carrying (i.e. carrying more burdens than before), et and coenum mud et tegulas and tiles ferens carrying (i.e. carrying mud and tiles).

Rursus again, igitur therefore, ut that mutaret he should change dominum his owner rogavit he asked (i.e. he asked to change his owner again), et and coriario to a tanner venundatus sold

quam prius, onera portans, et coenum et tegulas ferens.

Rursus igitur ut mutaret dominum rogavit, et coriario venundatus est.

210

est he is (i.e. he was sold to a tanner).

Pejorem a worse itaque and so (i.e. and so, a worse) prioribus (than) the former (owners) herum master nactus being obtained (i.e. and so, having obtained a worse master than the former ones), et and videns seeing, quae (those things) which ab by eo him fierent were done (i.e. and seeing the things done by him), cum suspiriis with sighs (i.e. sighing) ait he said, Hei woe mihi to me misero wretched (i.e. woe to poor me)! Melius better erat it was mihi for me apud at (i.e. with) priores (my) former heros masters manere to remain (i.e. it was better for me to remain with my former masters); hic this enim for (i.e. for this), ut as video I see, et and (i.e. also) pellem hide meam my

Pejorem itaque prioribus herum nactus, et videns, quae ab eo fierent, cum suspirius ait, Hei mihi misero! Melius erat mihi apud priores heros manere; hic enim, ut video, et pellem meam conficiet.

conficiet will finish (i.e. for this one will also finish my hide).

Fabula significat the fable signifies, *quod* that *tunc* then *maxime* greatly (i.e. mostly) *priores* former *dominos* masters *famuli* servants *desiderant* want (i.e. that people want their old bosses), *quum* when, *de* from *secundis* the second *periculum* a trial *fecerint* they have made (i.e. people want their old boss/situation once they've made a trial of the next).

Fabula significat, quod tunc maxime priores dominos famuli desiderant, quum, de secundis periculum fecerint.

212

Decoding Latin – Day 18

Don't forget the rules:

1. Don't try to memorise anything
2. Focus on the story, not the language – don't try to analyse!
3. Read one section from the left column and then the same from the right.
4. *Always read for speed and general gist, not for accuracy and perfection.*

AUCEPS THE BIRD-CATCHER ET GALERITA AND THE LARK	**AUCEPS ET GALERITA**
Auceps a bird-catcher avibus for birds struxerat had constructed laqueos pit-falls (i.e. a bird-catcher had constructed pit-falls for birds): Galerita a lark vero but (i.e. but a lark) hunc him procul at a distance conspicata having spied (i.e. but a lark, having seen him from a distance), rogavit asked (him), quidnam what	Auceps avibus struxerat laqueos: Galerita vero hunc procul conspicata, rogavit, quidnam faceret?

faceret he might do (i.e. what he was doing)?

Eo with him urbem a city se himself condere to build dicente saying (i.e. he said he was building a city); deinde then procul at a distance regresso having gone back (i.e. having gone back at a distance), et and abscondito having hidden, galerita the lark, viri of the man verbis in the words credens believing (i.e. believing the man's words) accessit approached ad cassem to the net, et and capta captured est is (i.e. and was captured);

at but, aucupe with the bird-catcher accurrente running up, illa she (i.e. the lark) dixit said, Heus tu hey you, si if talem such urbem a city condes you build, non multos not many invenies you will find

Eo urbem se condere dicente; deinde procul regresso, et abscondito, galerita, viri verbis credens accessit ad cassem, et capta est;

at, aucupe accurrente, illa dixit, Heus tu, si talem urbem condes, non multos invenies incolentes.

214

incolentes inhabitants (i.e. you won't find many inhabitants).

Fabula significat the fable signifies, *tunc* then *maxime* mostly *domos* houses *et urbes* and cities *desolari* to be desolated (i.e. that those houses and cities are most desolate), *quum* when *praefecti* (their) governors *molesti* troublesome *fuerint* shall have been (i.e. the fable signifies that when their governors are troublesome, that's when houses and cities are most deserted).

VIATOR A TRAVELLER

Viator a traveller, *multa* with much *confecta* completed *via* way (i.e. having gone a long way), *vovit* vowed, *si quod* (that) if anything *invenisset* he might have

Fabula significat, tunc maxime domos et urbes desolari, quum praefecti molesti fuerint.

VIATOR

Viator, multa confecta via, vovit, si quod invenisset, dimidium Mercurio ejus se dedicaturum.

215

found (i.e. that if he found anything), dimidium half Mercurio to Mercury ejus of it (i.e. half of it to Mercury) se himself dedicaturum about to devote (i.e. that if he found anything, he would devote half to Mercury).

Nactus having obtained igitur therefore, peram a bag plenam full cariotarum of dates et amygdalarum and almonds, atque and ea with it (i.e. the bag) accepta being received, eas them (i.e. the dates and almonds) comedit he ate up:

Nactus igitur peram plenam cariotarum et amygdalarum, atque ea accepta, eas comedit:

Sed but cariotarum of the dates ossa the bones (i.e. the bones/stones of the dates), et amygdalarum and of the almonds cortices the rinds (i.e. and the shells of the almonds), super upon quodam a certain imposuit he placed

Sed cariotarum ossa, et amygdalarum cortices, super quodam imposuit altari, inquiens, Habes, O Mercuri, votum; nam rei inventae exteriora et interiora dividendo tibi dono.

216

upon **altari** altar (i.e. he placed them upon a certain altar), **inquiens** saying, **Habes** you have, **O Mercuri** O Mercury, **votum** (my) vow; **nam** for **rei** of the thing **inventae** found (i.e. of the found thing) **exteriora** the outers **et interiora** and the inners **dividendo** by dividing (i.e. for, by dividing the outer and inner parts of the thing found), **tibi** to you **dono** I gift (i.e. I ive them to you).

Fabula the fable *in virum* into (i.e. against) *a man avarum* greedy, *et deos* and the gods *ob* on account of *cupiditatem* desire *fallentem* deceiving (i.e. the fable speaks against the greedy man, deceiving the gods for the sake of desire).

PUER A BOY ET MATER AND (HIS) MOTHER

Fabula in virum avarum, et deos ob cupiditatem fallentem.

PUER ET MATER

217

Puer a boy ex out of literatorio a literary ludo play (i.e. a school) condiscipuli a fellow student's librum book furatus having stolen (i.e. a boy, having stolen a fellow student's book from school), tulit brought (it) matri to (his) mother.

Quum when ea she vero but (i.e. but when she) non reprehendisset might not have rebuked (i.e. had not rebuked him), sed but potius rather amplexata embraced fuisset she might have been (i.e. she didn't rebuke him, but rather she embraced him), provectus having advanced aetate in age (i.e. having grown older) coepit he began et and (i.e. also) majora greater (things) furari to steal.

In in ipso the very same autem but (i.e. but in the

Puer ex literatorio ludo condiscipuli librum furatus, tulit matri.

Quum ea vero non reprehendisset, sed potius amplexata fuisset, provectus aetate coepit et majora furari.

In ipso autem furto aliquando deprehensus,

218

very same) furto theft aliquando sometime deprehensus being caught, ducebatur he was led recta straightaway ad to mortem death.

At but, sequente with following et lugente and mourning matre his mother (i.e. but with his mother following and mourning), ille he carnifices the executioners orabat prayed (i.e. he begged them), ut that pauca a few quaedam certain (things) matre to his mother colloqueretur he could speak together in into aurem her ear.

Quae who, quum when illico immediately ori to the mouth filii of (her) son se herself admovisset she had moved to (i.e. but when she brought herself immediately near her

ducebatur recta ad mortem.

At sequente et lugente matre, ille carnifices orabat, ut pauca quaedam matre colloqueretur in aurem.

Quae, quum illico ori filii se admovisset, ille aurem dentibus demorsam absecidit:

219

son's mouth), **ille** he **aurem** (her) ear **dentibus** with (his) teeth **demorsam** bitten off **absecidit** he cut off (i.e. he bit off her ear with his teeth):

Matre with the mother **autem** but (i.e. but with the mother), **et** and **aliis** the others **accusantibus** accusing (him), **quia** because **non solum** not only **furatus** stolen **fuisset** he might have been (i.e. because not only had he stolen), **sed** but **jam** now **et** and (i.e. also) **in** into (i.e. towards) **matrem** (his) mother **impius** impious (i.e. disrespectful) **esset** he might be (i.e, but now he was also disrespectful to his mother), **ille** he **ait** said, **Haec** this (i.e. she) **enim** for (i.e. for she) **mihi** to me **perditionis** of destruction **fuit** was **causa** the cause (i.e. for she was

Matre autem, et aliis accusantibus, quia non solum furatus fuisset, sed jam et in matrem impius esset, ille ait, Haec enim mihi perditionis fuit causa.

220

the cause of my destruction).

Si *if* enim *for* (i.e. *for if*), quum *when* librum *the book* furatus *stolen* fuissem *I might have been* (i.e. *for if, when I had stolen the book*), me *me* reprehendisst *she would have rebuked* (i.e. *if she'd rebuked me*), non *not*, ad *to* haec *these (things)* usque *as far as* progressus *advanced* (i.e. *not having advanced as far as to these things*), nunc *now* ducerer *I would (not) be led* ad mortem *to (my) death*.

Fabula significat the fable signifies, eorum of those, qui who non not in principio in the beginning puniuntur are punished, in majus into greater augeri to be increased mala the evil (things, i.e. deeds: i.e. the fable signifies that the evil

Si enim, quum librum furatus fuissem, me reprehendisst, non, ad haec usque progressus, nunc ducerer ad mortem.

Fabula significat, eorum, qui non in principio puniuntur, in majus augeri mala.

221

deeds of those who are not punished in the beginning, grow into greater).

Decoding Latin – Day 19

Don't forget the rules:

1. Don't try to memorise anything
2. Focus on the story, not the language – don't try to analyse!
3. Read one section from the left column and then the same from the right.
4. *Always read for speed and general gist, not for accuracy and perfection.*

PASTOR THE SHEPHERD ET MARE AND THE SEA

PASTOR ET MARE

Pastor a shepherd in in maritimo a maritime loco place gregem a flock pascens feeding (i.e. feeding a flock in a maritime region), viso being seen tranquillo the tranquil mari sea (i.e. having seen the calm sea), desideravit desired navigare to sail ad mercaturam for trading:

Pastor in maritimo loco gregem pascens, viso tranquillo mari, desideravit navigare ad mercaturam:

Venditis being sold, igitur therefore, ovibus his sheep, et and palmarum of palm trees fructibus the fruits emptis being bought, solvit he loosed (i.e. he loosed anchor, a Roman idiom for setting sail).	Venditis igitur ovibus, et palmarum fructibus emptis, solvit.
Tempestate with a storm vero but (i.e. but with a storm) vehementi vehement facta being made (i.e. but with a violent storm coming up), et and navis the ship in periculo in danger quum when esset it might have been (i.e. and when the ship was in danger), ne lest submergeretur it be submerged, omni with every onere burden ejecto thrown out in mare into the sea, vix barely vacua in the empty navi ship evasit he escaped incolumis safe (i.e. he barely escaped safe in the empty ship).	Tempestate vero vehementi facta, et navis in periculo quum esset, ne submergeretur, omni onere ejecto in mare, vix vacua navi evasit incolumis.

224

Post after vero but (i.e. but after) dies days non paucos not few (i.e. but after many days), transeunte with passing by quodam a certain (person, i.e. when a certain person was passing by), et maris and of the sea (erat it was enim for (i.e. for it was) id that forte by chance tranuillum tranquil) quietem the calm admirante admiring (i.e. admiring the calm of the sea), suscepto with taken up sermone the discourse, hic he (i.e. the shepherd) ait said, Cariotas dates iterum again, ut as videtur it seems, desiderat desires mare the sea (i.e. the sea desires dates again, so it seems), et and propterea on account of this (i.e. for this reason) videtur it seems quietum calm.

Fabula significat the fable signifies, calamitates calamities hominibus to

Post vero dies non paucos, transeunte quodam, et maris (erat enim id forte tranuillum) quietem admirante, suscepto sermone, hic ait, Cariotas iterum, ut videtur, desiderat mare, et propterea videtur quietum.

Fabula significat, calamitates hominibus documenta fieri.

people documenta instructions *fieri* to become (i.e. it signifies that calamities become instructions for people).

PUNICA THE POMEGRANATE ET MALUS AND THE APPLE

PUNICA ET MALUS

Punica a pomegranate et malus and an apple de about pulchritudine beauty contendebant did contend (i.e. debate/disagree).

Punica et malus de pulchritudine contendebant.

Multis with many vero but (i.e. but with many) contentionibus disputes interim meanwhile factis being made, rubus a briar ex out of proxima the nearest sepe hedge audiens hearing (i.e. a birar, listening from a nearby hedge), Desinamus let us cease, ait he said, O amicae O friends,

Multis vero contentionibus interim factis, rubus ex proxima sepe audiens, Desinamus, ait, O amicae, aliquando pugnare.

226

aliquando *some time* pugnare *to fight*.

Fabula significat the fable signifies, *in* in *praestantiorum* of the more excellent *seditionibus* disturbances *(i.e. in the disturbances of the more excellent)*, *vilissimos* the most vile *etiam* even *conari* to try *esse* to be *aliquos* some *(i.e. the fable signifies that even the lowest try to be someone/try to have a place in the troubles of the more excellent)*.

TALPA **THE MOLE**

Talpa *a mole*, caecum *blind* animal *animal* est *is (i.e. the mole is a blind animal)*.

Dicit *she says*, igitur *therefore*, aliquando *sometime (i.e. one day)* matri *to (her) mother*, Morum *a mulberry*, mater

Fabula significat, in praestantiorum seditionibus, vilissimos etiam conari esse aliquos.

TALPA

Talpa, caecum animal est.

Dicit igitur aliquando matri, Morum, mater, video:

227

mother, **video** I see (i.e. I see a mulberry, mother):

deinde then **rusus** again **ait** she says, **thuris** of frankincense **odore** with the smell **plena** full **sum** I am (i.e. I'm full of the smell of incense/I can smell incense)

deinde rusus ait, thuris odore plena sum

et and **tertio** thirdly (i.e. a third time) **iterum** again, **Aerei** of brazen, **inquit** she says, **lapilli** gem-stone **fragorem** the noise **audio** I hear (i.e. I hear the sound of a brazen gem).

et tertio iterum, Aerei, inquit, lapilli fragorem audio.

Mater (her) mother **vero** but (i.e. but her mother), **respondens** answering, **ait** says, **O filia** O daughter, **ut** as **jam** now **percipio** I perceive (i.e. as I now perceive), **non solum** not only **visu** from sight **privata deprived es** you are (i.e. not only are you deprive of sight), **sed et**

Mater vero respondens ait, O filia, ut jam percipio, non solum visu privata es, sed et auditu et olfactu.

228

but and *(i.e. but also)* auditu *from (i.e. of) hearing* et olfactu *and smell*.

Fabula significat the fable signifies, *nonnullus* not none (i.e. some) *jactabundos* beautiful (people) *impossibilia* impossible (things) *profiteri* to profess, *et* and *in minimis* in the least *redargui* to be refuted (i.e. the fable signifies that some beautiful people profess impossible things, and are refuted/proved wrong in the smallest things).

Fabula significat, nonnullus jactabundos impossibilia profiteri, et in minimis redargui.

Decoding Latin – Day 20

Don't forget the rules:

1. Don't try to memorise anything
2. Focus on the story, not the language – don't try to analyse!
3. Read one section from the left column and then the same from the right.
4. Always read for speed and general gist, not for accuracy and perfection.

VESPAE THE WASPS ET PERDICES AND THE PARTRIDGES	**VESPAE ET PERDICES**
Vespae wasps et perdices and partridges siti with thirst laborantes labouring ad agricolam to a farmer iverunt went (i.e. wasps and partridges, struggling with thirst, went to a farmer), ab from eo him rogantes asking potum a drink (i.e. asking for a drink from him), promittentes promising pro for (i.e. in place of/in exchange for) aqua the water se themselves hanc this gratiam favour	Vespae et perdices siti laborantes ad agricolam iverunt, ab eo rogantes potum, promittentes pro aqua se hanc gratiam reddituras:

230

reddituras about to return (i.e promising that in exchange for the water they would give back this favour):

Perdices the partridges quidem indeed fodere to dig vineas the vines (i.e. the partridges would dig/turn over the soil around the vines):

Vespae the wasps autem but (i.e. but the wasps), circumcirca round about eundo going (i.e. the wasps, by going around), aculeis with (their) stings arcere to drive away fures thieves (i.e. the was, going around, would drive away thieves with their stings).

At but agricola the farmer inquit said, Sed but mihi to me sunt are duo two boves oxen (i.e. I have

Perdices quidem fodere vineas:

Vespae autem, circumcirca eundo aculeis arcere fures.

At agricola inquit, Sed mihi sunt duo boves, qui, nihil promittentes, omnia faciunt.

231

two oxen)⁹, qui who, nihil nothing promittentes promising (i.e. promising nothing), omnia all (these) things faciunt do.

Melius better, igitur therefore, est it is (i.e. it's better, therefore), ilis to them dare to give (i.e. to give water to them), quam than vobis to you.

Fabula a fable in into (i.e. against) viros men perniciosos pernicious (i.e a fable against dangerous men), promittentes promsiing, quidem indeed, juvare to help, laedentes injuring autem but admodum very much (i.e. but injuring very much).

PAVO THE PEACOCK ET

Melius igitur est ilis dare, quam vobis.

Fabula in viros perniciosos, promittentes, quidem juvare, laedentes autem admodum.

PAVO ET MONEDULA

---

⁹ A very common Latin idiom is to say 'there is something to me', meaning 'I have something', e.g. in this case, the Latin says 'there are two oxen to/for me', but in English the sense is 'I have two oxen'

232

MONEDULA AND THE JACKDAW

Avibus *with birds* volentibus *wanting* creare *to create* regem *a king*, pavo *a peacock* rogabat *asked*, ut *that*, se *himself* ob *on account of* pulchritudinem *(his) beauty* eligerent *they would choose*.

Eligentibus *with electing* autem *but* eum *him* omnibus *all (i.e. but with all electing him)*, monedula *a jackdaw*, suscepto *having taken up* sermone *the discourse*, ait *said*,

Sed *but* si *if*, te *with you* regnante *reigning*, Aquila *an eagle* nos *us* persequi *to pursue* aggressa attempted fuerit *shall have been (i.e. but if, with you reigning, an eagle should attempt to pursue us)*, quomodo *in what way*

Avibus volentibus creare regem, pavo rogabat, ut se ob pulchritudinem eligerent.

Eligentibus autem eum omnibus, monedula, suscepto sermone, ait,

Sed si, te regnante, Aquila nos persequi aggressa fuerit, quomodo nobis opem feres?

233

nobis to us **opem assistance feres** will you bring (i.e. how will you help us)?

Fabula significat the fable signifies, *principes* chiefs *non modo* not only *propter* on account of *pulchritudinem* (their) beauty, *sed et* but and (i.e. but also) *fortitudinem* bravery, *et prudentiam* and prudence, *eligere* to choose *oportere* to behove (i.e. one should: the fable signifies that one should choose leaders not only for their beauty but for their bravery and prudence also).

APER THE WILD BOAR ET VULPES AND THE FOX

Aper a wild boar, **cuidam** to a certain **adstans** standing near **arbori** to a tree (i.e. standing near t a certain tree), **dentes** (his)

Fabula significat, principes non modo propter pulchritudinem, sed et fortitudinem, et prudentiam, eligere oportere.

APER ET VULPES

Aper, cuidam adstans arbori, dentes acuebat.

234

teeth **acuebat** sharpened (i.e. he sharpened his teeth).

Vulpe with a fox **autem** but (i.e. but with a fox) **rogante** asking **causam** the cause (i.e. the reason), **quare** for what reason (i.e. why), **nulla** with no **proposita** being proposed **necessitate** necessity (i.e. without any need being present), **dentes** his teeth **acueret** he should sharpen (i.e. when a fox asked why he would sharpen his teeth without there being any need)? **Inquit** he said:

Non not **sine** without **causa** cause (i.e. not without reason) **hoc** this **facio** do I do (i.e. I don't do this without cause):

nam for **si** if **me** me **periculum** danger **invaserit** should have attacked me (i.e. for if danger should

Vulpe autem rogante causam, quare, nulla proposita necessitate, dentes acueret? inquit:

Non sine causa hoc facio:

nam si me periculum invaserit, minime me tunc acuendis dentibus occupatum esse

235

come against me), minime by no means me me tunc then acuendis in to-be-sharpened dentibus teeth occupatum occupied esse to be oportebit it will behove (i.e. it will by no means befit me to be occupied in teeth needing to be sharpened), sed but potius rather paratis with (them) prepared (already) uti to be used.

Fabula significat the fable signifies, adversus against periculum danger praeparatum to be prepared for esse to be oportere to behove (i.e. one should: the fable signifies that one should be prepared against danger).

oportebit, sed potius paratis uti.

Fabula significat, adversus periculum praeparatum esse oportere.

Decoding Latin – Day 21

Don't forget the rules:

1. Don't try to memorise anything
2. Focus on the story, not the language – don't try to analyse!
3. Read one section from the left column and then the same from the right.
4. *Always read for speed and general gist, not for accuracy and perfection.*

CASSITA THE LARK

Cassita a lark, a by laqueo a snare capta being captured (i.e. being caught in a trap), plorans lamenting dicebat did say, Hei woe mihi to me misere wretched (i.e. woe to poor me) et and infelici unfortunate volucri bird!

Non aurum not the gold surripui have I stolen cujusquam of anyone (i.e. I haven't taken anyone's gold), non argentum not the silver, non aliud not other quicquam any

CASSITA

Cassita, a laqueo capta, plorans dicebat, Hei mihi misere et infelici volucri!

Non aurum surripui cujusquam, non argentum, non aliud quicquam pretiosum;

237

pretiosum precious (i.e. nor any other precious thing);

granum grain autem but tritici of wheat parvum a little (i.e. but a little grain of wheat) mortem death mihi for me conciliavit has procured.

Fabula a fable in into (i.e. against) eos those, qui who ob on account of vile mean (i.e. contemptible) lucrum gain, magnum a great subeunt undergo periculum danger (i.e. undergo a great danger).

HINNULUS THE FAWN

Hinnulus a fawn, aliquando some time (i.e. one day) cervo to a stag ait said (i.e. said to a stag), Pater father, tu you natus born es are (i.e. are born) et major and bigger et

granum autem tritici parvum mortem mihi conciliavit.

Fabula in eos, qui ob vile lucrum, magnum subeunt periculum.

HINNULUS

Hinnulus aliquando cervo ait, Pater, tu natus es et major et celerior canibus, et cornua praeterea ingentia gestas ad vindictam;

238

celerior and faster canibus than the dogs, et cornua and (your) horns praeterea moreover ingentia huge gestas you carry on (i.e. you carry huge horns) ad vindictam for revenge;

curnam why then igitur therefore, sic thus eos them times do you fear (i.e. why then do you fear them so much)?

Et ille and he, ridens lkaughing, ait said, Vera true quidem indeed haec these (things are) inquis you say, fili (my) son:

unum one thing vero but (i.e. but one thing) scio I know, quod that quum when canis of a dog latratum the barking audivero I will have heard (i.e. that when I hear the barking of a dog), statim immediately ad fugam to

curnam igitur sic eos times?

Et ille ridens ait, Vera quidem haec inquis, fili:

unum vero scio, quod quum canis latratum audivero, statim ad fugam, nescio quomodo efferor.

239

flight, **nescio** I know not **quomodo** how **efferor** I'm carried away.

Fabula significat the fable signifies, *quod* that *natura* by nature *timidos* the timid (i.e. those timid by nature) *nulla* no *admonitio* advice *confirmat* strengthens (i.e. the fable signifies that no advice strengthens those timid by nature).

LEPORES THE HARES ET RANAE AND THE FROGS

Lepores hares **aliquando** sometime (i.e. one day) **congregate** having flocked together, **sui** of their own **ipsorum** of themselves **deplorabant** they lamented **vitam** the life (i.e. they complained about their own life), **quod** because **foret** it might be (i.e. it was) **periculis** to dangers

Fabula significat, quod natura timidos nulla admonitio confirmat.

LEPORES ET RANAE

Lepores aliquando congregati, sui ipsorum deplorabant vitam, quod foret periculis obnoxis, et timoris plena:

240

obnoxis liable (i.e. liable to dangers), et and timoris of fear plena full (i.e., full of fear):

etenim for ab by omnibus all, et and (i.e. both) canibus by dogs, et aquilis and by eagles, et aliis and by other multis many (i.e. by many other [animals]) consumebantur they were consumed.

Melius better itaque and so (i.e. and so better) esse to be mori to die semel once dixerunt they said (i.e. and so they said it was better to die once), quam than toto in the whole vitae of life tempore time (i.e. in the whole time of life) timere to fear (i.e. they said it was better to die once than to be afraid their whole lifetime).

etenim ab omnibus, et canibus, et aquilis, et aliis multis consumebantur.

Melius itaque esse mori semel dixerunt, quam toto vitae tempore timere.

Hoc with this igitur therefore, confirmato being confirmed, impetum a charge fecerunt they made (i.e. they made a charge) simul together in into paludem a marsh, quasi as if in into eam it delapsuri about to slip et and suffocandi to be suffocated (i.e. they rushed into the marsh, to slip in and choke themselves/drown).

Sed but quum when ranae the frogs, quae which circum around paludem the marsh sedebant sat (i.e. which sat around the marsh), cursus of the running strepitu with the noise percepto being perceived (i.e. having heard the noise of the running), illico immediately in into hanc this (marsh) insiluissent might have leapt in (i.e. they leapt into the marsh immediately), ex out of

Hoc igitur confirmato, impetum fecerunt simul in paludem, quasi in eam delapsuri et suffocandi.

Sed quum ranae, quae circum paludem sedebant, cursus strepitu percepto illico in hanc insiluissent, ex leporibus quidam, sagacior esse visus aliis, ait, Sistite, O socii, nihil grave in vos ipsos molimini:

242

leporibus the hares quidam a certain (one, i.e. a certain one of the hares), sagacior more sagacious (i.e. wiser) esse to be visus seemed aliis (than) the others (i.e. who seemed wiser than the others), ait said, Sistite stop, O socii O companions, nihil nothing grave heavy (i.e. serious) in into vos you ipsos yourselves molimini devise (i.e. don't do anything serious to yourselves):

jam now enim for (i.e. for now), ut as videtis you see, et and (i.e. also) nobis (than) us alia other sunt there are animalia animals (i.e. there are other animals) timidiora more timid (i.e. for now, as you see, there are other animals more timid than us).

jam enim, ut videtis, et nobis alia sunt animalia timidiora.

243

Fabula significat the fable signifies, *miseros* (that) the wretched *ab* by *aliis* others, *graviora* heavier (i.e. more serious things) *patientibus* by suffering, *recreari* to be recreated/relieved (i.e. the fable signifies that the wretched are relieved by others suffering more serious/worse things).

ASINUS THE ASS ET EQUUS AND THE HORSE

Asinus an ass *equum* a horse *beatum* happy *putabat* thought (i.e. an ass thought a horse [was] happy), *utpote* inasmuch as *abunde* abundantly *nutritum* being fed, *et accurate* and carefully (i.e. inasmuch as the horse was fed abundantly and carefully), *quum* when (i.e. while) *ipse* he himself (i.e. the ass) *neque* neither *palearum* of straws (i.e. of

Fabula significat miseros ab aliis, graviora patientibus, recreari.

ASINUS ET EQUUS

Asinus equum beatum putabat, utpote abunde nutritum, et accurate, quum ipse neque palearum satis haberet, idque, plurimum defatigatus.

244

straw) satis enough haberet would have (i.e. while he didn't have enough straw), idque and that, plurimum very much defatigatus wearied.

Quum when autem but (i.e. but when) tempus time instaret would press on belli of war (i.e. but when a time of war came up), et and miles a soldier armatus armed (i.e. an armed soldier) ascendisset might have ascended (i.e. ascended) equum the horse, huc hither illuc (and) thither ipsum him impellens driving (i.e. driving him/the horse hither and thither), et and insuper moreover in into medios the middle hostes (of) the enemies insiluisset might have leapt in (i.e. and, moreover, had leapt into the middle of the enemy), et equus and the horse vulneratus wounded

Quum autem tempus instaret belli, et miles armatus ascendisset equum, huc illuc ipsum impellens, et insuper in medios hostes insiluisset, et equus vulneratus jacebat:

245

jacebat lay (i.e. and the horse lay wounded):

His with these (things) visis being seen, asinus the ass equum the donkey, mutata being changed sentential his opinion (i.e. having changed his opinion), miserum wretched existimabat thought (i.e. having seen these things, the ass thought, having changed his opinion, that the horse was wretched).

Fabula significat the fable signifies, non oportere not to behove (i.e. one shouldn't) principibus to princes et divitibus and riches invidere to envy (i.e. that we shouldn't envy princes and riches):

sed but in illos into (i.e. against) them invidia with the envy et periculo and danger consideratis being

His visis, asinus equum, mutate sentential, miserum existimabat.

Fabula significat, non oportere principibus et divitibus invidere:

sed in illos invidia et periculo consideratis, paupertatem amare.

246

considered (i.e. but with the envy and danger against them being considered), **paupertatem** *poverty* **amare** *to love (i..e but, having considered the danger and envy that's against the, one should rather love poverty).*

Decoding Latin – Day 22

Don't forget the rules:

1. Don't try to memorise anything
2. Focus on the story, not the language – don't try to analyse!
3. Read one section from the left column and then the same from the right.
4. *Always read for speed and general gist, not for accuracy and perfection.*

AVARUS THE GREEDY MAN

Avarus a greedy man quidam a certain (i.e. a certain greedy man), quum when omnia all things sua his own bona good (i.e. all his own good things) in into pecuniam money vertisset might have turned (i.e. when he'd turned all his good things into money), et and auream a golden massam heap fecisset he might have made (i.e. and when he'd made a golden heap), in in loco a place quodam a certain (i.e. in a certain

AVARUS

Avarus quidam, quum omnia sua bona in pecuniam vertisset, et auream massam decisset, in loco quodam defodit, una defosso illic et animo suo, et mente;

248

place) **defodit** he buried (it), **una** in one (i.e. together) **defosso** being buried **illic** there **et** and (i.e. also) **animo** (his) soul **suo** his own (i.e. and with his own soul being buried with it), **et mente** and (his) mind;

atque and **quotidie** daily (i.e. every day) **eundo** by going **ipsam** it (i.e. the heap) **videbat** he saw (i.e. and he saw it every day, by going).

atque quotidie eundo ipsam videbat.

Quum when **autem** but (i.e. but when) **ex** out of **operariis** the working (men) **quidam** a certain one **eum** him **observasset** might have observed (i.e. but when one of the workers had observed him), **et** and **quod** what **factum** done **erat** was **recognovisset** he might have recognized (i.e. and when he

Quum autem ex operariis quidam eum observasset, et quod factum erat recognovisset, refossam massam sustulit.

249

recognised/realised what had been done), **refossam** having dug up **massam** the heap **sustulit** he took it up (i.e. he took away the heap, having dug it up).

Post after **haec** these (things) **et** and (i.e. also) **ille** he **profectus** having set out (i.e. after these things, he also set out), **et** and **vacuum** and empty **locum** place **conspicatus** having caught sight of (i.e. and having seen the place empty), **lugere** to mourn **coepit** he began (i.e. he began to mourn), **et** and **capilllos** (his) hairs **evellere** to pull out.

Hunc this (man, i.e. him) **vero** but **quum** when **quidam** a certain **vidisset** might have seen (i.e. but when a certain persn had seen him) **sic** thus **plorantem** wailing, **et causam** and the cause (i.e.

Post haec et ille profectus, et vacuum locum conspicatus, lugere coepit, et capilllos evellere.

Hunc vero quum quidam vidisset sic plorantem, et causam audivisset,

250

the reason) **audivisset** he might have heard (i.e. and when he'd heard the reason),

Ne not **sic** thus, **ait** he said, **heus tu** hey you, **tristare** to be sad (i.e. hark, don't be sad), **neque** not **enim** for (i.e. for not) **habens** having **aurum** gold **habebas** did you have (it, i.e. for, when you had the gold, you didn't have it):

Lapidem a stone **igitur** therefore, **pro** for (i.e. in place of) **auro** the gold **acceptum** taken **reconde** hide away (i.e. hide away a stone instead of the gold) **et puta** and think **tibi** to you **aurum** gold **esse** to be (i.e. hide a stone and think/pretend it's gold for yourself):

eundem the same **enim** for (i.e. for the same) **tibi** for you **praestabit** it will

Ne sic, ait heus tu, tristare, neque enim habens aurum habebas:

Lapidem igitur pro auro acceptum reconde et puta tibi aurum esse:

eundem enim tibi praestabit usum.

afford **usum** use (i.e. for it will give you the same use/it will be just as useful for you).

Ut as **video** I see **enim** for (i.e. for as I see it), **neque** neither, **quum** when **aurum** the gold **erat** was there, **in usu** in use **eras** you were **possessionis** of the possession (i.e. for, as I see it, when there was gold, you didn't make any use of it).

Fabula significat the fable signifies, **nihil** (that) nothing **esse** to be **possessionem** possession (i.e. that possession is nothing), **nisi** unless **usus** the use (of it) **adfuerit** shall have been present (i.e. possession is nothing, unless it's use is present too/unless it's used).

Ut video enim, neque, quum aurum erat, in usu eras possessionis.

Fabula significat, nihil esse possessionem, nisi usus adfuerit.

252

AUSERES THE GEESE ET GRUES AND THE CRANES	**AUSERES ET GRUES**
Auseres geese et grues and cranes in in eodem the same prato field pascebantur were grazed/fed.	Auseres et grues in eodem prato pascebantur.
Venatoribus with hunters autem but (i.e. but with hunters) visis being seen, grues the cranes, quod because essent they might be (i.e. they were) leves light, statim immediately avolaverunt flew away:	Venatoribus autem visis, grues, quod essent leves, statim avolaverunt:
Auseres the geese vero but (i.e. but the geese), ob on account of onus the burden (i.e. the weight) corporum of (their) bodies, quum when (i.e. since) mansissent they might have remained (i.e. since they remained), capti taken fuerunt they	Auseres vero, ob onus corporum, quum mansissent, capti fuerunt.

were (i.e. they were taken).

Fabula significat the fable signifies, *et* and (i.e. also) *in* in *expugnatione* the attacking *urbis* of a city *inopes* the poor *facile* easily *fugere* to flee (i.e. that the poor easily flee in the attacking of a city), *divites* the wealthy *vero* but (i.e. but the wealthy) *servire* to serve (i.e. to be slaves) *captos* (are) taken.

TESTUDO THE TORTOISE ET AQUILA AND THE EAGLE

Testudo a tortoise orabat prayed (i.e. begged) aquilam an eagle, ut that se herself (i.e. the tortoise) volare to fly doceret she (i.e. the eagle) would teach (i.e. a

Fabula significat, et in expugnatione urbis inopes facile fugere, divites vero servire captos.

TESTUDO ET AQUILA

Testudo orabat aquilam, ut se volare doceret.

254

tortoise begged an eagle to teach her to fly).

Ea she **autem** but (i.e. but she) **admonente** warning (her), **procul** at a distance (i.e. very far) **hoc** this a **from natura** the nature **ipsius** of her (i.e. her nature) **esse** to be (i.e. but she, warning her that it was very far from being in her nature), **illa** she (i.e. the tortoise) **magis** the more **precibus** with prayers **instabat** stood by (i.e. urged; but the tortoise urged the eagle all the more with her prayers).

Ea autem admonente, procul hoc a natura ipsius esse, illa magis precibus instabat.

Accepit she took, **ergo** therefore, **ipsam** her (i.e. the tortoise) **unguibus** in (her) talons, **et** and **in** into **altum** high (i.e. high up) **sustulit** took (her) up, **inde** thence (i.e. from there) **demisit** sent down (i.e. let her fall).

Accepit ergo ipsam unguibus, et in altum sustulit, inde demisit.

Haec this (woman, i.e. the tortoise) autem but (i.e. but she) in into (i.e. onto) petras rocks cecidit fell (i.e. she fell onto the rocks), et and contrita crushed est is (i.e. and was crushed).

Fabula significat the fable signifies, multos (that) many, quia because in contentionibus in (their) contentions (i.e. disagreements) prudentiores more prudent (people) non audierint they might not have heard (i.e. didn't hear/listen to), seipsos they themselves laesisse to have injured (i.e. the fable signifies that many have injured themselves because they didn't hear/listen to more prudent people).

PULEX THE FLEA

Haec autem in petras cecidit, et contrita est.

Fabula significat, multos, quia in contentionibus prudentiores non audierint, seipsos laesisse.

PULEX

256

Pulex a flea, **aliquando** some time (i.e. one day) **cum** when **saltasset** might have leapt (i.e. when a flea had leapt one day), **viri** of a man **pede** on the foot (i.e. on the foot of a man) **insedit** he sat on (i.e. he settled on the foot of a man).	Pulex, aliquando cum saltasset, viri pede insedit.
Hic this (man, i.e. he) **autem** but (i.e. but he) **Herculem** Hercules **in auxilium** into (i.e. for) help **invocabat** invoked:	Hic autem Herculem in auxilium invocabat:
at but, **quum** when **illinc** from there **rursus** again **saltasset** he (i.e. the flea) might have leapt (i.e. but when the flea had leapt from there again), **suspirans** sighing **ait** he (i.e. the man) said,	at, quum illinc rursus saltasset, suspirans ait,
O Hercules O Hercules, **si** if **contra** against **pulicem** a flea **non auxiliatus** not helped **es** you are (i.e. if	O Hercules, si contra pulicem non auxiliatus es,

257

you haven't helped [me] against a flea), **quomodo** in what way (i.e. how) **contra** against **majores** greater **adversarios** adversaries **adjuvabis** will you help?

Fabula significat the fable signifies, *non oportere* not to behove (i.e. that one shouldn't) *in minimis* in the least *deum* god *rogare* to ask (i.e. that one shouldn't ask god in the least/smallest things), *sed* but *in necessariis* in the necessary.

quomodo contra majores adversarios adjuvabis?

Fabula significat, non oportere in minimis deum rogare, sed in necessariis.

Decoding Latin – Day 23

Don't forget the rules:

1. Don't try to memorise anything
2. Focus on the story, not the language – don't try to analyse!
3. Read one section from the left column and then the same from the right.
4. *Always read for speed and general gist, not for accuracy and perfection.*

CERVA A DOE

Cerva a doe, altero with the other obcaecato being blinded oculo eye (i.e. with one eye blinded), in litore in (i.e. on) the shore pascebatur was fed (i.e. was fed on the shore) sanum the healthy oculum eye ad to terram land propter on account of venatores hunters habens having (i.e. having the healthy eye on the land on account of/in case of hunters), alterum the other vero but (i.e. but the other) ad mare to the sea, unde whence (i.e.

CERVA

Cerva, altero obcaecato oculo, in litore pascebatur sanum oculum ad terram propter venatores habens, alterum vero ad mare, unde nihil suspicabatur:

259

from which) nihil nothing suspicabatur she suspected (i.e. she had her bad eye to the sea, from which direction she suspected nothing):

praeternavigantes sailing by autem but quidam certain (persons, i.e. but, certain people sailing by), et and hoc this conjectantes guessing (i.e. and guessing the situation), ipsam her (i.e. the doe) sagittarunt they shot,	praeternavigantes autem quidam, et hoc conjectantes, ipsam sagittarunt,
Haec this (woman, i.e. the doe) autem but (i.e. but she) seipsam herself lugebat mourned, ut that quae (those things) which, unde whence (i.e. from which) timuerat she had feared, nihil nothing passa suffered foret she might have been (i.e. that she had suffered nothing from	Haec autem seipsam lugebat, ut quae, unde timuerat, nihil passa foret;

260

the place from which she'd feared);

quod (that) which vero but (i.e. but that which) non putabat she didn't think malum evil allaturum about to bring (i.e. that place which she didn't think would bring evil), ab eo from it prodita betrayed foret she might have been (i.e. she was betrayed by it).

quod vero non putabat malum allaturum, ab eo prodita foret.

Fabula significat the fable signifies, saepe often quae (those things) which nobis to us noxia noxious (i.e. harmful) videntur seem, utilia useful fieri to become (i.e. those things which seem harmful to us, often become useful); quae (those things) which vero but (i.e. but those things which) utilia (seem) useful, noxia (become) harmful.

Fabula significat, saepe quae nobis noxia videntur, utilia fieri; quae vero utilia, noxia.

261

CERVA **THE DOE** ET LEO **AND THE LION**

Cerva **a doe** venatores **hunters** fugiens **fleeing (i.e. a doe, fleeing hunters)** in **into** speluncam **a cave** ingressa **entered** est **is (i.e. entered a cave)**:

in **into** leonem **a lion** autem **but** cum **when (i.e. but when into a lion)** ibi **there** incidisset **she might have fallen (i.e. but when she'd fallen/run into a lion there)**, ab **by** eo **him** comprehensus **seized** est she is **(i.e. she was seized)**:

moriens **dying** autem **but (i.e. but dying)** dicebat **she said**, Hei mihi **woe to me**! Quod **because**, homines **men** fugiens **fleeing (i.e. fleeing from men)**, in **into** ferarum **of wild beasts** immitissimum **the cruelest (i.e. into the cruelest of**

CERVA ET LEO

Cerva venatores fugiens in speluncam ingressa est:

in leonem autem cum ibi incidisset, ab eo comprehensus est:

moriens autem dicebate, Hei mihi! quod, homines fugiens, in ferarum immitissimum incidi.

262

wild animals) incidi I have fallen.

Fabula significat the fable signifies, *multos many homines people*, *dum while parva small pericula dangers fugiunt they flee (i.e. while they flee small dangers)* *in into magna great incurrere to run into (i.e. the fable signifies that many people, while they flee small dangers, run into great dangers)*.

CERVA THE DOE ET VITIS AND THE VINE

Cerva *a doe* venatores *hunters* fugiens *fleeing (i.e. fleeing hunters)*, sub *under* vite *a vine* delituit *lay hidden*.

Quum *when* praeteriisent *they might have passed by (i.e. they had passed by)* autem *but* parumper *a little* illi *they (i.e. but when*

CERVA ET VITIS

Cerva venatores fugiens, sub vite delituit.

Quum praeteriisent autem parumper illi, cerva, prorsus jam latera

263

they had passed by a little way), **cerva** a doe, **prorsus** altogether **jam** now **latera** to lie hidden **arbitrata** having thought (i.e. having thought now to stay hidden altogether), **vitis** of the vine **folia** the leaves **despasci** to feed on **incepit** began (i.e. began to feed on the leaves of the vine).

Illis with them **vero** but (i.e. but with them) **agitatis** being shaken (i.e. with the leaves being shaken), **venatores** the hunters **conversi** being turned (i.e. the hunters turned), **et** and **quod** what **erat** was **verum** true **arbitrati** having judged (i.e. and having realised what was the case), **animal** (that) an animal **aliquod** some (i.e. that some animal) **sub** under **foliis** the leaves **occultari** to be hidden (i.e. was hidden), **sagittis** with arrows

arbitrata, vitis folia despasci incepit.

Illis vero agitatis, venatores conversi, et quod erat verum arbitrati, animal aliquod sub foliis occultari, sagittis confecerunt cervam.

confecerunt they finished (off) cervam the doe.

Haec this (woman, i.e. the doe) autem but (i.e. but she), moriens dying, talia such (words) dicebat did say (i.e. but she, dying, said these words):

Haec autem moriens talia dicebat:

Justa just (things) passa suffered sum I am (i.e. I suffer just things), non not enim for offendere to offend (i.e. for not to offend) oportebat it behoved (i.e. one shouldn't) eam that (i.e. for one shouldn't/I shouldn't offend that), quae which me me servaret preserved (i.e. I suffer justly, because I oughtn't to have offended that [the vine] which kept me safe).

Justa passa sum, non enim offendere oportebat eam, quae me servaret.

Fabula significat the fable signifies, *eos* those, *qui* who *injuria* with injury *benefactores* (their) *benefactors afficiunt affct* (i.e. those who injure their benefactors), *a deo* by god *puniri* to be punished (i.e. the fable signifies that those who treated their benefactors with injury, are punished by god).

ASINUS THE ASS ET LEO AND THE LION

Cum asino with an ass *gallus* a rooster *aliquando* sometime (i.e. one day) *pascebatur* was fed:

leone with a lion *autem* but (i.e. but with a lion) *aggresso* having attacked *asinum* the ass, *gallus* the rooster *exclamavit* cried out, *et* and *leo* the lion (*aiunt* they say *enim* for (i.e. for they say) *hunc* him *galli* the rooster's *vocem*

Fabula significat, eos, qui injuria benefactores afficiunt, a deo puniri.

ASINUS ET LEO

Cum asino gallus aliquando pascebatur:

leone autem aggresso asinum, gallus exclamavit, et leo (aiunt enim hunc galli vocem timere) fugit.

266

voice **timere** to fear (i.e. for they say he was afraid of the rooster's voice) **fugit** he fled.

At but **asinus** the ass **ratus** having thought **eum** him (i.e. the lion) **propter** on account of **se** himself **fugisse** to have fled (i.e. the ass, thinking the lion had fled because of him), **aggressus** attacked **est** is (i.e. he attacked) **statim** immediately **leonem** the lion:

At asinus ratus eum propter se fugisse, aggressus est statim leonem:

ut as (i.e. when) **vero** but (i.e. but when) **procul** at a distance (i.e. far off/a long way) **hunc** him (i.e. the lion) **persecutus** having followed **est** he is (i.e. but when he'd followed the lion a long way), **quo** to where **non amplius** no more **galli** the rooster's **perveniebat** came through **vox** voice (i.e. to where the rooster's voice didn't

ut vero procul hunc persecutes est, quo non amplius galli perveniebat vox, conversus leo, eum devoravit.

267

reach), **conversus** having turned **leo** the lion (i.e. the lion, having turned), **eum** him (i.e. the ass) **devoravit** devoured.

Hic this (i.e. the ass) **vero** but (i.e. but he) **moriens** dying, **clamabat** cried, **Me me** miserum wretched (i.e. wretched me) **et dementem** and insane (i.e. wretched and insane me)!

ex out of **pugnacibus** fightings **enim** for **non natus** not born **parentibus** (my) parents (i.e. I wasn't born from fighting parents), **cujus** of what **gratia** by the grace (i.e. for what reason) **in** into **aciem** edge (i.e. into battle) **irrui** have I rushed (i.e. why did I rush into battle)?

Fabula significat the fable signifies, *plerosque* most (people) *homines* people *inimicos* hostile, *qui* who *se*

Hic vero moriens clamabat, Me miserum et dementem!

ex pugnacibus enim non natus parentibus, cujus gratia in aciem irrui?

Fabula significat, plerosque homines inimicos, qui se de industria humiliarunt,

268

themselves **de** *from* **industria** *industry* **humiliarunt** *have humbled (i.e. who have humbled themselves through industry/by design),* **aggredi** *to attack (i.e. the fable signifies that most people attack those who have humbled themselves/made themselves look weak by design),* **atque** *and* **ita** *so* **ab illis** *by them* **occidi** *to be killed (i.e. are killed).*

aggredi, atque ita ab illis occidi.

Decoding Latin – Day 24

Don't forget the rules:

1. Don't try to memorise anything
2. Focus on the story, not the language – don't try to analyse!
3. Read one section from the left column and then the same from the right.
4. Always read for speed and general gist, not for accuracy and perfection.

OLITOR THE HERB-SELLER ET CANIS AND THE DOG	**OLITOR ET CANIS**
Olitoris of a herb-seller canis the dog (i.e. a herb-seller's dog) in into puteum a well decidit fell down:	Olitoris canis in puteum decidit:
olitor the herb-seller autem but (i.e. but the herb-seller), volens wanting ipsum him (i.e. the dog) illinc from there extrahere to draw out (i.e. wanting to pull him out of there), descendit descended et and (i.e.	olitor autem, volens ipsum illinc extrahere, descendit et ipse in puteum.

also) **ipse** himself **in** into **puteum** the well.

Ratus having thought **autem** but (i.e. but, having thought) **canis** the dog (i.e. but, the dog having thought), **eum** him **ut** that **se** himself **inferius** lower **magis** more **accessisse** to have approached **obrueret** he could overwhelm (i.e. sink: the dog, thinking that he/the herb-seller had approached so that he could force the dog lower), **olitorem** the herb-seller, **conversus** having turned, **momordit** he bit (i.e. having turned around, he bit the herb-seller).

Hic he **autem** but (i.e. but he/the herb-seller) **cum dolore** with pain **reversus** having turned back (i.e. having turned back with pain), **Justa** just (i.e. rightly/rightly), **inquit** he said, **patior** do I suffer:

Ratus autem canis, eum ut se inferius magis accessisse obrueret, olitorem conversus momordit.

Hic autem cum dolore reversus, Justa, inquit, patior:

271

nam *for* cur *why* unquam *ever* sui *of himself* interfectorem *a killer* servare *to save* studui *have I endeavoured* (i.e. for whyever have I tried to preserve someone who is his own murderer)?

Fabula *a fable* in *into* (i.e. against/for) injustos *the unjust*, et ingratos *and the ungrateful*.

SUS *THE SOW (I.E. FEMAIL PIG)* ET CANIS *AND THE DOG*

Sus *a sow* et canis *and a dog* mutuo *mutually* conviatiabantur *railed* (i.e. they fought/insulted eachother).

Et *and* sus *the sow* jurabat *swore* per *through* venerem *Venus* (i.e. she swore on Venus), procul *far* dubio *from doubt* (i.e.

nam cur unquam sui interfectorem servare studui?

Fabula in injustos, et ingratos.

SUS ET CANIS

Sus et canis mutuo conviatiabantur.

Et sus jurabat per venerem, procul dubio dentibus se discissuram canem.

272

doubtless) **dentibus** with (her) teeth **se** herself **discissuram** about to tear apart **canem** the dog (i.e. she swore on Venus that she would tear the dog apart with her teeth).

Canis the dog **vero** but (i.e. but the dog) **ad** to **haec** these (words) **per** through **ironiam** irony (i.e. ironically) **dixit** he said, **Bene** well **per Venerem** through Venus **nobis** to us **juras** do you swear (you swear rightly to call on Venus), **significas** you signifiy **enim** for (i.e. for you signify/suggest) **ab** by **ipsa** her **vehementer** vehemently **te** you **Amari** to be loved (i.e. for you signify that you're loved strongly by her), **quae** (she) who **impuras** impure **tuas** your (i.e. your impure) **carnes** fleshes **degustantem** (someone) tasting (i.e. she who, someone tasting your

Canis vero ad haec per ironiam dixit, Bene per venerem nobis juras, significas enim ab ipsa vehementer te Amari, quae impuras tuas carnes degustantem, nullo pacto in sacellum admittit.

impure flesh), **nullo** by no **pacto** agreement (i.e. in no way) **in sacellum** into (her) chapel **admittit** admits (i.e. you suggest she loves you strongly, she who admits nobody into her chapel who tastes your impure flesh).

Et sus and the sow (said), **Propter** on account of **hoc** this, **igitur** therefore, **magis** more **prae** before **se** herself **fert** carries (i.e. professes: carries before herself = professes[10]) **dea** the goddess (i.e. on account of this the goddess professes) **amare** to love **me** me:

nam for **occidentem** (the one) killing, **aut** or **alio** in other **quovis** in any **modo** way (i.e. or in any other way) **laedentem** injuring (i.e. for anyone killing or in any other way injuring

Et sus, Propter hoc igitur magis prae se fert dea amare me:

nam occidentem, aut alio quovis modo laedentem, omnino aversatur:

---

[10] Akin to the English 'wears his heart on his sleeve'

me), **omnino** wholly (i.e. completely) **aversatur** she avoids (i.e. for she avoids anyone killing or in any other way hurting me):

tu you, **tamen** however, **male** badly **oles** you stink, **et** and (i.e. both) **viva** alive **et mortua** and dead.

Fabula significat the fable signifies, **prudentes** prudent (i.e. skillfull) **oratores** orators, **quae** which **ab inimicis** from (their) enemies **objiciuntur** are thrown against (i.e. objected/cast out at them) **convicia** the reproaches (i.e. that skillfull orators, the reproaches/criticisms which are cast against them by their enemies), **artificiose** artfully **in laudem** into praise **convertere** to turn (i.e. the fable signifies that skillfull orators turn the reproaches which are cast at them by their enemies into praise).

tu tamen male oles, et viva et mortua.

Fabula significat, prudentes oratores, quae ab inimicis objiciuntur convicia, artificiose in laudem convertere.

SUS THE SOW ET CANIS AND THE DOG

Sus a sow et canis and a dog de about foecunditate (their) fruitfulness certabant contended (i.e. they argued about which was more fruitful).

Dixit said autem but canis the dog (i.e. but the dog said) foecundam fruitful se herself esse to be maxime the most (i.e. she said she was the most fruitful) pedestrium of the pedestrian omnium of all animalium of the animals (i.e. the most fruitful of all of the pedestrian/walking-on-foot animals):

et and sus the sow, occurrens meeting (i.e. answering) ad to haec these (words) inquit said, Sed but quum when hoc this dicis you say (i.e. but

SUS ET CANIS

Sus et canis de foecunditate certabant.

Dixit autem canis foecundam se esse maxime pedestrium omnium animalium:

et sus occurrens ad haec inquit, Sed quum hoc dicis, scito et caecos tuos te catulos parere.

276

when you say this), **scito** know **et** and (i.e. know also) **caecos** blind **tuos** your **te** you **catulos** whelps **parere** to bring forth (i.e. know that you bring forth your pups blind).

Fabula significat the fable signifies, *non* not *celeritate* by speed *res* things, *sed* but *perfection* by perfection, *judicari* to be judged (i.e. the fable signifies that things aren't judged by their speed but by their perfection).

SERPENS THE SERPENT ET CANCER AND THE CRAB

Serpens a serpent **una** in one (i.e. together) **cum** with **cancro** a crab **vivebat** lived (i.e. lived together with a crab), **inita** having

Fabula significat, non celeritate res, sed perfectione, judicari.

SERPENS ET CANCER

Serpens una cum cancro vivebat, inita cum eo sociatate.

entered **cum** with **eo** him **sociatate** in an alliance.

Itaque and so **cancer** the crab, **simplex** simple **moribus** in (his) manners, **ut** that **et** and (i.e. also) **ille** he (i.e. the snake) **mutaret** would change, **admonebat** he (i.e. the crab), **astutiam** (his) cunning (i.e. and so the crab, simple/honest in his dealings, warned the snake to change his cunning/stop being so crafty/dishonest):

hic he (i.e. the snake) **autem** but (i.e. but he) **minime** by no means **se** himself **praebuit** afforded **obedientem** obedient (i.e. he in know way made himself obedient to this advice).

Quum when **observasset** might have observed, **igitur** therefore, **cancer**

Itaque cancer simplex moribus, ut et ille mutaret, admonebat, astutiam:

hic autem minime se praebuit obedientem.

Quum observasset igitur cancer ipsum dormientem, et pro

278

the crab (i.e. when the crab had observed) ipsum him (i.e. the snake) dormientem sleeping, et and pro according to viribus (his) strengths (i.e. with all his strength) compressisset he might have squeezed (i.e. when he'd squeezed the snake with all his strength), occidit he killed (him).

At but, serpens the serpent, post after mortem death extensor being stretched out, ille he (i.e. the crab) ait said, Sic thus oportebat it behoved (i.e. thus you should) antehac before this rectum straight et simplicem and simple esse to be (i.e. you should have been this straight and simple before);

neque not enim for (i.e. for not) hanc this poenam punishment dedisses you

viribus compressisset, occidit.

At, serpens post mortem extenso, ille ait, Sic oportebat antehac rectum et simplicem esse;

neque enim hanc poenam dedisses.

279

would have given (i.e. suffered: for then you wouldn't have suffered this punishment).

Fabula significat the fable signifies, *qui* (those) who *cum dolo* with deceit *amicos* friends *adeunt* come to (i.e. those who come to their friends with trickery), *ipsos* they themselves *potius* rather *offendi* to be (i.e. will be) injured.

Fabula significat, qui cum dolo amicos adeunt, ipsos potius offendi.

Decoding Latin – Day 25

Don't forget the rules:

1. Don't try to memorise anything
2. Focus on the story, not the language – don't try to analyse!
3. Read one section from the left column and then the same from the right.
4. *Always read for speed and general gist, not for accuracy and perfection.*

PASTOR THE SHEPHERD ET LUPUS AND THE WOLF	**PASTOR ET LUPUS**
Pastor a shepherd nuper recently natum born lupi of a wolf catulum a whelp reperit found (i.e. a shepherd found a recently born pup of a wolf) ac sustulit and took it up, unique and together cum with canibus (his) dogs nutrivit he nourished (it).	Pastor nuper natum lupi catulum reperit ac sustulit, unique cum canibus nutrivit.
At but, quum when adolevisset it might have grown up (i.e. but when	At, quum adolevisset, si quando Lupus ovem

it'd grown up), si quando if anytime lupus a wolf ovem a sheep rapuisset might have snatched (i.e. whenever a wolf had snatched a sheep), cum canibus with the dogs et and (i.e. also) ipse he himself persequebatur pursued (i.e. he himself pursued the wolf with the dogs).

Quum when canes the dogs vero but (i.e. but when the dogs) aliquando sometime (i.e. one day) non possent weren't able assequi to catch lupum the wolf, atque and ideo on that account reverterentur they might turn back (i.e. and for that reason they went back), ille he (i.e. the young wolf pup) sequebatur followed donec until, quum when ipsum him (i.e. the wolf) assecutus having caught esset he might be (i.e. until, when he'd caught

rapuisset, cum canibus et ipse persequebatur.

Quum canes vero aliquando non possent assequi lupum, atque ideo reverterentur, ille sequebatur donec, quum ipsum assecutus esset, utpote lupus, particeps foret venationis, deinde redibat.

the wolf), **utpote** as (i.e. being) **lupus** a wolf, **particeps** a sharer **foret** he might be (i.e he was a sharer) **venationis** of the hunt (i.e. he shared in eating the sheep), **deinde** then **redibat** he returned.

Sin but if **autem** but (i.e. but if) **lupus** the wolf **extra** outside **non rapuisset** might not have snatched **ovem** a sheep (i.e. but if the wolf hadn't carried away a sheep), **ipse** he himself (i.e. the wolf pup), **clam** secretly **occidens** killing (one), **una** together **cum** with **canibus** the dogs **comedebat** ate (it) up, **donec** until **pastor** the shepherd, **quum** when **conjectasset** he might have guessed (i.e. when he'd guessed), **et intellexisset** and understood **rem** the matter (i.e. what was happening), **de** from **arbore** a tree **ipsum** him

Sin autem lupus extra non rapuisset ovem, ipse, clam occidens, una cum canibus comedebat, donec pastor, quum conjectasset, et intellexisset rem, de arbore ipsum suspendit, et occidit.

(i.e. the wolf pup) suspendit he (i.e. the shepherd) suspended, et occidit and killed (him).

Fabula significat the fable signifies, naturam a nature pravam depraved (i.e. a depraved nature) bonos good mores manners non nutrire not to nourish (i.e. the fable signifies that a corrupt nature doesn't nourish/nurture good morals/habits).

LEO THE LION ET LUPUS AND THE WOLF

Leo a lion, quum when consenuisset it might have grown old (i.e. when it had grown old), aegrotabat was sick, jacens lying in in antro a cavern.

Fabula significat, naturam pravam bonos mores non nutrire.

LEO ET LUPUS

Leo, quum consenuisset, aegrotabat, jacens in antro.

Accesserunt they approached autem but (i.e. but they approached) visitatura about to visit (i.e. to visit) regem the king (i.e. the king of animals/the lion), praeter except vulpem the fox, caetera the rest animalia (of) the animals (i.e. all the other animals, except the fox, went to visit the king).

Lupus the wolf, igitur therefore, capta having taken occasione the opportunity, accusabat accused apud at (i.e. to) leonem the lion vulpem the fox (i.e. he condemned the fox in front of the lion), quasi as if nihil nothing facientem making (i.e. as if he were making nothing of) suum their own omnium of all dominum lord (i.e. as if he weren't giving any respect to their lord of all), et and propterea on account of

Accesserunt autem visitatura regem, praeter vulpem, caetera animalia.

Lupus igitur, capta occasione, accusabat apud leonem vulpem, quasi nihil facientem suum omnium dominum, et propterea neque ad visitationem profectam

285

this (i.e. for this reason) neque not ad to (i.e. for) visitationem a visit profectam having set out (i.e. he accused him of not respecting their king, and therefore not coming to visit)

Interim meanwhile adfuit was present et and (i.e. also) vulpes the fox (i.e. the fox was also there), et and ultima the last audivit she heard lupi of the wolf verba the words (i.e. and she heard the wolf's last words).

Leo the lion, igitur therefore, contra against eam her infremuit growled;

sed but defensionis of defence tempore with the time petito being sought (i.e. having asked for time/opportunity to defend herself), Et quis

Interim adfuit et vulpes, et ultima audivit lupi verba.

Leo igitur contra eam infremuit;

sed defensionis tempore petito, Et quis, inquit, eorum, qui convenerunt, tantum profuit, quantum ego, quae in omnem partem circuivi, et

286

and who, inquit she said, eorum of those, qui who convenerunt have come together, tantum so much profuit has profited, quantum as much as ego I (i.e. who of those who have come here has profited as much as I), quae who in into omnem every partem part (i.e. into all parts/everywhere) circuivi I have gone about, et and medicamentum a medicine pro for te you a medico from a doctor quaesivi I've sought, et didici and I've learnt (it, i.e. who has benefitted more than I, who have gone around everywhere looking for a medicine for you, and have found one)?

Quum when autem but (i.e. but when) leo the lion statim immediately, ut that medicamentum the medicine diceret she should say, imperasset might have commanded medicamentum pro te a medico quaesivi, et didici?

Quum autem leo statim, ut medicamentum diceret, imperasset, illa inquit, Si, lupo vivente excoriato, ipsius calidam pellem indueris.

287

(i.e. but when the lion commanded her to say the cure), illa she inquit said, Si if, lupo with a wolf vivente living excoriato being flayed (i.e. if, having flayed a wolf alive), ipsius of the same (wolf) calidam the warm pellem skin indueris you will have put on (i.e. if you put on the warm skin/hide of a wolf flayed alive).

Et and, lupo with the wolf statim immediately mortuo dead jacente lying (i.e. and with the wolf immediately lying dead), vulpes the fox, ridens laughing, ait said, Sic thus non oportet it does not behove (i.e. thus one ought not) dominum a lord ad malevolentiam to malevolence movere to move (i.e. one shouldn't move/incite a lord to anger), sed but ad benevolentiam to

Et, lupo statim mortuo jacente, vulpes ridens ait, Sic non oportet dominum ad malevolentiam movere, sed ad benevolentiam.

benevolence (i.e. but to goodwill).

Fabula significat the fable signifies *eum* (that) him, *qui* who *contra* against *alium* another *machinatur* plots (i.e. that he who plots against another), *in* into (i.e. against) *seipsum* himself *laqueum* a noose *vertere* to turn (i.e. he who plots against another, turns a noose against himself).

MULIER THE WOMAN

Mulier a woman *quaedam* a certain (i.e. a certain woman) *virum* a man (i.e. a husband) *ebrium* drunken *habebat* had (i.e. a certain woman had a drunken husband):

ipsum him *autem* but *a morbo* from the disease *liberare* to free *volens* wanting (i.e. but, wanting

Fabula significate um, qui contra alium machinatur, in seipsum laqueum vertere.

MULIER

Mulier quaedam virum ebrium habebat:

ipsum autem a morbo liberare volens, tale quid comminiscitur.

to free him from the disease), **tale** such **quid** anything (i.e. some such thing) **comminiscitur** she devises.

Gravatum oppressed **enim** for **ipsum** him (i.e. for him oppressed) **ab ebrietate** by drunkenness **quum** when **observasset** she might have observed (i.e. for when she'd observed him oppressed by drunkenness), **et** and **mortui** of a dead (man) **instar** like **insensatum** senseless (i.e. and senseless like of a dead man/like a dead man), **in** into (i.e. onto) **humeros** (her) shoulders **elevatum** having lifted up **in** into **sepulcretum** a tomb **allatum** having brought to (i.e. having lifted him onto her shoulders and brought him to a tomb) **deposuit** she put (him) down, **et abiit** and went away.

Gravatum enim ipsum ab ebrietate quum observasset, et mortui instar insensatum, in humeros elevatum in sepulcretum allatum deposuit, et abiit.

290

Quum when vero but (i.e. but when) ipsum him jam now sobrium sober esse to be conjectata having guessed esset she might be (i.e. but when she guessed he was now sober), januam the door pulsavit she beat (i.e. she knocked the door) sepulcreti of the tomb:	Quum vero ipsum jam sobrium esse conjectata esset, januam pulsavit sepulcreti:
ille he autem but (i.e. but he) quum when diceret he might say (i.e. but when he said), Quis who est is it, qui who pulsat beats (i.e. knocks at) januam the door?	ille autem quum diceret, Quis est, qui pulsat januam?
Uxor the wife respondit answered, Mortuis to the dead cibaria meats (i.e. food) ferens bringing (i.e. bringing food for the dead), ego I adsum I'm present.	Uxor respondit, Mortuis cibaria ferens, ego adsum.

Et ille and he (said), Non not mihi for me comesse to eat, sed but bibere to drink, O optime O best (friend), potius rather affer bring (i.e. bring not something to eat, but rather to drink):

molestus troublesome enim for mihi to me es you are (i.e. for you're a pain for me), quum when cibi of food, non potus (but) not of drink meministi you have remembered (i.e. for you pain me when you remember food but not drink).

Haec this (woman, i.e. she) autem but (i.e. but she), pectore with (her) breast percusso being struck (i.e. beating her breast), Hei alas mihi misere to wretched me! Inquit she said:

Et ille, Non mihi comesse, sed quum cibi, non potius affer:

molestus enim mihi es, quum cibi, non potus meministi.

Haec autem, pectore percusso, Hei mihi misere! inquit:

292

nam for neque not astu by craft profui have I profited (i.e. for my planning hasn't helped):

tu you enim for (i.e. for you), vir man (i.e. husband), non solum not only non not emendatus amended es you are (i.e. not only are you not fixed), sed but pejor worse quoque also te ipso you yourself evasisti you have escaped (i.e. but you've come out worse), cum when in habitum into a habit tibi for you deductus brought sit might be (i.e. has brought) morbus the disease (i.e. for the disease has made a habit for you).

Fabula significat the fable signifies, non oportere not to behove (i.e. that one shouldn't) malis in evil actibus acts immorari to continue in (i.e. that one

nam neque astu profui:

tu enim, vir, non solum non emendatus es, sed pejor quoque te ipso evasisti, cum in habitum tibi deductus sit morbus.

Fabula significat, non oportere malis actibus immorari:

293

shouldn't continue in bad acts):

nam for *aliquando* sometime (i.e. one day) *etiam* even *nolentem* unwilling *hominem* a man *consuetudo* habit *invadit* seizes (i.e. for habit sometimes seizes/overcomes a man even when he's unwilling).

CYGNUS THE SWAN

Vir a man *dives* wealthy (i.e. a wealthy man) *et* and (i.e. both) *anserem* a goose *simul* at the same time *et* and *cygnum* a swan *nutriebat* nourished (i.e. a rich man nourished/fed a goose and a swan at the same time), *non* not *ad* to *eadem* the same thing (i.e. not for the same purpose) *tamen* however, *sed* but *alterum* the other (i.e. the one/the first) *cantus* of song, *alterum* the other *mensae*

nam aliquando etiam nolentem hominem consuetudo invadit.

CYGNUS

Vir dives et anserem simul et cygnum nutriebat, non ad eadem tamen, se alterum cantus, alterum mensae gratia.

294

of the able **gratia** for the favour (i.e. one for the sake/purpose of its song, the other for the sake/purpose of the table/to eat it).

Quum when **autem** but (i.e. but when) **oporteret** it behoved **anserem** the goose (i.e. but when the goose had to) **ea** those things **pati** to suffer (i.e. but when the goose had to suffer those things), **quorum** of which **causa** for the sake (i.e. for the sake of which) **nutriebatur** he was nourished, **nox** night **erat** it was (i.e. it was night), **ac** and **discernere** to distinguish **tempus** time **non permisit** didn't permit **utrmque** each (i.e. and there wasn't time to tell them apart).

Cygnus the swan **autem** but (i.e. but the swan), **pro** for (i.e. in place of)

Quum autem oporteret anserem ea pati, quorum causa nutriebatur, nox erat, ac discernere tempus non permisit utrmque.

Cygnus autem pro ansere abductus, cantat cantum

295

ansere *the goose* abductus *being taken away (i.e. but the swan being taken in place of the goose)*, cantat *it sings* cantum *a song* quondam *a certain (i.e. sings a certain song)*, mortis *of death* exordium *the beginning (i.e. the beginning of death)*:	quondam, mortis exordium:
ac *and* cantu *by song* quidem *indeed* exprimit *he presses out (i.e. he expresses)* naturam *(his) nature (i.e. and, indeed, he expresses his nature by song)*, mortem *death* vero *but (i.e. but death)* effugit *he escapes* suavitate *by the sweetness* canendi *of (his) singing.*	ac cantu quidem exprimit naturam, mortem vero effugit suavitate canendi.
Fabula significat the fable signifies, saepe *often* musicen *music* differre *to carry away (i.e. put off)* mortem *death (i.e. the fable signifies that music often puts off death).*	*Fabula significat, saepe musicen differre mortem.*

Decoding Latin – Day 26

Don't forget the rules:

1. Don't try to memorise anything
2. Focus on the story, not the language – don't try to analyse!
3. Read one section from the left column and then the same from the right.
4. *Always read for speed and general gist, not for accuracy and perfection.*

EQUUS THE HORSE ATER BLACK (I.E. THE BLACK HORSE)	**EQUUS ATER**
Equum a horse atrum black (i.e. a black horse) quidam a certain (person) emit bought (i.e. a certain man bought a black horse), talem such ei to him colorem colour inesse to be in ratus having thought (i.e. and thinking that such a colour/black was in him/the horse), negligentia by the negligence ejus of him, qui who prius before habuit had (i.e. he thought the black colour was	Equum atrum quidam emit, talem ei colorem inesse ratus, negligentia ejus, qui prius habuit.

298

because of the negligence of the previous owner).

Ac and, **assumpto** being taken up in into **domum** (his) house **omnes** all **adhibuit** he applied **abstersiones** the cleansings (i.e. he applied all his cleanses), **omnibusque** and by all **lavaveris** washes (i.e. kinds of washing) **tentavit** he tried **mundare** to clean (i.e. to whiten the horse):

et and **colorem** the colour, **quidem** indeed, **transmutare** to change **non potuit** he wasn't able (i.e. he wasn't able to change the colour), **sed** but **morbum** a disease **vexatio** the harassing (i.e. all the rubbing) **paravit** prepared (i.e. but all the bother brought on a disease).

Ac assumpto in domum omnes adhibuit abstersiones, omnibusque lavaveris tentavit mundare:

et colorem quidem transmutare non potuit, sed morbum vexatio paravit.

Fabula significat the fable signifies, *manere* to remain *naturas* natures (i.e. that natures remain), *ut* as *a principio* from the beginning *provenerunt* they came forth (i.e. the fable signifies that nature stays as it started).

HIRUNDO THE SWALLOW ET CORNIX AND THE CROW

Hirundo a swallow *et cornix* and a crow *de* about *pulchritudine* (their) beauty *contendebant* contended (i.e. argued).

Respondens answering *autem* but *cornix* the crow i.e. but the crow, answering), *ei* to him *dixit* said (i.e. said to him), *Sed* but *tua* your *pulchritudo* beauty *verno* in spring *tempore* time *floret* flourishes;

Fabula significat, manere naturas, ut a principio provenerunt.

HIRUNDO ET CORNIX

Hirundo et cornix de pulchritudine contendebant.

Respondens autem cornix ei dixit, Sed tua pulchritudo verno tempore floret;

meum *my* vero *but* corpus *body* (i.e. but my body) etiam *even* hyeme *in winter* durat *lasts*.

Fabula significat the fable signifies, durationem *duration* corporis *of the body* decore *(than) decoration (i.e. beauty)* meliorem *better* esse *to be (i.e. the fable signifies that lastingness of body is better than its beauty)*.

BUTALIS THE BUZZARD

Butalis *a buzzard* a *from* quadam *a certain* fenestra *window* pendebat *hung (i.e. a buzzard hung from a certain window)*:

vespertilio *a bat* autem *but (i.e. but a bat)*, cum *when* accessisset *he might have approached (i.e. but when a bat had approached)*, rogavit *he*

meum vero corpus etiam hyeme durat.

Fabulae significat, durationem corporis decore meliorem esse.

BUTALIS

Butalis a quadam fenestra pendebat:

vespertilio autem, cum accessisset, rogavit causam, quare die quidem silet, nocte vero canit?

301

asked **causam** the reason, **quare** why **die** by day **quidem** indeed **silet** she is silent, **nocte** by night **vero** but (i.e. but by night) **canit** she sings?

Ea with her **vero** but (i.e. but she), **non temere** not rashly (i.e. not without reason) **hoc** this **facere** to do, **dicente** saying (i.e. but she said she didn't do it without reason):

nam for **die** by day **canens** singing (i.e. singing by day), **olim** once **capta** taken **fuerat** she had been (i.e. she'd once been captured), **et** and **propterea** on account of this **ex illo** from that (time) **prudens** prudent **evasit** she has come off (i.e. she'd become prudent):

vespertillio the bat **ait** says, **Sed** but **non** not **te**

	Ea vero non temere hoc facere, dicente:
	nam die canens, olim capta fuerat, et propterea ex illo prudens evasit:
	vespertillio ait, Sed non te cavere nunc oportet,

302

you cavere to beware nunc now oportet it behoves (i.e. but you shouldn't be wary now), quum when nulla no utilitas use est there is (i.e. when there's no use), sed but antequam before capereris you were taken.

Fabula significiat the fable signifies, in in infortuniis misfortunes inutilem useless esse to be *penitentiam repentence (i.e. the fable signifies that regret/repentenance is useless in misfortunes)*[11].

quum nulla utilitas est, sed antequam capereris.

Fabula significiat, in infortuniis inutilem esse penitentiam.

COCHLEAE THE SNAILS

COCHLEAE

Rustici of a rustic filius the son (i.e. the son of a countryman) assabat roasted cochleas snails:

Rustici filius assabat cochleas:

---

[11] Equivalent to the English 'no use crying over spilt milk'

quum *when* autem *but (i.e. but when)* audiret *he might have heard* eas *them (i.e. but when he heard them)* stridentes *hissing*, ait *he said*, O pessime *O worst* animantes *living things*, domibus *with houses* vestris *your (i.e. with your houses)* incensis *being burned*, vos *you* canitis *do you sing (i.e. O, lowest animals, are you singing with your houses being burnt)*?

Fabula significat *the fable signifies*, omne *every (thing)* intempestive *unseasonably* factum *done* vituperabile *blameable (i.e. able to be criticised)* esse *to be (i.e. the fable signifies that everything done out of season/in an inappropriate time can be criticised)*.

quum autem audiret eas stridentes, ait, O pessime animantes, domibus vestris incensis, vos canitis?

Fabula significat, omne intempestive factum vituperabile esse.

304

Decoding Latin – Day 27

Don't forget the rules:

1. Don't try to memorise anything
2. Focus on the story, not the language – don't try to analyse!
3. Read one section from the left column and then the same from the right.
4. *Always read for speed and general gist, not for accuracy and perfection.*

MULIER THE WOMAN ET ANCILLAE AND THE SERVANT GIRLS

Mulier a woman vidua a widow operosa laborious (i.e. a laborious widow woman), ancillas servant girls habens having (i.e. having servant girls), has them solebat tended noctu by night excitare to rouse up (i.e. awaken) ad to opera (their) works/tasks (i.e. she would wake them up in the night to do their jobs), ad to gallorum of the roosters cantus the song

MULIER ET ANCILLAE

Mulier vidua operosa ancillas habens, solebat noctu excitare ad opera, ad gallorum cantus.

(i.e. at the crowing of the roosters).

His *with this* vero *but (i.e. but with these girls)* assidue *assiduously (i.e. constantly)* defatigatis *being exhausted* labore *from the work,* visum *seen* est *it is (i.e. it seemed)* oportere *to behove (i.e. i.e. it seemed they ought)* domesticum *the domestic* occidere *to kill* gallum *the rooster (i.e. it seemed they ought to kill the domestic rooster),* tanquam *as if* illum *(it were) him,* qui *who* noctu *by night* excitaret *would rouse* heram *(their) mistress.*

| Hiis vero assidue defatigatis labore, visum est oportere domesticum occidere gallum, tanquam illum, qui noctu excitaret heram. |

Evenit *came out (i.e. it happened)* autem *but (i.e. but it happened)* ipsis *to them,* hoc *with this* facto *being done,* ut *that* in *into* grandiora *greater* inciderent *they wuld fall*

Evenit autem ipsis, hoc facto, ut in grandiora inciderent mala.

306

mala evils (i.e. but it happened to them that, with this being done, they fell into greater troubles).

Nam for hera (their) mistress, ignorans not knowing gallorum of the roosters horam the hour (i.e. not knowing whether it was the hour of the roosters or not), magis more de from nocte night eas them excitabat did rouse (i.e. she roused them even more by nght).

Fabula significat the fable signifies, plerisque to most hominibus people consilia the advices (i.e. plans) malorum of evils causas the causes (i.e. the causes of evils/troubles) esse to be (i.e. the fable signifies that their plans are the causes of troubles for most people).

MULIER THE WOMAN VENEFICA

Nam hera, ignorans gallorum horam, magis de nocte eas excitabat.

Fabula significat, plerisque hominibus consilia malorum causas esse.

MULIER VENEFICA

307

ENCHANTRESS (I.E. THE ENCHANTRESS WOMAN)

Mulier *a woman* venefica *enchantress (i.e. an enchantress woman)* et *and* divinarum *of the divine* irarum *angers* propulsiones *the expulsions* promittens *promising (i.e. promising to get rid of the divine rages)*, multa *many (things)* perseverabat *persevered (i.e. tried)* facere *to do*, et *and* lucrum *profit* inde *thence* facere *to make (i.e. and thus to make a prophet)*.

Quidam *some (people)* vero *but (i.e. but some people)* accusaverunt *accused* eam *her* impietatis *with (i.e. of) impiety*, et convicerunt *and convicted (her)*, et *and* damnatam *condemned* ducebant *they*

Mulier venefica et divinarum irarum propulsiones promittens, multa perseverabat facere, et lucrum inde facere.

Quidam vero accusaverunt eam impietatis, et convicerunt, et damnatam ducebant ad mortem.

led (i.e. they led her condemned) **ad mortem** to death.

Conspicatus having spotted **autem** but **quidam** a certain (person) **eam** her **duci** to be led (i.e. but, a certain person having spotted her being led away), **ait** said,

Tu you, **quae** who **deorum** of the gods **iras** the angers (i.e the angers of the gods) **avertere** to turn away **promittebas** you promised (i.e. you, who promised to turn away the angers of the gods), **quomodo** how **neque** not **hominum** of people **consilium** the sounsel (i.e. the plan of people) **mutare** to change **potuisti** you were able (i.e. how were you not able to change the plans of people)?

Conspicatus autem quidam eam duci, ait,

Tu, quae deorum iras avertere promittebas, quomodo neque hominum consilium mutare potuisti?

Fabula significat the fable signifies, multos many (people) magna great (things) promittere to promise (i.e. that many promise great things), ne not parva small (things) quidem indeed (i.e. not even small things) facere to do valentes being strong/able (i.e. the fable signifies that many promise great things, not being strong enough/capable to do even small things).

Fabula significat, multos magna promittere, ne parva quidem facere valentes.

MUSTELA THE WEASEL

MUSTELA

Mustela *a weasel* in *into* officinam *the workshop* ingressa *having entered* ferarii *of a smithy (i.e. having entered the workshop of a smithy)*, ibi *there* jacentem *lying* circumlambebat *licked around (i.e. licked all over)* limam *a file (i.e. the weasel licked a file lying there all over).*

Mustela in officinam ingressa ferarii, ibi jacentem circumlambebat limam.

310

Rasa being scraped autem but lingua (her) tongue (i.e. but, with her tongue being scraped), sanguis blood multus much (i.e. much blood/a lot of blood) ferebatur was brought (out).

Haec this (woman, i.e. she) autem but (i.e. but she) laetabatur rejoiced, rata having thought ex out of ferro the iron aliquid something auferre to have brought away (i.e. thinking she'd bring/lick something off the file), donec until penitus entirely totam the whole linguam tongue absumpsisset she might have consumed (i.e. she kept licking it up until she'd eaten/filed down her whole tongue).

Fabula a fable in into (i.e. against) eos those, qui who contentionibus in disputes seipsos themselves

---

Rasa autem lingua, sanguis multus ferebatur.

Haec autem laetabatur, rata ex ferro aliquid auferre, donec penitus totam linguam absumpsisset.

Fabula in eos, qui contentionibus seipsos offendunt.

offendunt offend (i.e. a fable for those who hurt themselves in disputes).

AGRICOLA THE FARMER

Agricola a farmer quidam a certain (i.e. a certain farmer) fodiens digging, aurum gold reperit found (i.e. found gold);

quotidie every day igitur therefore terram the earth, ut as ab by ea it beneficio with goodwill/kindness affectus being affected coronbabat he crowned (i.e. every day he crowned/paid respect to the earth, as he was affected by it with kindness).

Huic to this (man) autem but (i.e. but to him) Fortuna Fortune adstans standing near, inquit said (i.e. but Fortune, standing

AGRICOLA

Agricola quidam fodiens, aurum reperit;

quotidie igitur terram, ut ab ea beneficio affectus coronbabat.

Huic autem Fortuna adstans, inquit, Heus tu, cur terrae mea munera

312

near, said to this man), Heus tu *hey you*, cur *why* terrae *to the earth* mea *my* munera *gifts* attribuis *do you attribute* (i.e. why do you attribute my gifts to the earth), quae *(the gifts) which* ego *I* tibi *to you* dedi *I've given* (i.e. the gifts which I've given you), ditare *to enrich* te *you* volens *wanting* (i.e. the gifts which I gave to you, wanting to enrich you)?

nam *for* si *if* tempus *time* immutetur *were changed*, et *and* in *into* alias *other* manus *hands* hoc *this* tuum *your* aurum *gold* veniat *would come* (i.e. for if times changed, and this your gold came into other hands), scio *I know* te *you* tunc *then* (i.e. at that time) me *me*, Fortunam *Fortune*, accusaturum *about to accuse* (i.e. I know that

attribuis, quae ego tibi dedi, ditare te volens?

nam si tempus immutetur, et in alias manus hoc tuum aurum veniat, scio te tunc me, Fortunam, accusaturum.

then you would accuse me, Fortune).

Fabula significat the fable signifies, *oportere* to behove (i.e. one ought) *benefactorem* a benefactor *cognoscere* to know (i.e. one should know a benefactor), *atque* and *huic* to this *gratiam* favour (i.e. thanks) *referre* to give back (i.e. the fable signifies, one should know their benefactor, and give them thanks).

Fabula significat, oportere benefactorem cognoscere, atque huic gratiam referre.

Decoding Latin – Day 28

Don't forget the rules:

1. Don't try to memorise anything
2. Focus on the story, not the language – don't try to analyse!
3. Read one section from the left column and then the same from the right.
4. *Always read for speed and general gist, not for accuracy and perfection.*

VIATORES THE TRAVELLERS

VIATORES

Duo two quidam certain (i.e. certain two people) una in one (i.e. together) iter a journey faciebant made (i.e. two people made a journey together).

Duo quidam una iter faciebant.

Et and quum when alter the other (i.e. the one/the first) securim an axe reperisset might have found (i.e. and when one found an axe), alter the other, qui who non invenerat had not found (it), admonebat reminded

Et quum alter securim reperisset, alter, qui non invenerat, admonebat ipsum, ne diceret, Inveni, sed Invenimus.

ipsum him, ne lest diceret he should say (i.e. that he shouldn't say), Inveni 'I've found (it)', sed but (rather) Invenimus 'We've found (it)'.

Sed but paulo a little post after (i.e. a little while later), quum when obviam towards venissent might come ipsis to them illi those (i.e. when those people came towards them), qui who securim the axe perdiderant had lost (i.e. when the people who had lost the axe came towards them), qui (he) who habebat had illam it (i.e. the axe) cursu in the course pressus being pressed (i.e. being closely chased), qui (he) who non invenerat hadn't found (it), comiti to his companion dicebat said (i.e. he said to his companion, who hadn't found it), Periimus we

Sed paulo post, quum obviam venissent ipsis illi, qui securim perdiderant, qui habebat illam cursu pressus, cui non invenerat, comiti dicebat, Periimus.

have perished (i.e. we're done for).

Hic this (man, i.e. he) autem but (i.e. but he) ait said, Perii 'I've perished' dic say (i.e. say 'I've perished'), non not Periimus 'we've perished':

etenim for et and (i.e. also) tunc then, quum when securim the axe invenisti you found, Inveni 'I've found (it)', dixisti you said, non Invenimus not 'we've found (it)'.

Fabula significat the fable signifies, eos those, qui who non fuerunt were not participes sharers felicitatum of happinesses (i.e. sharers in good fortune), neque neither in calamitatibus in calamities firmos firm esse to be amicos friends (i.e. the fable signifies that those who were not sharers in

Hic autem ait, Perii dic, non Periimus:

etenim et tunc, quum securim invenisti, Inveni, dixisti, non Invenimus.

Fabula significat, eos, qui non fuerunt participes felicitatum, neque in calamitatibus firmos esse amicos.

good fortune, aren't firm friends in misfortunes).

RANAE THE FROGS | RANAE

Duae two ranae frogs vicinae neighbouring sibi to themselves erant they were (i.e. two frogs were neighbours).

Duae ranae vicinae sibi erant.

Pascebantur they were fed autem but (i.e. but they were fed), altera the other (i.e. one) in in profundo a deep, et and procul far a via from the way (i.e. the road) stagno pond (i.e. but they were fed, one in a deep pond, far from the road);

Pascebantur autem, altera in profundo, et procul a via stagno;

altera the other in via on the way (i.e. on the road), parum little aquae of water habens having (i.e. the other was fed on the road, having little water).

altera in via, parum aquae lhabens.

Verum but, quum when quae (she) who in stagno in the pond erat was (i.e. but when the one who was in the pond), alteram the other admoneret advised (i.e. but when the one who was in the pond advised the other), ut that ad to se herself migraret she should migrate (i.e. told the other to move over to the pond), ut so that tutiore with safer cibo food frueretur she could enjoy (i.e. so that she could enjoy safer food), illa she (i.e. the frog on the road) non paruit didn't obey, dicens saying, Firmissima by a very strong teneri to be held hujusce of this loci place consuetudine custom (i.e. saying she was held by a very strong habit of the place/she was used to being there), usque dum until at last obtigeret it might happen (i.e. until at last it happened), currum	Verum, quum quae in stagna erat, alteram admoneret, ut ad se migraret, ut tutiore cibo frueretur, illa non paruit, dicens, Firmissima teneri hujusce loci consuetudine, usque dum obtigeret, currum praetereuntem ipsam contundere.

a carriage **praetereuntem** passing over **ipsam** her **contundere** to crush (i.e. until it happened that a passing carriage crushed her).

Fabula significat the fable signifies, *homines* people *quoque* also, *prava* depraved (things) *aggredientes* attempting (i.e. attempting to do bad things), *citius* more quickly *mori* to die (i.e. they die more quickly), *quam* than *in* into *melius* better *mutari* to be changed (i.e. the fable signifies that people attempting bad things, die sooner than they change).

APIARIUS THE BEE-KEEPER

In into **mellarium** an apiary **ingressus** having entered **quidam** a certain (person), **domino** with (its) owner **absente** being absent,

Fabula significat, homines quoque, prava aggredientes, citius mori, quam in melius mutari.

APIARIUS

In mellarium ingressus quidam, domino absente, favum abstulit.

320

favum a honeycomb abstulit he took away (i.e. he stole some honeycomb).

Hic this (man, i.e. he) autem but (i.e. but he), reversus having returned, ut as (i.e. when) alveolos (his) hives vidit he saw inanes empty (i.e. when he saw his hives empty), stabat he stood, quod what in in his them erat was, perscrutans examining (i.e. slooking for what was in them).

Apes the bees autem but (i.e. but the bees) e out of pastu feeding redeuntes coming back (i.e. returning from feeding), ut as (i.e. when) deprehenderunt they seized ipsum him, aculeis with (their) stings percutiebant they struck (him), pessimeque and terribly tractabant they treated (him).

Hic autem reversus, ut alveolos vidit inanes, stabat, quod in his erat, perscrutans.

Apes autem e pastu redeuntes, ut deprehenderunt ipsum, aculeis percutiebant, pessimeque tractabant.

Hic he autem but (i.e. but he) eis to them dixit said O pessimae oh worst animantes creatures, furatum the [person] having taken (i.e. the one who's taken) vestros your favos honeycombs illaesum uninjured dimisistis you've sent away (i.e. you've let the one who's taken your honeycombs go unharmed), me me vero but (i.e. but me) satagentem being busy vestri of you (i.e. on your behalf) percutitis you strike (i.e. but me, who is attentive to your needs, you strike)!

Fabula significat the fable signifies, sic thus hominum of people quosdam some (i.e. some people) *per through* imprudentiam *imprudence* inimicos (their) enemies non caventes not bewaring (i.e. not watching out for their enemies),

Hic autem eis dixit O pessimae animantes, furatum vestros favos illaesum dimisistis, me vero satagentem vestri percutitis!

Fabula significat, sic hoinum quosdam per imprudentiam inimicos non caventes, amicos, ut insidiatores, repellere.

amicos (their) friends, *ut* as *insidiatores* plotters, *repellere* to drive back (i.e. the fable signifies that some people, through imprudence, not watching out for their enemies, drive away their friends as plotters).

ALCEDO THE KINGFISHER

Alcedo the kingfisher **avis** a bird **est** is **solitaria** solitary (i.e. the kingfisher is a solitary bird), **semper** always **in** in **mari** the sea **vitam** (its) life **degens** spending (i.e. always spending its life in the sea).

Hanc this (bird) **aiunt** they say, **hominum** of people **venationes** the huntings **caventem** bewaring (i.e. being wary of the huntings of men), **in** in **scopulis** cliffs **maritimis** maritime (i.e. the sea-side cliffs)

ALCEDO

Alcedo avis est solitaria, semper in mari vitam degens.

Hanc aiunt, hominum venationes caventem, in scopulis maritimis nidum aedificare;

nidum (its) nest aedificare to build (i.e. they say this bird, being careful of human hunting builds its nest on the sea-cliffs);

et and aliquando some time (i.e. one day) jam now paritura about to bring forth (i.e. about to give birth), nidum (its) nest fecit it made (i.e. it made its nest).

Egressa having gone out autem but ea she (i.e. but, with her having gone out) ad to (i.e. for) pabulum food, evenit it came out (i.e. happened) mare (that) the sea, a by vehementi a vehement concitatum roused up (i.e. roused up by a vehement) vento wind, elevatum being lifted up supra above nidum the nest fuisse to have been (i.e. it rose above the nest), atque and, hoc with this

et aliquando jam paritura, nidum fecit.

Egressa autem ea ad pabulum, evenit mare, a vehementi concitatum vento, elevatum supra nidum fuisse, atque, hoc submerse, pullos perdisse.

324

(nest) **submerse** submerged, **pullos** the chicks **perdisse** to have been lost (i.e. the chicks were lost).

Haec she (i.e. the bird) **vero** but (i.e. but she), **reversa** being returned, **re** with the matter **cognita** being known (i.e. realizing what had happened), **ait** said, **Me miserum** wretched me! **quae** (I) who **terram** the earth, **ut** as **insidiatricem** a plotress (i.e. a plotter), **cavens** bewaring (i.e. I, watching out for the earth as if it were a plotter), **ad** to **hoc** this (place) **confugi** I've fled, **quod** which **mihi** for me **longe** by far **est** is insidious more plotting.

Fabula significat the fable signifies, *homines* people *etiam* also *quosdam* some (i.e. some people also) *ab* from *inimicis* (their) enemies

Haec vero reversa, re cognita, ait, Me miserum! quae terram, ut insidiatricem, cavens, ad hoc confugi, quod mihi longe est insidius.

Fabula significat, homines etiam quosdam ab inimicis cavendo, ignaros in multo graviores inimicis amicos incidere.

325

cavendo bewaring (i.e. watching out for their enemies), **ignaros** *ignorant* **in** *into* **multo** *by much* **graviores** *heavier (i.e. more serious)* **inimicis** *(than) enemies* **amicos** *friends* **incidere** *to fall on (i.e. the fable signifies that some people also, watching out for their enemies, fall on friends much worse than enemies).*

Decoding Latin – Day 29

Don't forget the rules:

1. Don't try to memorise anything
2. Focus on the story, not the language – don't try to analyse!
3. Read one section from the left column and then the same from the right.
4. *Always read for speed and general gist, not for accuracy and perfection.*

PISCATOR THE FISHERMAN

Piscator a fisherman in in fluvio a river quodam a certain (i.e. in a certain river) piscabatur did fish (i.e. a fisherman was fishing in a certain river).

Extensis being stretched autem but retibus with the nets (i.e. but with the nets stretched out), et and fluxu the stream comprehenso being seized utrinque on either side, funi to a rope alligato being bound lapide with a

PISCATOR

Piscator in fluvio quodam piscabatur.

Extensis autem retibus, et fluxu comprehenso utriinque, funi alligato lapide, aquam verberabat, ut pisces, fugientes incaute, in retia inciderent.

327

stone (i.e. with a stone tied to a rope), **aquam** the water **verberabat** he struck (i.e. he struck the water with a rock tied to a rope), **ut** so that **pisces** the fish, **fugientes** fleeing **incaute** incautiously, **in** into **retia** the nats **inciderent** would fall (i.e. so that the fish, running away in a panic, would fall into the nets).

Cum when **quidam** a certain (one) **vero** but **ex** out of **iis** them (i.e. but when one of them), **qui** who **circa** around **locum** the place **habitabant** lived (i.e. but one of he people who lived around that place), **id** that **eum** him **facere** to do **videret** might see (i.e. saw him/the fisherman do that), **increpabat** told (him) off, **utpote** as **fluvium** the river **turbantem** disturbing (i.e. he told him off for disturbing the river), **et**

Cum quidam vero ex iis, qui circa locum habitabant, id eum facere videret, increpabat, utpote fluvium turbantem, et claram aquam non sinentem bibere.

328

and claram clear aquam water non sinentem not allowing bibere to drink (i.e. and for not allowing him to drink clear water).

Et and is he respondit answered, Sed but, nisi unless sic thus fluvius the river perturbetur be (i.e. is) disturbed, me me oportebit it will be hove esurientem hungry mori to die (i.e. I'll have to die hungry).

Fabula significat the fable signifies, civitatum of states etiam also rectores the rulers tunc then (i.e. at that time) maxime mostly quaestum profit facere to make (i.e. that rulers make profits most), quum when patrias (their) fatherlands in into seditionem treacheries induxerint they will have led in (i.e. the fable signifies that rules make the most profit

Et is respondit, Sed, nisi sic fluvius perturbetur, me oportebit esurientem mori.

Fabula significat, civitatum etiam rectores tunc maxime quaestum facere, quum patrias in seditionem induxerint.

when they lead their countries into treachery).

SIMIUS **THE APE** ET DELPHIN **AND THE DOLPHIN**

Mos *a custom* quum *when* esset *it might be* navigantibus *to (those) sailing (i.e. when it was a custom for those sailing)*, melitenses *Militensian* catulos *puppies* et simios *and apes* adducere *to lead* in *into* solamen *consolation* navigationis *of the voyage (i.e. when it was a custom for sailors to bring Militensian puppies and apes with them as a consolation for the voyage)*, navigans *sailing* quidam *a certain (person)* habebat *had (i.e. a certain person, sailing, had)* secum *with him* et *and (i.e. also)* Simium *an ape*.

SIMIUS ET DELPHIN

Mos quum esset navigantibus, melitenses catulos et simios adducere in solamen navigationis, navigans quidam habebat secum et Simium.

330

Quum when autem but (i.e. but when) pervenissent he might have arrived ad to Sunium Sunium (i.e. when he'd arrived at Sunium), Atticae of Attica promontorium a promontory (i.e. a promontory of Attica), tempestatem a storm vehementem vehement (i.e. a vehement/strong storm) contigit happened fieri to be made.

Navi with the ship autem but (i.e. but with the ship) eversa being turned over, et and omnibus with all (i.e. with everyone) enatantibus swimming out, natabat swam et and (i.e. also) simius the ape (i.e. the ape also swam):

delphin a dolphin autem but aliquis some ipsum him conspicatus having caught sight (i.e. but some

Quum autem pervenissent ad Sunium, Atticae promontorium, tempestatem vehementem contigit fieri.

Navi autem eversa, et omnibus enatantibus, natabat et simius:

delphin autem aliquis ipsum conspicatus, et hominem esse ratus

331

dolphin, having caught sight of him), et and hominem a person esse to be ratus having thought (i.e. and thinking he was a person) suppositus being placed under sustinebat he held (him) up, perferens carrying (him) through ad to terram the land.

Ut as vero but (i.e. but when) in in Piraeo the Piraeus fuit he was (i.e. but when he was in the Piraeus), Atheniensium of the Athenians navale a dock (i.e. a dock of the Athenians), rogavit he (i.e. the dolphin) asked simium the ape, an whether genere by race (i.e. by birth) esset he might be Atheniensis Athenian (i.e. he asked the ape whether he was Athenian by birth)?

suppositus sustinebat, perferens ad terram.

Ut vero in Piraeo fuit, Atheniensium navale, rogavit simium, an genere esset Atheniensis?

332

Quum when autem but (i.e. but when) hic he diceret said se himself esse to be (i.e. but when he said he was), et and claris with clear (i.e. well-known) ibi there esse to be parentibus parents (i.e. and that there were/he had well-known parents there);

rogavit he (i.e. the dolphin) asked, an whether et and (i.e. also) Piraeum the Piraeus nosset me might have known (i.e. the dolphin asked him if he knew the Piraeus also)?

Ratus having thought autem but simius the ape (i.e. but the ape, having thought) de about homine a person eum him (i.e. the dolphin) dicere to say (i.e. but the ape, thinking he was speaking about a person), ait said, Et and

Quum autem hic diceret se esse, et claris ibi esse parentibus;

rogavit, an et Piraeum nosset?

Ratus autem simius de homine eum dicere, ait, Et valde amicum esse ei, et familiarem:

333

(i.e. also) valde very much amicum a friend esse to be ei to him, et and familiarem intimate (i.e. he said he was also very much a friend to him, and good friends):

et delphin and the dolphin, tanto by such mendacio a lie indignatus enraged, submergens sinking, ipsum him occidit killed (i.e. killed him).

Fabula a fable in into (i.e. against) viros men, qui who, veritatem the truth ignorantes not knowing, decipere to deceive sperunt hope (i.e. who, not knowing the truth, hope to deceive).

MUSCAE THE FLIES

In in cella a cell (i.e. a pantry) quadam a certain melle with honey effuse being poured out (i.e. with honey being spilt in a

et delphin, tanto mendacio indignatus, submergens, ipsum occidit.

Fabula in viros, qui, veritatem ignorantes, decipere sperunt.

MUSCAE

In cella quadam melle effuse, muscae advolantes comedebant.

334

certain pantry), **muscae** flies **advolantes** flying to (it) **comedebant** ate (it) up.

Implicitis being entangled **autem** but **earum** of them **pedibus** with the feet (i.e. but with their feet being entangled [in the honey]), **evolare** to fly away **non poterant** they weren't able (i.e. they couldn't fly away).

Quum when **vero** but (i.e. but when) **suffocarentur** they might be choked (i.e. but when they were choked), **dicebant** they said, **Misere nos** wretched us, **qui** who **ob** on account of **modicum** a little **cibum** food **perimus** we perish.

Fabula significat the fable signifies, *multis* for many (people) *gulam* the throat (i.e. gluttony/greed/desire) *multorum* of many *malorum*

Implicitis autem earum pedibus, evolare non poterant.

Quum vero suffocarentur, dicebant, Misere nos, qui ob modicum cibum perimus.

Fabula significat, multis gulam multorum malorum causam esse.

evils causam *the cause* esse *to be (i.e. the fable signifies that greed is the cause of many evils for many people).*

MERCURIUS *MERCURY* ET STATUARIUS *AND THE STATUE MAKER*

Mercurius *Mercury* scire *to know* volens *wanting (i.e. wanting to know)*, in *in* quanto *how much* honore *honour* apud *at (i.e. among)* homines *people* esset *he might be (i.e. wanting to know in how much honour he was held by people)*, ivit *went* in *into* statuarii *a statue-maker's* domum *home*, eum *him* se *himself* assimilasset *he might have likened* homini *to a man (i.e. having made himself look like a man)*, et *and*, visa *being seen* statua *a statue* Jovis *of Jupiter*, rogabat *asked*, Quanti *of*

MERCURIUS ET STATUARIUS

Mercurius scire volens, in quanto honore apud homines esset, ivit in statuarii domum, eum se assimilasset homini et visa statua Jovis, rogabat, Quanti quis ipsam emere posset?

(i.e. for) how much quis anyone ipsam it emere to by posset would be able (i.e. for how much would one be able to buy it)?

Hic he **autem** but **quum** when **dixisset** he (i.e. the statue maker) might have said, **Drachma** 'With a drachma', **risit** he (i.e. Mercury) laughed:

Hic autem quum dixisset, Drachma, risit:

et and, **Quanti** of (i.e. for) how much **eam** this (statue) **Junonis** of Juno, **ait** he (i.e. Mercury) said, **quum** when **dixisset** he (i.e. the statue maker) said, **Pluris** of (i.e. for) more (than the statue of Jupiter):

et, Quanti eam Junonis, ait quum dixisset, Pluris:

visa having seen **et** and (i.e. also) **sua** his own **ipsius** of himself **statua** statue (i.e. having seen a statue of himself), **ac** and **opinatus** having imagined **quum** when (i.e. since)

visa et sua ipsius statua, ac opinatus quum nuntius sit Deorum, et lucro praesit, maximam de se apud homines haberi rationem, rogavit de ea.

337

nuntius a messenger sit he might be Deorum of the gods (i.e. since he was a messenger of the gods), et and lucro to profuit praesit presides (over), maximam the greatest de about se himself apud at (i.e. among) homines people haberi to be held rationem regard (i.e. having imagined he would be held in the highest regard by people), rogavit he asked de about ea it.

Statuarius the statue maker vero but (i.e. but the statue maker) ait said, Si if hasce these emeris you buy (i.e. if you buy these statues), et and (i.e. also) hanc this additamentum (as) an addition tibi to you do I give.

Fabula a fable in into (i.e. against) virum a man gloriosum boastful (i.e.

Statuarius vero ait, Si hasce emeris, et hanc additamentum tibi do.

Fabula in virum gloriosum, qui in nullo apud alios est honore

338

against a boastful man), **qui** *who* **in nullo** *in nothing* **apud at** *(i.e. among)* **alios** *others* **est** *is* **honore** *with honour (i.e. who is valued at nothing among others)*

Decoding Latin – Day 30

Don't forget the rules:

1. Don't try to memorise anything
2. Focus on the story, not the language – don't try to analyse!
3. Read one section from the left column and then the same from the right.
4. *Always read for speed and general gist, not for accuracy and perfection.*

MERCURIUS MERCURY ET TIRESIAS AND TIRESIAS

Mercurius Mercury, volens wanting Tiresiae Tiersias's vaticinium prophecying, an whether verum true esset it might be (i.e. whether it was true), cognoscere to find out (i.e. wanting to find out whether Tiresias's prophecies were true), furatus having stolen ipsius his boves oxen ex from rure the country, venit he came ad ipsum to him in urbem into the city, similis

MERCURIUS ET TIRESIAS

Mercurius volens Tiresiae vaticinium, an verum esset, cognoscere, furatus ipsius boves ex rure, venit ad ipsum in urbem, similis factus homini, et ad ipsum divertit.

340

like **factus** being made **homini** to a man (i.e. having made himself look like a human), **et** and **ad ipsum** to him **divertit** he turned.

Boum the oxen **autem** but **amissione** with the loss **renunciata** being announced **Tiresiae** to Tiersias (i.e. but with the loss of the oxen being announced to Tiresias), **ille** he, **assumpto** having taken **Mercurio** Mercury (with him), **exivit** went out, **augurium** divination **aliquod** some **de fure** about the thief **consideraturus** he was about to consider (i.e. and he was about to consider some divination about the thief), **et** and **huic** to him **jubet** he ordered **dicere** to say (i.e. speak) **sibi** to himself, **quamnam** what **avem** bird **viderit** he might have seen?

Boum autem amissione renunciata Tiresiae, ille, assumpto Mercurio, exivit, augurium aliquod de fure consideraturus, et huic jubet dicere sibi, quamnam avem viderit?

Mercurius autem *but Mercury*, primum *first* conspicatus *having caught sight of* aquilam *an eagle* sinistris *from the left* ad dextram *to the right* velantem *flying (i.e. flying from the left to the right)*, ei *to him (i.e. to Tiresias)* dixit *said (it, i.e. he told him what he saw)*.

Hic *he* non ad se *not to himself* eam *it* attinere *to relate*, quum *when*, dixisset *he might have said (i.e. when he said it didn't relate to him)*, secondo *secondly (i.e. secondly after the eagle)*, cornicem *a crow* vidit *he saw* super *upon* arbore *a tree* quadam *a certain (i.e. a certain crow he saw)* sedentem *sitting (i.e. sitting upon a tree)*, et *and* modo *now* superius *higher* aspicientem *looking (i.e. and now, looking higher)*, modo *now* ad terram *to the earth*

Mercurius autem, primum conspicatus aquilam sinistris ad dextram velantem, ei dixit.

Hic non ad se eam attinere, quum, dixisset, secondo, cornicem vidit super arbore quadam sedentem, et modo superius aspicientem, modo ad terram declinatam, et vati refert.

342

declinatam bent, et and vati to the prophet refert he reported (it).

Et and is he, re with the matter cognita being known, inquit he says;

Et is, re cognita, inquit;

Sed but haec this cornix crow jurat swears to et coelum both heaven, et terram and earth, si if tu velis you wish, meas my me me recepturum about to recover boves oxen (i.e. that I will recover my oxen if you choose[12]).

Sed haec cornix jurat et coelum, et terram, sit u velis, meas me recepturum boves.

Hoc this sermone speech uti to use (i.e. to use this speech) quispiam anyone poterit should be able (i.e. anyone should be able to use this speech) adversus against virum a man furacem thieving (i.e. against a thieving man).

Hoc sermone uti quispiam poterit adversus virum furacem.

---

[12] Thus indicating that Tiersias knew Mercury was the one who had his oxen.

CANES **THE DOGS**

Habens *having* quidam *a certain man* duos Canes *two dogs* (i.e. a certain man, having two dogs), alterum *the other* (i.e. one) venari *to hunt* docuit *he taught* (i.e. he taught one to hunt), alterum *the other* domum *the home* servare *to keep* (i.e. he taught the other to keep the home).

Caeterum *but*, si quando *if anytime* venaticus *the hunting* (dog) caperet *would catch* aliquid *something*, et *and* (i.e. also) domus *the house* custos *guard* particeps *sharer* erat *was* una *together* cum *with* eo *him* dapis *of the feast* (i.e. the house dog was a sharer in the feast together with him).

CANES

Habens quidam duos Canes, alterum venari docuit, alterum domum servare.

Caeterum, si quando venaticus caperet aliquid, et domus custos particeps erat una cum eo dapis.

344

Aegre ill ferente bearing autem but venatico with the hunting (dog; i.e. but with the hunting dog taking it badly), et and illi to him objiciente objecting quod because ipse he himself quotidie daily laboraret laboured, ille he vero but (i.e. but he) nihil nothing laborans labouring (i.e. doing nothing), suis by his own nutrietur might be nourished laboribus labours (i.e. the house dog was nourished by his/the hunting dog's labours);

respondens answering ipse he ait said, Non me not me, sed but herum (our) owner reprehende blame (i.e. don't blame me, but our owner), qui who non laborare not to labour me me docuit has taught, sed but labores labours alienos others' comedesse to eat up (i.e.

Aegre ferente autem venatico, et illi objiciente quod ipse quotidie laboraret, ille vero nihil laborans, suis nutrietur laboribus;

respondens ipse ait, Non me, sed herum reprehende, qui non laborare me docuit, sed labores alienos comedesse.

345

but to eat up other people's labours).

Fabula significat the fable signifies, *adolescentes* (that) youths *qui* who *nihil* nothing *sciunt* know (i.e. who know nothing), *haud* not *esse* to be *reprehendendos* should be blamed (i.e. should not be blamed), *quum* when *eos* them *parentes* (their) parents *sic* thus *educaverint* might have brought up (i.e. when their parents brought them up this way).

MARITUS THE HUSBAND ET UXOR AND THE WIFE

Habens having *quidam* a certain (man, i.e. a certain man having) *uxorem* a wife, *quae* who *domesticis* to the domestics *omnibus* all *inimica* unfriendly *erat* was (i.e. who was unfriendly to all the domestic servants), *voluit*

Fabula significat, adolescentes qui nihil sciunt, haud esse reprehendendos, quum eos parentes sic educaverint.

MARITUS ET UXOR

Habens quidam uxorem, quae domesticis omnibus inimica erat, voluit scire, an etiam erga paternos domesticos ita afficeretur:

346

wanted scire to know, an whether etiam also erga towards paternos (her) paternal domesticos domestics (i.e. her father's servants) ita thus afficeretur she was affected (i.e. he wanted to know whether she acted that way towards her father's servants):

quapropter on account of which cum rationabili with a reasonable praetextu pretext ad suum to her owm ipsam her mittit he sent patrem father (i.e. he sent her to her own father with some reasonable pretext).

quapropter cum rationabili praetextu ad suum ipsam mittit patrem.

Paucis in a few vero but post after diebus days (i.e. but after a few days) ea she reversa having returned, rogavit he asked, Quomodo in what way erga towards illos them se she herself

Paucis vero post diebus ea reversa, rogavit, Quomodo erga illos se habuisset.

347

habuisset **might have held** (i.e. he asked how she held/carried herself towards them).

Haec vero **but she** quum **when** dixisset **she might have said** (i.e. but when she said), Quod **that** bubulci **the herdsmen**, et pastores **and shepherds** me **me** suspectabant **suspected**, ait **he said**, Sed **but**, O uxor **O wife**, si **if** eis **to them** odiosa **hateful** es **you are** (i.e. but if you're hateful to them), qui **who** mane **early** greges **the flocks** agunt **act** (i.e. who drive the flocks out early), sero **late** autem **but** revertuntur **return** (i.e. but return late), quid **what** sperare **to hope** oportet **ought one** (i.e. what should one hope) de **about** iis **them**, quibuscum **with whom** toto **in the whole** conversaris **you spoke** die **day** (i.e. with

Haec vero quum dixisset, Quod bubulci, et pastores me suspectabant, ait, Sed, O uxor, si eis odiosa es, qui mane greges agunt, sero autem revertuntur, quid sperare oportet de iis, quibuscum toto conversaris die?

whom you spoke the whole day)?

Fabula significat the fable signifies, *sic* thus *saepe* often *ex paris* from small (things) *magna* great, *et* and *ex manifestis* from obvious (things) *incerta* uncertain *cognosci* to be known (i.e. the fable signifies that thus often great things are known from small, and uncertain things from obvious).

HOEDUS THE KID (I.E. BABY GOAT) ET LUPUS AND THE WOLF

Hoedus a kid *derelictus* being deserted *a grege* by the flock, *agitabatur* was hunted *a lupo* by a wolf.

Conversus vero but having turned *ad eum* to him *dixit* he said, *O lupe* O fox, *quoniam* since *persuasus sum* I'm

Fabula significat, sic saepe ex paris magna, et ex manifestis incerta cognosci.

HOEDUS ET LUPUS

Hoedus derelictus a grege, agitabatur a lupo.

Conversus vero ad eum dixit, O lupe, quoniam persuasus sum, me tuum cibum futurum, ne

349

persuaded, me (that) myself tuum your cibum food futurum about to be (i.e. that I'll end up as your food), ne lest injucunde unpleasantly moriar I may die (i.e. lest I die unpleasantly), cane sing (i.e. play) tibia with a pipe primum first, ut so that saltem I may dance.

Lupo autem but the wolf canente singing (i.e. playing) tibia on the pipe, atque and haedo the kid saltante dancing, canes the dogs, quum when audivissent they'd heard (it), lupum the wolf persecuti sunt they chased.

Hic vero but he conversus having turned, haedo to the kid inquit said, Merito deservedly haec these things mihi to me accidunt happen; oportebat enim me for I ought, coquus a

injucunde moriar, cane tibia primum, ut saltem.

Lupo autem canente tibia, atque Haedo saltante, canes, quum audivissent, lupum persecuti sunt.

Lupo autem canente tibia, atque Haedo saltante, canes, quum audivissent, lupum persecuti sunt.

cook **quum** when **sim** I might be, **tibicinem** a flute-player **non imitari** not to imitate (i.e. for, when I'm a cook I shouldn't pretend to be a flautist).

Fabula significat the fable signifies, *eos* those, *qui* who *ea* those things, *quibus* for which *natura* by nature *apti sunt* they're suited, *negligunt* neglect (i.e. those who neglect the things for which they're suited by nature), *quae vero* but (those things) which *aliorum* (are characteristic) of others *sunt* are, *exercere* to exercise *conantur* they try (i.e. but they endeavour to work in those things which are the lot of others), *in infortunia* into misfortunes *incidere* to fall (i.e. they'll fall).

Fabula significat, eos, qui ea, quibus natura apti sunt, negligunt, quae vero aliorum sunt, exercere conantur, in infortunia incidere.

Decoding Latin – Day 31

Don't forget the rules:

1. Don't try to memorise anything
2. Focus on the story, not the language – don't try to analyse!
3. Read one section from the left column and then the same from the right.
4. *Always read for speed and general gist, not for accuracy and perfection.*

CANCER THE CRAB ET VULPES AND THE FOX	**CANCER ET VULPES**
Cancer a crab e mari from the sea quum when ascendisset it might have come up (i.e. when a crab had come up from the sea), in quodam in a certain pascebatur it grazed loco place (i.e. it grazed in a certain place).	Cancer e mari quum ascendisset, in quodam pascebatur loco.
Vulpes the fox vero but esuriens being hungry (i.e. but the fox, being hungry), ut when cospexisset it might have (i.e. had)	Vulpes vero esuriens, ut cospexisset, accessit, ac eum rapuit.

352

caught sight of (the crab), accessit approached, ac and eum him rapuit snatched (i.e. snatched him).

Ille vero but he devorandus to be devoured (i.e. the one who was to be eaten), ait said, Sed ego but I justa justly patior suffer, qui (I) who, marinus a marine (animal) quum since sim I might be (i.e. since I'm a marine animal), terrestris terrestrial (i.e. land-based) volui I wanted esse to be.

Ille vero devorandus, ait, Sed ego justa patior, qui, marinus quum sim, terrestris volui esse.

Fabula significat the fable signifies, ex hominibus out of people etiam also eos those, qui who propriis their own derelicta having abandoned exercitiis exercises (i.e. the fable signifies those people who, having abandoned their own activities), ea those things, quae which nihil nothing conveniunt suit

Fabula significat, ex hominibus etiam eos, qui propriis derelicta exercitiis, ea, quae nihil conveniunt, aggrediuntur, merito infortunatos esse.

(i.e. which don't suit them at all), **aggrediuntur** *they attempt*, **merito** *deservedly* **infortunatos** *unfortunate* **esse** *to be (i.e. they are deservedly unfortunate)*.

CITHAROEDUS THE HARPER

Citharoedus *a harper (i.e. harp player/guitar player)* **rudis** *unskillful* **in domo** *in a house* **calce** *with lime* **incrustata** *plastered (i.e. an unskillful harpist, in a house plastered with lime)*, **ut solebat** *as he tended (to do)*, **canens** *(was) singing (i.e. playing the harp)*, **et contra** *and on the other hand* **resonante** *re-echoing* **in se** *against himself* **voce** *(his won) voice (i.e and with his own voice echoing back to him)*, **putabat** *he thought* **valde** *exceedingly* **canorus** *musical* **esse** *to*

CITHAROEDUS

Citharoedus rudis in domo calce incrustata, ut solebat, canens, et contra resonante in se voce, putabat valde canorus esse:

354

be (i.e. he thought he was very musical):

itaque and so elatus puffed up ob on account of id this, cogitavit he thought oportere to behove (i.e. he thought he ought) etiam even theatro to the theatre sese himself committere to commit (i.e. he thought he ought to put himself in the theatre).	itaque elatus ob id, cogitavit oportere etiam theatro sese committere.
Profectus vero but having set out ad se for himself ostendendum to be shown (i.e. to show himself), quum when male badly admodum very caneret he sang (i.e. when he played very badly), lapidibus with stones ipsum him explosum scared off abegerunt they drove (him) away (i.e. they drove him away with stones, scared off).	Profectus vero ad se ostendendum, quum male admodum caneret, lapidibus ipsum explosum abegerunt.

355

Fabula significat the fable signifies, *sic* thus *ex rhetoribus* out of the rhetoricians *quosdam* some (i.e. in this way some rhetoricians), *qui* who *in scholis* in schools *videntur* seem *esse* to be *aliqui* some (i.e. who seem to be something in the schools), *quum* when *ad res publicas* to public affairs *venerint* they come, *nullius* of no *pretii* value *esse* to be (i.e. they seem to be of no value in the real world).

FURES THE THIEVES

Fures theves *in domum* into a house *quamdam* a certain *ingress* having entered (i.e. having entered into a certain house), *nihil* nothing *invenerunt* they found (i..e they found nothing), *nisi except* *gallum* a rooster;

Fabula significat, sic ex rhetoribus quosdam, qui in scholis videntur esse aliqui, quum ad res publicas venerint, nullius pretii esse.

FURES

Fures in domum quamdam ingressi, nihil invenerunt, nisi gallum;

356

atque and, hoc this capto being taken, abierunt they went away.

Hic vero but he (i.e. the rooster) ab eis by them occidendus to be killed rogabat asked (i.e. but the one who was to be killed/the rooster asked), ut that se himself dimitterent they would send away (i.e. that they'd let him go), dicens saying, se himself utilem useful esse to be hominibus to the men (i.e. that he was useful to people), noctu by night eos them ad opera to (their) works excitantem rousing (i.e. the rooster said it was useful to men, rousing/waking them by night to their works).

Hi vero but they dixerunt said, Sed but propter hoc because of this te you tanto only magis more

atque, hoc capto, abierunt.

Hic vero ab eis occidendus rogabat, ut se dimitterent, dicens, se utilem esse hominibus, noctu eos ad opera excitantem.

Hi vero dixerunt, Sed propter hoc te tanto magis occidimus:

357

occidimus we kill (i.e. but we kill you only more because of this):

illos enim for them excitans rousing (i.e. for, waking them), furari to steal nos us non sinis you don't allow (i.e. you don't let us steal).

illos enim excitans, furari nos non sinis.

Fabula significat the fable signifies, *ea those things* maxime *very greatly* pravis *to the depraved* esse *to be (i.e. that those things to the corrupt are very greatly)*, adversa *adverse (i.e. against)*, quae *which* bonis *to the good* sunt *are* beneficia *beneficent*.

Fabula significat, ea maxime pravis esse, adversa, quae bonis sunt beneficia.

CORNIX THE CROW ET CERVUS AND THE RAVEN

CORNIX ET CERVUS

Cornix a crow cervo to a raven invidens envying (i.e. being jealous of a raven), quod because is it per

Cornix cervo invidens, quod is per auguria hominibus vaticinaretur, ob idque crederetur, uti

358

through auguria divinations hominibus to men vaticinaretur he (the raven) prophecied, ob idque and because of this crederetur was believed, uti as futura future things (i.e. the future) praedicens predicting, conspicata having caught sight of viatores travelers quosdam some (i.e. having seen some travelers) praetereuntes passing by, ivit went super upon quamdam a certain arborem tree, stansque and standing (there) valde very strongly crocitavit cawed (i.e. and crowed very loudly).

Illis vero but they ad vocem to the voice conversis having turned, et stupefactis and being amazed;

re cognita with the thing being known (i.e. having

futura praedicens, conspicata viatores quosdam praetereuntes, ivit super quamdam arborem, stansque valde crocitavit.

Illis vero ad vocem conversis, et stupefactis;

re cognita, quidam inquit, Abeamus, heus vos,

359

found out what it was making the sound), quidam *a certain one* inquit *said*, Abeamus *let us go*, heus vos *hey you*, cornix enim *for a crow* est *it is (i.e. for it's a crow)* quae *which* corcitavit *cawed*, et augurium *and divination* non habet *he doesn't have*.

Fabula significat *the fable signifies*, eodem modo *in the same way* et *and (i.e. also)* homines *people* cum praestantioribus *with more excellent (i.e. with their betters)* certantes *contesting (i.e. in the same way people competing against their betters)*, praeterquam *besides* quod *that* non *not* ad aequa *to equal (rewards)* perveniunt *they arrive (i.e. besides not achieving equal success)*, risu *laughter* quoque *also* dignos *worthy*

cornix enim est quae corcitavit, et augurium non habet.

Fabula significat, eodem modo et homines cum praestantioribus certantes, praeterquam quod non ad aequa perveniunt, risu quoque dignos esse.

360

of esse *to be (i.e. they're also worthy of ridicule).*

CORNIX THE CROW ET CANIS AND THE DOG | CORNIX ET CANIS

Cornix *a crow* Minervae *to Minerva* sacrifans *sacrificing,* canem *a dog* ad epulas *to the feasts* invitavit *invited (i.e. invited a dog to the feasts).*

Cornix Minervae sacrifans, canem ad epulas invitavit.

Ille vero *but he* dixit *said,* Quid *why* frustra *in vain* sacrificia *the sacrifices* absumis *do you consume?*

Ille vero dixit, Quid frustra sacrificial absumis?

Dea enim *for the goddess (Minerva)* adeo *so much* te *you* odit *has hated (i.e. for the goddess has hated you so much),* ut *that* ex conviventibus *from the living together* tecum *with you* avibus *birds (i.e. for from the birds living with*

Ille vero dixit, Quid frustra sacrificial absumis?

361

you) fdem trust sustulerit has taken away.

Cui to which cornix the crow (said): Ob id on account of this magis more ei to her sacrificio do I sacrifice, ut so that reconcilietur she may be reconciled mihi to me.

Fabula significat the fable signifies, plerosque (that) most (people), ob on account of lucrum gain inimicos enemies, beneficiis with benefits prosequi to pursue non vereri not to fear (i.e. the fable signifies that most people fear not to follow up their enemies for gain).

Cui cornix: Ob id magis ei sacrificio, ut reconcilietur mihi.

Fabula significat, plerosque, ob lucrum inimicos, beneficiis prosequi non vereri.

Decoding Latin – Day 32

Don't forget the rules:

1. Don't try to memorise anything
2. Focus on the story, not the language – don't try to analyse!
3. Read one section from the left column and then the same from the right.
4. *Always read for speed and general gist, not for accuracy and perfection.*

CORVUS THE RAVEN ET SERPENS AND THE SERPENT	**CORVUS ET SERPENS**
Corvus a raven cibi of food indigens needing (i.e. a raven, needing food), ut when vidisset it had seen in in quodam a certain aprico sunny loco place serpentem a serpent dormientem sleeping, hunc this, devolando by flying down, rapuit he (the raven) siezed.	Corvus cibi indigens, ut vidisset in quodam aprico loco serpentem dormientem, hunc, devolando, rapuit.
Hic vero but he (the snake), quum when se himself vertisset had	Hic vero, quum se vertisset, atque momordisset ipsum,

363

turned, atque and momordisset had bitten ipsum him (the raven), corvus the raven moriturus about to die dixit said, Me miserum poor me! qui (I) who tale such reperi I've found lucrum gain (i.e. I, who have found such profit), ex quo from which etiam also pereo I perish.

corvus moriturus dixit, Me miserum! qui tale reperi lucrum, ex quo etiam pereo.

Fabula a fable in virum against the man, qui who, ob on account of thesaurorum of treasures inventionem the finding (i.e. having found treasure), de salute about (his) health periclitatus sit might have endangered (i.e. who risks his health on account of finding treasures).

Fabula in virum, qui, ob thesaurorum inventionem, de salute periclitatus sit.

MONEDULA THE JACKDAW ET COLUMBAE AND THE DOVES

MONEDULA ET COLUMBAE

Monedula *a jackdaw* in quodam *in a certain* columbario *dove house* columbas *the doves* conspicata *having seen* bene *well* nutritas *fed* (i.e. a jackdaw, having seen the doves in a certain dovehouse being well-fed), dealbavit *whitened* sese *herself*, ivitque *and went*, ut *so that* et *and* (i.e. also) ipsa *herself* eodem *in the same* cibo *food* impertiretur *might share*.

Hae vero *but they (the doves)*, donec *while* tacebat *she was silent*, ratae *having thought* columbam *a dove* eam *her* esse *to be* (i.e. having thought she was a dove while she was silent), admiserunt *admitted (her, i.e. let her in)*.

Sed *but* quum *when* aliquando *sometime*

Monedula in quodam columbario columbas conspicata bene nutritas, dealbavit sese, ivitque, ut et ipsa eodem cibo impertiretur.

Hae vero, donec tacebat, ratae columbam eam esse, admiserunt.

Sed quum aliquando oblita vocem emisisset, tunc,

365

(later) **oblita** having forgot **vocem** (her) voice **emisisset** she sent forth (i.e. she made a sound with her voice), **tunc** then, **ejus** her **cognita** being known, **natura** nature (i.e. her nature/who she really was being found out), **expulerunt** they (the doves) expelled (her) **percutientes** striking (her);

eaque and she, **privata** being deprived of **eo** that **cibo** food, **rediit** went back **ad monedulas** to the jackdaws **rursum** again.

Et illae and they, **ob** on account of **colorem** her colour **quum** when **ipsam** her **non nossent** they didn't know (i.e. and when they didn't recognise her because of her whitened colour), **a suo** from their own **cibo** food **abegerunt** they drove (her) away, **ita ut** so that, **duorum** (the

ejus cognita, natura, expulerunt percutientes;

eaque, privata eo cibo, rediit ad monedulas rursum.

Et illae, ob colorem quum ipsam non nossent, a suo cibo abegerunt, ita ut, duorum appetens, neutro potiretur.

366

food) of two **appetens** seeking, **neutro** neither **potiretur** she possessed.

Fabula significat the fable signifies, **oportere** *to behove (i.e. one ought)* **et** *also* **nos** *us (i.e. we also ought)* **nostris** *with our own (affairs)* **contentos** *content* **esse** *to be (i.e. that we also ought to be content with our own affairs),* **considerantes** *considering,* **habendi** *of having* **cupiditatem** *the desire (i.e. the desire of having),* **praeterquam** *besides* **quod** *that* **nihil** *nothing* **juvat** *it helps (i.e. not only does it help nothing),* **auferre** *(but) to take away* **et** *also* **quae** *(those things) which* **adsunt** *are present (i.e. we have)* **bona** *the good things* **saepe** *often (i.e. the desire of having not only doesn't help, but often takes away also the good things we have).*

Fabula significat, oportere et nos nostris contentos esse, considerantes, habendi cupiditatem, praeterquam quod nihil juvat, auferre et quae adsunt bona saepe.

MONEDULA THE JACKDAW

Monedulam a jackdaw quum when quis someone cepisset had taken (i.e. when someone had taken a jackdaw), et and aligasset bound pedem (its) feet filio with thread, suo to his own tradidit he handed it over filio to the son (i.e. he handed it over to his son).

Haec vero but she (the jackdaw), non passa not having suffered inter among homines people victum food (i.e. having no food among the people), ubi when parumper a little while (later) liberantem librty nacta est she obtained, fugit she fled, in suumque and into her own nidum nest se herself contulit she bore (i.e. she took herself back to her own nest).

MONEDULA

Monedulam quum quis cepisset, et aligasset pedem filio, suo tradidit filio.

Haec vero, non passa inter homines victum, ubi parumper liberantem nacta est, fugit, in suumque nidum se contulit.

368

Circumvoluto vero *but being entwined* vinculo *the tie* ramis *with the branches* (i.e. the tie on her foot got tangled with the branches), evolare *to fly away* haud *not* valens *being able*, quum *when* moritura *about to die* esset *she was*, secum *with herself* loquebatur *she spoke* (i.e. she spoke to herself), Me miserum *poor me*! quae *who* apud homines *among people* non passa *suffered not* servitutem *slavery*, incaute *uncautiously* me *me* vita *from live* privavi *I've deprived* (i.e. I've deprived myself of life).

Fabula significat the fable signifies, quosdam *some (people)* nonnumquam *sometimes*, dum *when* se *themselves* a mediocribus *from mediocre* periculis *dangers* student *they strive* liberare *to free* (i.e. when they try to free themselves

Circumvoluto vero vinculo ramis, evolare haud valens, quum moritura esset, secum loquebatur, Me miserum! quae apud homines non passa servitutem, incaute me vita privavi.

Fabula significat, quosdam nonnumquam, dum se a mediocribus periculis student liberare, in majora incidere.

from moderate dangers), *in* majora *into greater* incidere *to fall (i.e. they fall)*.

JUPITER JUPITER ET MERCURIUS AND MERCURY

JUPITER ET MERCURIUS

Jupiter *Jupiter* Mercurio *to Mercury* jussit *ordered*, ut *that* omnibus *to all* artificibus *artists* mendacii *of falsehood* medicamentum *a medicine* infunderet *he might infuse* (i.e. Jupiter ordered Mercury to give a potion of lying to all artists).

Jupiter Mercurio jussit, ut omnibus artificibus mendacii medicamentum infunderet.

Hic vero *but he*, eo *it* trito *being ground* (i.e. having found out the poweder to make them liars), et *and* ad mensuram *to measure* facto *made* (i.e. made to measure), aequabiliter *equally* singulis *to each (artist)* infudit *he infused (it)*.

Hic vero, eo trito, et ad mensuram facto, aequabiliter singulis infudit.

Quum vero *but when*, solo *with only* sutore *the shoemaker* relicto *being left*, multum *much (i.e. a lot)* superesset *remained* medicamenti *of the medicine*, totum *the whole* acceptum *taken up* mortarium *mortar (i.e. everything left in the mortar)* ei *to him (to the shoemaker)* infudit *he infused*.

Atque *and* hinc *hence* confugit *it happened*, artifices *(that) artists* omnes *all* mentiri *lie*, maxime vero *but mostly* omnium *of all* sutores *the shoemakers*.

Fabula a fable *in mendaces* against lying *artifices* artists.

JUPITER JUPITER

Quum vero, solo sutore relicto, multum superesset medicamenti, totum acceptum mortarium ei infudit.

Atque hinc confugit, artifices omnes mentiri, maxime vero omnium sutores.

Fabula in mendaces artifices.

JUPITER

Jupiter Jupiter nuptias nuptials celebrans celebrating, omnia all animalia the animals convivio to the banquet excipiebat received (i.e. Jupiter, celebrating a wedding, received all the animals to the banquet).	Jupiter nuptias celebrans, omnia animalia convivio excipiebat.
Sola vero but alone testudine the tortoise sero later profecta having set out (i.e. but the tortoise, having set out alone late), admiratus having wondered at causam the cause tarditatis of her slowness, rogavit he (Jupiter) asked eam he, quamobrem for what reason ipsa she ad convivium to the banquet non accessisset hadn't approached (i.e. he asked why she hadn't come to the banquet).	Sola vero testudine sero profecta, admiratus causam tarditatis, rogavit eam, quamobrem ipsa ad convivium non accessisset.

Quum vero *but when* haec *she* dixisset *said*, Domus *home* chara *dear* (i.e. dear home), domus *home* optima *best* (i.e. he was at his home, which is a dear home, and the best home);

iratus *being angry* ipsi *to* (i.e. with) *her*, damnavit *he condemned (her)*, ut *that* domum *(her) home* bajulans *carrying* circumferret *she should bear about* (i.e. he condemned her always to carry her home around).

Fabula significat the fable signifies, plerosque *most* homines *people* eligere *choose* potius *rather* parce *sparingly* apud se *at themselves* vivere *to live,* quam *than* apud alios *with others* laute *lavishly* (i.e. the fable signifies that many, like the tortoise, are happier

Quum vero haec dixisset, Domus chara, domus optima;

iratus ipsi, damnavit, ut domum bajulans circumferret.

Fabula significat, plerosque homines eligere potius parce apud se vivere, quam apud alios laute.

with little by themselves than a lot with others).

Decoding Latin – Day 33

Don't forget the rules:

1. Don't try to memorise anything
2. Focus on the story, not the language – don't try to analyse!
3. Read one section from the left column and then the same from the right.
4. *Always read for speed and general gist, not for accuracy and perfection.*

LUPUS THE WOLF ET OVIS AND THE SHEEP	**LUPUS ET OVIS**
Lupus a wolf a canibus by (some) dogs morsus being bitten, et and male badly affectus affected, abjectus downcast jacebat lay down.	Lupus a canibus morsus, et male affectus, abjectus jacebat.
Cibi vero but of food idigens needing (i.e. but needing food), conspicatus having caught sight of ovem a sheep, rogabat he asked, ut so that potum a drink ex out of praeterfluente the flowing	Cibi vero idigens, conspicatus ovem, rogabat, ut potum ex praeterfluente flumine sibi afferret:

375

past **flumine** river **sibi** for himself **afferret** she would bring (i.e. he asked her to bring him a drink from the river flowing by):

Si enim for if **tu** you **mihi** to me, **inquit** he (the wolf) said, **dederis** you will have given **potum** a drink (i.e. for if you give me a drink), **ego** I **cibum** food **mihi ipsi** for me myself **inveniam** I will find (i.e. I'll find my own food).

Si enim tu mihi, inquit, dederis potum, ego cibum mihi ipsi inveniam.

Illa vero but she **respondit** answered **et ait** and said, **Sed** but, **si ego** if I **potum** a drink **dedero** will have given **tibi** to you, **tu** you **et** also **cibo** for food **me** me **uteris** you'll use (i.e. you'll also use me for food).

Illa vero respondit et ait, Sed, si ego potum dedero tibi, tu et cibo me uteris.

Fabula a fable *in virum* against the man *maleficem* malicious (i.e. against a malicious man) *per* through

Fabula in virum maleficem per simulationem insidiantem.

376

simulationem pretence insidiantem plotting.

LEPORES THE HARES | LEPORES

Lepores the hares olim once, belligerantes warring cum aquilis with the eagles, invocarunt called on in auxilium into help vulpes the foxes (i.e. called on the foxes to help):

Lepores olim, belligerantes cum aquilis, invocarunt in auxilium vulpes:

Hae autem but they dixerunt said, Non auxiliateremur we will not help vobis you, nisi unless sciremus we might know, qui who vos you estis are, et and cum with quibus what bellamini you war?

Hae autem dixerunt, Non auxiliateremur vobis, nisi sciremus, qui vos estis, et cum quibus bellamini?

Fabula significat the fable signifies, eos those, qui who cum praestantioribus with their betters certant fight,

Fabula significat, eos, qui cum praestantioribus certant, suam salutem contemnere.

suam *their own* salutem safety contemnere *despise*.

FORMICA THE ANT

Formica *the ant* quae *which* nunc *now* est *is (i.e. that which is now an ant)*, olim *once* homo *a person* fuit *was*, et *and* agriculturae *at agriculture* assidue *constantly* incumbens *plying (i.e. working hard)*, non propriis *not with his own* erat *was* contentus *he content* laboribus *with his labours (i.e. he wasn't content with his own labours)*, sed et *but also* vicinorum *of (his) neighbours* fructus *the fruits* surripiebat *he stole*.

Jupiter autem *but Jupiter* indignatus *enraged* hujus *of him* habendi *of having* cupiditate *with the desire (i.e. enraged with his desire of having things)*,

FORMICA

Formica quae nunc est, olim homo fuit, et agriculturae assidue incumbens, non propriis erat contentus laboribus, sed et vicinorum fructus surripiebat.

Jupiter autem indignatus hujus habendi cupiditate, transmutavit eum in hoc animal, quae Formica appellatur.

378

transmutavit transformed eum him in into hoc this animal animal, quae which Formica the ant appellatur is called.

Verum but quum when mutasset he'd changed formam (its) form, non et not also affectum (his) passion mutavit he changed (i.e. but changing his form/his body he didn't change his desire):

Nam for hucusque until now arva the lands circumeundo by going about (i.e. for by wandering around through the lands up to the present day), aliorum others' labores labours colligit he collects, et and sibi ipsi for himself recondit he lays (it) up.

Fabula significat the fable signides, natura by nature pravos the corrupt, ut

Verum quum mutasset formam, non et affectum mutavit:

Nam hucusque arva circumeundo, aliorum labores colligit, et sibi ipsi recondit.

Fabula significat, natura pravos, ut maxime speciem

379

though maxime *mostly* speciem *(their) face (i.e. their appearance)* transmutaverint *they may have transformed,* mores *(their) manners* non mutare *not to change (i.e. the fable signifies that the corrupt by nature, though they change their appearance, don't change their habits).*

VESPERTILIO **THE BAT** ET MUSTELA **AND THE WEASEL**

Vespertilio *a bat,* in terram *onto the ground* cum *when* cecidisset *it'd fallen (i.e. when it'd fallen to the ground),* a *by* mustela *a weasel* capta est *was captured,* et *and* quum *when* occidenda *to be killed* foret *she might be (i.e. and when she/the bat was to be killed),* pro salute *for (her) safety* rogabat *she asked (begged).*

transmutaverint, mores non mutare.

VESPERTILIO ET MUSTELA

Vespertilio, in terram cum cecidisset, a mustela capta est, et quum occidenda foret, pro salute rogabat.

Hac vero *but she (the weasel)* dicente *saying*, non posse *not to be able* ipsam *her (the bat)* dimittere *to send away (i.e. she said she couldn't let her go)*, quod *because* natura *by nature* volucribus *to birds* omnibus *all (i.e. to all birds)* inimica *hostile* foret *she was*;	Hac vero dicente, non posse ipsam dimittere, quod natura volucribus omnibus inimica foret;
illa ait *she (the bat) said*, Non avem *not a bird*, sed murem *but a mouse* esse *to be (i.e. she said she wasn't a bird but a mouse)*:	illa ait, Non avem, sed murem esse:
et sic *and so* dimissa est *she was sent away (i.e. let go)*.	et sic dimissa est.
Postremo autem *but finally*, quum *when* iterum *again* cecidisset *she'd fallen*, et *and* ab alia *by another* capta *captured* mustela *weasel* fuisset *she*	Postremo autem, quum iterum cecidisset, et ab alia capta mustela fuisset, ne voraretur, orabat.

was (i.e. she was captured by another weasel), ne lest voraretur she be devoured, orabat she begged (i.e. she begged not to be devoured).	
Hac autem but she dicente saying, cunctis to all inimicam hostile esse to be muribus to mice (i.e. but she said she was hostile to all mice);	Hac autem dicente, cunctis inimicam esse muribus;
se herself non murem not a mouse, sed vespertilionem but a bat dicebat said esse to be (i.e. she said she wasn't a mouse but a bat):	se non murem, sed vespertilionem dicebat esse:
et rursus and again dimissa est she was sent away (let go).	et rursus dimissa est.
Atque ita and so evenit it came about, bis twice mutato with a changed nomine name, eam her salutem safety consecutam	Atque ita evenit, bis mutato nomine, eam salutem consecutam fuisse.

382

fuisse *to be obtained (i.e. was obtained)*.

Fabula significat the fable signifies, *neque* neither *nos oportere* it behoves us (i.e. that neither ought we), *in eisdem* in the same (states) *semper* always *permanere* to remain, *considerantes* considering, *eos* those *qui* who *ad tempus* for a time *mutatur* are changed *plerumque* generally *pericula* dangers *effugere* escape.

VIATORES THE TRAVELLERS

Viatores travellers *juxta* near *littus* a shore *quoddam* a certain (i.e. near a certain shore) *iter* a journey **facientes** making (i.e. some travellers, making a journey near a particular shore), **venerunt** came *in speculam* into a watch-

Fabula significat, neque nos oportere, in eisdem semper permanere, considerantes, eos qui ad tempus mutatur plerumque pericula effugere.

VIATORES

Viatores juxta littus quoddam iter facientes, venerunt in speculam quandam;

383

tower quondam a certain (i.e. came into a certain watchtower);

et and illinc from there conspicati having caught sight of sarmenta branches procul far off natantia floating, navem a ship esse to be magnum a great existimarunt they thought (i.e. they thought it was a great ship);

et illinc conspicati sarmenta procul natantia, navem esse magnum existimarunt;

quamobrem for which reason expectarunt they waited, tanquam as though appulsura about to land ea it esset was (i.e. as though it were about to land).

quamobrem expectarunt, tanquam appulsura ea esset.

Quum vero but when a vento by the wind lata borne sarmenta the twigs propius nearer forent might be (i.e. but when the branches were brought by the wind nearer), non navem not a

Quum vero a vento lata sarmenta propius forent, non navem amplius, sed scapham videbantur videre.

ship **amplius** (any)more, **sed** but **scapham** a skiff (a small boat) **videbantur** they seemed **videre** to see.

Advecta autem but being brought to **illa** it (i.e. but it, being brought near), **quum** when **sarmenta** branches **esse** to be **vidissent** they saw (i.e. when they saw it was branches), **inter se** among themselves **dixerunt** they said, **Ut** how **igitur** therefore **frustra** in vain **nos** we, **quod** what **nihil** nothing **est** is (for that which is nothing), **expectabamus** we've awaited!

Fabula significat the fable signifies, *nonnullos* some *homines* people, *ex improviso* suddenly *terribiles terrible* *esse* to be *visos having seemed* (i.e. that some men, having seemed

Advecta autem illa, quum sarmenta esse vidissent, inter se dixerunt, Ut igitur frustra nos, quod nihil est, expectabamus!

Fabula significat, nonnullos homines, ex improviso terribiles esse visos, quum periculum feceris, nullius inveniri esse pretii.

385

suddenly terrible), **quum** *when* **periculum** *a trial* **feceris** *you've made (i.e. when you've tried them out),* **nullius** *of no* **inveniri** *you find (them)* **esse** *to be* **pretii** *of value (i.e. you find them to be of no value).*

Decoding Latin – Day 34

Don't forget the rules:

1. Don't try to memorise anything
2. Focus on the story, not the language – don't try to analyse!
3. Read one section from the left column and then the same from the right.
4. *Always read for speed and general gist, not for accuracy and perfection.*

ASINUS THE ASS **SYLVESTRIS WOODLAND (I.E. THE WILD DONKEY)**

ASINUS SYLVESTRIS

Asinus an ass sylvestris woodland (i.e. from the wild) asinum an ass conspicatus having caught sight of domesticum a domestic (i.e. a wild ass, having caught sight of a domestic ass) in in quodam a certain aprico sunny loco place, profectus set out ad ipsum to him, beatum happy dicebat did say, et corporis both the body's bona good habitudine

Asinus sylvestris asinum conspicatus domesticum in quodam aprico loco, profectus ad ipsum, beatum dicebat, et corporis bona habitudine, et cibi perceptione.

condition, et and cibi of food perceptione the enjoyment (i.e. he said that the other seemed happy both in the good condition of his body and the enjoyment of food).

Deinde vero but then, quum when vidisset he'd seen, eum him ferentem bearing onera burdens, et and agasonem a groom a tergo from the back (i.e. from behind) sequentem following (i.e. following behind a groom), et and baculis with sticks ipsum him percutionem striking (i.e. and striking him/the ass with sticks), ait he (the wild ass) said, Ast but ego I non amplius not more beatum happy te you existimo I think (i.e. I don't think you're happy anymore);

Deinde vero, quum vidisset, eum ferentem onera, et agasonem a tergo sequentem, et baculis ipsum percutionem, ait, Ast ego non amplius beatum te existimo;

video enim *for I see*, quod *that* non sine *not without* malis *evils* magnis *great (i.e. great evils)* felicitatem *happiness* habes *you have*.

Fabula significat the fable signifies, *non esse* not to be *aemulanda* to be emulated, *cum periculis* with dangers *et miseris* and miseries, *lucre* gains (i.e. the fable signifies that gains with dangers and miseries are not to be emulated).

ASINUS THE ASS ET VULPES AND THE FOX

Asinus *an ass* indutus *clothed* pele *with the hide* leonis *of a lion* circuibat *went about*, reliqua *the rest (of)* bruta *the brutes (animals)* perterrens *frightening*.

video enim, quod non sine malis magnis felicitatem habes.

Fabula significat, non esse aemulanda, cum periculis et miseris, lucra.

ASINUS ET VULPES

Asinus indutus pele leonis circuibat, reliqua bruta perterrens.

389

Ceterum *but* conspicatus *having caught signt of* vulpem *a fox*, tentavit *he tried* et *also* hanc *her* perterrefacere *to make afraid*.	Ceterum conspicatus vulpem, tentavit et hanc perterrefacere.
Haec autem *but she* (casu enim *for by chance* ipsum *him* rudentem *braying* audiverat *had heard*) ei *to him* ait *said*,	Haec autem (casu enim ipsum rudentem audiverat) ei ait,
Sed *but* bene *well* scito *do I know (you)*, quod *that* et ego *I also* te *you* timuissem *I would fear*, nisi *if not* rudentem *the braying* audivissem *I've heard* (i.e. I'd have been frightened of you too, if I hadn't heard your braying).	Sed bene scito, quod et ego te timuissem, nisi rudentem audivissem.
Fabula significat the fable signifies, nonnullos *some* indoctos *uneducated (people)*, qui *who* videntur *seem* exteris *to foreign (people, i.e. to others)* aliqui	*Fabula significat*, nonnullos indoctos, qui videntur exteris aliqui esse, ex sua loquacitate redargui.

390

someone **esse** *to be (i.e. who seem to be interesting to others),* **ex sua** *by their own* **loquacitate** *babbling* **redargui** *are refuted*.

ASINUS THE ASS ET RANAE AND THE FROGS | ASINUS ET RANAE

Asinus *an ass* ligna *logs (i.e. wood)* ferens *carrying* pertransibat *passed through* quandam *a certain* paludem *marsh*.

Asinus ligna ferens pertransibat quandam paludem.

Lapsus autem *but having slipped*, ut *as* decidit *he fell down*, surgere *to rise* non valens *not being able*, lamentabatur *he lamented*, ac *and* suspirabat *sighed*.

Lapsus autem, ut decidit, surgere non valens, lamentabatur, ac suspirabat.

Ranae autem *but the frogs*, quae *who* erant *were* in palude *in the marsh*, suspiriis *the sighs* ejus *of him* auditis *having heard (i.e. having heard his sighs)*, Heus tu *hey you*,

Ranae autem, quae erant in palude, suspiriis ejus auditis, Heus tu, dixerunt, et quid faceres, si tanto hic tempore mansisses, quanto nos, quum, quia in

dixerunt *they said*, et *and* quid *what* faceres *would you do*, si *if* tanto *in so great* hic *here* tempore *a time* mansisses *you'd remain*, quanto *as great* nos *(as) we (i.e. what would you do if you had to stay in this marsh for a long time like us)*, quum *when*, quia *because* in *in (i.e. for)* breve *a short* tempus *time* lapsus sis *you've slipped*, sic *thus (i.e. in such a way)* lamentaris *you complain?*

breve tempus lapsus sis, sic lamentaris?

Hoc sermone *this speech* uti *to use* poterit *should be able*, quisquam *anyone (i.e. anyone should be able to use this speech)* in virum *against a man* segnem *lazy (i..e against a lazy man)*, qui *who* ob *on account of* minimos *the least* labores *labours* tristatur *is saddened*, quum *when* ipse *he himself* majoribus *to greater*

Hoc sermone uti poterit, quisquam in virum segnem, qui ob minimos labores tristatur, quum ipse majoribus facile resistat.

392

(labours) **facile** *easily* **resistat** *resists*.

ASINUS **THE ASS** ET CORVUS **AND THE RAVEN** | ## ASINUS ET CORVUS

Asinus *an ass*, ulcerato *being ulcered* dorso *on (its) back (i.e. having ulcers on its back)*, in quodam *in a certain* prato *field* pascebatur *grazed*.

Asinus, ulcerato dorso, in quodam prato pascebatur.

Corvo autem *but a raven* incidente *perching on* ei *him*, et *and* ulcus *the ulcer* percutiente *striking*, asinus *the ass* rudebat *brayed*, ac *and* saltabat *danced (i.e. leapt about)*.

Corvo autem incidente ei, et ulcus percutiente, asinus rudebat, ac saltabat.

Sed *but* agasone *a groom* procul *at a distance* stante *standing*, ac *and* ridente *laughing*, lupus *a wolf* praeteriens *passing by* ipsum *him* vidit *saw (i.e. saw the man laughing at the ass)*, et dixit *and said*,

Sed agasone procul stante, ac ridente, lupus praeteriens ipsum vidit, et dixit, Miseri nos! qui, si tantum videamur, agitamur, hunc autem rident.

Miseri nos *poor us*! Qui *who*, si tantum *if only* videamur *we're seen*, agitamur *we're hunted*, hunc autem *but him (i.e. the ass)* rident *they laugh at*.

Fabula significat the fable signifies, maleficos malicious homines people, si tantum if only appareant they appear, dignosci (are) distinguished.

ASINUS THE ASS ET VULPES AND THE FOX	**ASINUS ET VULPES**
Asinus *an ass* et vulpes *and a fox*, societate *in an alliance* inita *having entered* inter se *between themselves (i.e. having entered an alliance between them)*, exiverunt *went out* ad venationem *for hunting*.	Asinus et vulpes, societate inita inter se, exiverunt ad venationem.
Leo vero *but a lion* quum *when* occurrisset *he'd run*	Leo vero quum occurrisset ipsis, vulpes,

394

into ipsis them, vulpes the fox, imminens the impending videns seeing periculum danger (i.e. seeing the impending danger), profecta (and) having gone ad leonem to the lion, se himself tradituram about to hand over ei to him asinum the ass pollicita est he promised (i.e. he promised he'd give him the ass), si if sibi for himself impunitatem impunity promiserit he'd promise.

Qui who, quum when se himself dimisurum about to dismiss (i.e. let go) eam he dixisset he'd said (i.e. when he'd said he'd let the fox go), illa she, adducto being led asino the ass in cases into nets quosdam certain (i.e. she, the ass, accidentally coming up to some nets), ut that incideret he'd fall

imminens videns periculum, profecta ad leonem, se tradituram ei asinum pollicita est, si sibi impunitatem promiserit.

Qui quum se dimisurum eam dixisset, illa, adducto asino in cases quosdam, ut incideret, fecit.

395

in, fecit *he made (i.e. he looked like he'd fall in).*

Sed leo *but the lion,* videns *seeing* illum *him* fugere *to flee* minime *by no means* posse *to be able (i.e. seeing that the ass couldn't get away),* primam *first* vulpem *the fox* comprehendit *grabbed,* deinde *then* sic *thus* ad asinum *to the ass* versus est *he turned.*

Fabula significat *the fable signifies,* eos *those,* qui *who* sociis *for (their) allies* insidiantur *plot,* saepe *often* et seipsos *themselves also* perdere *lose (i.e. those who plot against their friends often also lose themselves).*

Sed leo videns illum fugere minime posse, primam vulpem comprehendit, deinde sic ad asinum versus est.

Fabula significat, eos, qui sociis insidiantur, saepe et seipsos perdere.

Decoding Latin – Day 35

Don't forget the rules:

1. Don't try to memorise anything
2. Focus on the story, not the language – don't try to analyse!
3. Read one section from the left column and then the same from the right.
4. *Always read for speed and general gist, not for accuracy and perfection.*

GALLINA THE HEN ET HIRUNDO AND THE SWALLOW	**GALLINA ET HIRUNDO**
Gallina a hen, serpentis a serpent's ovis eggs inventis being found, diligenter diligently calefacta warmed excludit shut out (i.e. hatched them: a hen, having found a snake's eggs, warmed them carefully and hatched them).	Gallina, serpentis ovis inventis, diligenter calefacta excludit.
Hirundo autem but a swallow, quum when eam he vidisset had seen (i.e. when he'd seen her), ait	Hirundo autem, quum eam vidisset, ait, O demens, quid haec nutris, quae cum excreverint, a

sad, O demens O mad (creature), quid why haec these (eggs) nutris do you nourish, quae which, cum when excreverint they've grown up, a te from you prima first injuriam injury auspicabuntur will commence (i.e. who will end up hurtiung you first)?

Fabula significat the fable signifies, implacabilem implacable esse to be pravitatem corruption (i.e. the fable signifies that corruption is implacable), licet although afficiatur it might be affected maximis by the greatest beneficiis benefits.

CAMELUS THE CAMEL

Quum when primum first visa est was seen camelus the camel (i.e. when a camel was first seen), homines people perterriti

te prima injuriam auspiciabuntur?

Fabula significat, implacabilem esse pravitatem, licet afficiatur maximis beneficiis.

CAMELUS

Quum primum visa est camelus, homines perterriti, et

398

(were) terrified, et and magnitudinem (its) size admirati having admired, fugiebant they fled;

ubi vero but when, procedente advancing tempore time (i.e. over time), cognoverunt they knew ipsius its mansuetudinem tameness, confisi sunt they trusted eo usque to such an extent, ut that ad eam to her (i.e. to the camel) accederent they approached.

At but intellecto having understood paulo post a little later, Belluam the beast non bilam no bile habere to have (i.e. that the beast had no bile), eo to that (level) contemptus of contempt iere they went, ut that et also frena the bits (of a bridle) ei to it (the camel) imponerent they placed upon (i.e. they

magnitudinem admirati, fugiebant;

ubi vero, procedente tempore, cognoverunt ipsius mansuetudinem, confisi sunt eo usque, ut ad eam accederent.

At intellecto paulo post, Belluam non bilam habere, eo contemptus iere, ut et frena ei imponerent, et pueris agendam traderent.

399

were so little afraid of it they put a saddle and bridle on it), **et** and **pueris** by boys **agendam** to be driven **traderent** they handed (it) over (i.e. and they turned it into a pack animal driven by young boys).

Fabula significat the fable signifies, *ut that* **terribiles** *terrible* **res** *matters* **consuetudo** *custom* **contemptibiles** *contemptible* **faciat** *may make (i.e. that habit makes terrible things contemptible – 'familiarity breeds contempt')*.

SERPENS THE SNAKE

Serpens a snake **a multis** by many **hominibus** people **conculcatus** being trampled **Jovem** Jupiter **supplex** humbly begging

Fabula significat, ut terribiles res consuetudo contemptibiles faciat.

SERPENS

Serpens a multis hominibus conculcatus Jovem supplex adiit.

400

adiit he went to (i.e. he went to Jupiter begging).

Jupiter autem but Jupiter **ei** to him **dixit** said:

Sed but, **si** if, **qui** who **prior** first **conculcavit** trampled (you), **pupugnisses** you have pricked (i.e. if you'd bitten the first person who trampled on you), **nequaquam** by no means **secundus** the second **id** iut **facere** to do **aggressus fuisset** would have attempted.

Fabula significat the fable signifies, *eos* those, *qui* who *prius* first *invadentibus* to invaders *resistunt* resist, *aliis* to others *formidolosos* formidable *fieri* become (i.e. those who resist the first people to invade them become fearsome in the eyes of others).

Jupiter autem ei dixit:

Sed, si, qui prior conculcavit, pupugnisses, nequaquam secundus id facere aggressus fuisset.

Fabula significat, eos, qui prius invadentibus resistunt, aliis formidolosos fieri.

401

COLUMBA THE DOVE

Columba a dove siti by thirst correpta being seized, ut when vidit she saw in quodam in a certain loco place poculum a cup aquae of water depictum painted (i.e. a painted cup of water), putavit thought esse to be (i.e. thought it was) verum true (i.e. real), atque and, multo by much impetu force allata borne (i.e. carried by much force), imprudens imprudent(ly) in tabulam against the picture offendit dashed, ut so that, et also pennis the feathers ipsius of her perfractuis being broken (i.e. having broken her wings), in terram into the earth decideret she fell down, atque and a quodam by a certain (person) occurrentium of those meeting (her, i.e. by

COLUMBA

Columba siti correpta, ut vidit in quodam loco poculum aquae depictum, putavit esse verum, atque, multo impetu allata, imprudens in tabulam offendit, ut, et pennis ipsius perfractuis, in terram decideret, atque a quodam occurrentium caperetur.

one of those who found her) **caperetur** she was taken.

Fabula significat the fable signifies, *nonnullos* some *homines* people, *ob* on account of *vehementem* their passionate *alacritatem* speed, *inconsulto* unthinkingly *res aggredientes* attempting things, *injicere* cast *sese* themselves *in perniciem* into destruction.

Fabula significat, nonnullos homines, ob vehementem alacritatem, inconsulto res aggredientes, injicere sese in perniciem.

COLUMBA THE DOVE ET CORNIX AND THE CROW

COLUMBA ET CORNIX

Columba a dove, **in quodam** in a certain **columbario** dovehouse **nutrita** being fed, **fecunditate** in (her) fruitfulness **superiebat** prided (i.e. she prided herself on her fertility).

Columba, in quodam columbario nutrita, fecunditate superiebat.

Cornix vero *but a crow*, ea *her* audita *having heard (i.e. having heard her)*, ait *said*:	Cornix vero, ea audita, ait:
Sed *but*, heus tu *hey you*, desine *cease* hac re *about this matter* gloriari *to boast (i.e. stop boasting about this matter)*;	Sed, heus tu, desine hac re gloriari;
nam *for* quo plures *how much more* paries *you give birth*, eo plures *by that much more* Dolores *griefs* accumulas *do you accumulate*.	nam quo plures paries, eo plures Dolores accumulas.
Fabula significat the fable signifies, ex famulis *among servants* quoque *also* eos *those* infelicissimos *very unfortunate* esse *be (i.e. that those servants are very unfortunate),* qui *who* in servitute *in servitude* multos *many* liberos *children* procreant *procreate*	*Fabula significat, ex famulis quoque eos infelicissimos esse, qui in servitute multos liberos procreant.*

404

(because they're born into slavery).

Decoding Latin – Day 36

Don't forget the rules:

1. Don't try to memorise anything
2. Focus on the story, not the language – don't try to analyse!
3. Read one section from the left column and then the same from the right.
4. Always read for speed and general gist, not for accuracy and perfection.

DIVES THE RICH (LADY)	**DIVES**
Dives a rich (lady) duas two filias daughters habens having (i.e. having two daughters), altera the other (i.e. one of them) mortua having died, praeficas mourners conduxit she hired (i.e. she paid people to mourn her daughter):	Dives duss filias habens, altera mortua, praeficas conduxit:
altera vero but the other filia daughter, dicente saying, Ut how nos misere wretched we (are), quae who ipsae ourselves,	altera vero filia dicente, Ut nos misere, quae ipsae, quarum est dolor, lamentari nescimus, hae

quarum whose est it is dolor the grief, lamentari to lament nescimus we don't how (i.e. how wretched are those, who don't lament their own grief), hae vero but these non necessariae non-acquaintances sic thus vehementer passionately plangent wail?

Mater (her) mother ait said, Ne mirare don't wonder, filia (my) daughter, si if hae these (women) ita so (i.e. in this way) lamentatur lament, nam for nummorum of moneys gratia for the sake id it agunt they do (i.e. for they do it for the sake of money).

Fabula significat the fable signifies, nonnullos some homines people, propter on account of pecuniae money's amorem love, non dubitare don't hesitate ex

vero non necessariae sic vehementer plangunt?

Mater ait, Ne mirare, filia, si hae ita lamentatur, nam nummorum gratia id agunt.

Fabula significat, nonnullos homines, propter pecuniae amorem, non dubitare ex alienis calamitatibus quaestum facere.

alienis out of others' calamitatibus misfortunes quaestum gain facere to make (i.e. some people make a profit from others' misfortunes because of their love of money).

PASTOR THE SHEPHERD

Pastor *a shepher*, actis *being driven* in quercetum *into an oak-grove* quoddam *a certain* ovibus *his sheep (i.e. with his sheep being driven into a certain oak-grove)*, strata *having spread* sub *under* quercu *an oak* veste *(his) clothe(s)*, ascendit *he went up (the tree)*, et fructum *and (its) fruit* decutiebat *he shook off.*

Oves vero *but the sheep* edentes *eating* glandes *acorns*, nesciae *unknowing* et *also* vestes *(his) clothes* una *together (with the*

PASTOR

Pastor, actis in quercetum quoddam ovibus, strata sub quercu veste, ascendit, et fructum decutiebat.

Oves vero edentes glandes, nesciae et vestes una devorarunt.

acorns) devorarunt devoured.	
At but, quum when pastor the shepherd descendisset came down, et and, quod what erat was factum done, vidisset he'd seen (i.e. when he'd seen what had been done);	At, quum pastor descendisset, et, quod erat factum, vidisset;
O pessima O worst, ait he said, Animalia animals (i.e. O worst animals), vos you caeteris to others vellera fleeces ad vestes for clothes praebetis you afford, a me vero but from me, qui who vos you nutria I feed, etiam even vestem (my) clothes surripuistis you've stolen (i.e. you give your fleece to others for clothes, but from me, who feeds you, you've even stolen my clothes).	O pessima, ait, animalia, vos caeteris vellera ad vestes praebetis, a me vero, qui vos nutrio, etiam vestem surripuistis.
Fabula significat the fable signifies, plerosque most	*Fabula significat*, plerosque homines, ob stultitiam, eos,

homines *people*, ob *on account of* stultitiam *(their) stupidity*, eos *those*, qui *who* nihil *nothing* ad se *for themselves* attinent *relate*, beneficio *with kindness* afficientes *affecting (i.e. treating)* in domesticos *against (their) domestics* male *badly* tractare *treating (i.e. most people treat those who have nothing to do with them with kindness, but those close to them they treat badly)*.

PISCATOR THE FISHERMAN ET CERRUS AND THE PILCHARD

Piscator *a fisherman*, demisso *having sent down* reti *(his) net* in mare *into the sea*, rettulit *brought back* cerrum *a pilchard*:

qui *which*, parvus *small* quum *since* esset *it was* (i.e. since it was small),

qui nihil ad se attinent, beneficio afficientes in domesticos male tractare.

PISCATOR ET CERRUS

Piscator, demisso reti in mare, rettulit cerrum:

qui, parvus quum esset, suppliciter rogabat, ipsum, tunc ne quidem se

410

suppliciter suppliantly rogabat it begged, ipsum him, tunc then ne quidem not indeed se himself caperet he should take (i.e. he begged him, saying he/the fisherman should take him/the fish just yet), sed but dimitteret he should let him go, quod because parvus small essset he was (i.e. because he was small):

At but, quum when crevero I've grown, et magnus and big, inquit he said, evasero I'll have come off (i.e. when I've turned out big), me me capere to seize poteris you'll be able, quoniam since et also majori greater tibi to you ero I'll be utilitati for use (i.e. I'll be greater use to you).

Et piscator and the fishermen ait said, Sed ego but I demens mad fuerim

caperet, sed dimitteret, quod parvus essset:

At, quum crevero, et magnus, inquit, evasero, me capere poteris, quoniam et majori tibi ero utilitati.

Et piscator ait, Sed ego demens fuerim, si, quod in manibus est, misso lucro,

411

would be, si if, quod what in manibus in (my) hands est there is, misso having sent (lost) lucro the gain, licet although sit it might be parvum small, expectatum (for the expected), licet although magnum laught fuerit it would have been, sperem I'd hope (i.e. I'd be mad if, letting go the gain which is in my hands go, however small, I hoped for an expected gain, however large).

licet sit parvum, expectatum, licet magnum fuerit, sperem.

Fabula significat the fable signifies, inconsideratum thoughtless esse to be (i.e. that they're thoughtless), qui who, spe with the hope majoris of a greater rei thing, quae what in manibus in (their) hands sunt are amittat they lose, quod because parva small sint they may be (i.e. that those people are thoughtless who let go what's in their hands,

Fabula significat, inconsideratum esse, qui, spe majoris rei, quiae in manibus sunt amittat, quod parva sint.

412

however small, in the hope of of something bigger).

EQUUS THE HORSE ET ASINUS AND THE ASS

Homo a man quidam a certain (i.e. a certain man) habebat had equum a horse et asinum and an ass.

Quum autem but when iter a journey facerent they made in via on the way, ait said asinus the ass equo to the horse, Tolle take partem part ex meo from (i.e. of) my onere burden, si if vis you want esse to be me me salvum saved (i.e. if you want me to be safe/okay).

Ille vero but he non persuasus est wasn't persuaded.

EQUUS ET ASINUS

Homo quidam habebat equum et asinum.

Quum autem iter facerent in via, ait asinus equo, Tolle partem ex meo onere, si vis esse me salvum.

Ille vero non persuasus est.

Asinus vero *but the ass* cecidit *fell*, atque *and* e labore *from the labour (i.e. the effort)* mortuus est *he died*.

Ab hero autem *but by the master* omnibus *all things (i.e. everything)* impositis *being placed upon* ei *him (the horse)*, et ipsa *and the very* asini *ass's* pelle *hide*, conquerens *complaining* equus *the horse* clamabat *cried out*, Hei mihi *woe to me* miserrimo *most wretched*! quid *what* mihi *to me* evenit *has happened* afflict *afflicted (i.e. for what has happened to me, afflicted in this way)*?

quia enim *for because* nolui *I didn't want* parum *a little* oneris *of the burden* accipere *to receive*, ecce *behold* omnia *all (the burdens)*

Asinus vero cecidit, atque e labore mortuus est.

Ab hero autem omnibus impositis ei, et ipsa asini pelle, conquerens equus clamabat, Hei mihi miserrimo! quid mihi evenit afflicto?

quia enim nolui parum oneris accipere, ecce omnia gesto, et pellem.

414

gesto *I carry*, et pellem *and the hide*.

Fabula significat the fable signifies, si if magni great cum parvis with small jungantur are joined, utrosque both servari (should be) preserved in vita in life.

HOMO THE MAN ET SATYRUS AND THE SATYR

Homo quidam *a certain man*, cum satyro *with a styr* inita *having entered into* societate *an alliance*, una *together* cum eo *with him* comedebat *ate (i.e. he ate with him)*.

Hyems vero *but winter*, et frigus *and the cold* quum accessisset *when it'd approached*, homo *the man* manus suas *his hands* admovens *moving to* ori

Fabula significat, si magni cum parvis jungantur, utrosque servari in vita.

HOMO ET SATYRUS

Homo quidam, cum satyro inita societate, una cum eo comedebat.

Hyems vero, et frigus quum accessisset, homo manus suas admovens ori afflabat.

415

to (his) mouth **afflabat** he blew (on them).

Sciscitato autem but having inquired **satyro** the satyr (i.e. but with satyr asking), **quam ob rem** for what reason **hoc** this **faceret** he might do (i.e. why he did this)? **Ait** he said, **Manus meas** my hands **calefacio** I'm warming **propter** on account of **frigus** the cold.

Sed but **paulo post** a little later, **edulio** food **calido** hot **allato** being brought (i.e. hot food having brought), **homo** the man **admovens** moving (it) **ori** to (his) mouth **insufflabat** blew on **ipsum** it.

Rogante vero but asking **rursus** again **satyro** the satyr (i.e. but the satyr, asking again), **quare** for what reason **id** this **faceret** he did? **Ait** he said,

Sciscitato autem satyro, quam ob rem hoc faceret? ait, Manus meas calefacio propter frigus.

Sed paulo post, edulio calido allato, homo admovens ori insufflabat ipsum.

Rogante vero rursus satyro, quare id faceret? ait, Ferculum frigefacio.

Ferculum *the meat-dish* frigefacio *I'm cooling*.

Suscepto vero *but having taken up* sermone *the subject*, satyrus *the styr*, Sed ego *but I*, ait *he said*, posthac *after this* renuncio *I renounce* tuam *your* amicitiam *friendship*;

| Suscepto vero sermone, satyrus, Sed ego, ait, posthac renuncio tuam amicitiam; |

quia *because* ex eodem *out of the same* ore *mouth* et calidum *both hot* et frigidum *and cold* emittis *you emit*.

quia ex eodem ore et calidum et frigidum emittis.

Fabula significat the fable signifies, *oportere* to behove *fugere* to flee *nos* us (i.e. that we ought to flee) *amicitias* friendships, *quarum* of which *anceps* doubtful *est affectio* is the affection.

Fabula significat, oportere *fugere nos amicitias,* quarum anceps est affectio.

417

Decoding Latin – Day 37

Don't forget the rules:

1. Don't try to memorise anything
2. Focus on the story, not the language – don't try to analyse!
3. Read one section from the left column and then the same from the right.
4. *Always read for speed and general gist, not for accuracy and perfection.*

VULPES THE FOX ET LIGNATOR AND THE WOOD-CUTTER	**VULPES ET LIGNATOR**
Vulpes a fox venatores hunters fugiens fleeing (i.e. a fox, running away from hunters), et and in deserto in a desert multa much decursa having run via way (i.e. having run a long way in the desert), virum a man, lignatorem a wood-cutter, invenit she found in eo in it (in the desert), cui to whom supplicabat she begged, ut that se herself absconderet he would	Vulpes venatores fugiens, et in deserto multa decursa via, virum lignatorem invenit in eo, cui supplicabat, ut se absconderet.

418

hide (i.e. she begged the wood-cutter to hide her).

A quo *by whom* ei *to her* ostenso *having shown* suo *his own* tugurio *bed*, ingressa *having entered* delituit *she lay hid* in angulis *in the corners*.

A quo ei ostenso suo tugurio, ingressa delituit in angulis.

Ac *but* venatoribus *with the hunters* profectis *having set out*, et *and* rogantibus *asking* virum *the man*, hic *he* voce *with his voice*, quidem *indeed,* negabat *denied* quidquam *anything* scire *to know* (i.e. he denied that he knew anything), sed *but* manu sua *with his hand* locum *the place* (where she was hidden) demonstrabat *he pointed out*.

Ac venatoribus profectis, et rogantibus virum, hic voce quidem negabat quidquam scire, sed manu sua locum demonstrabat.

Hi vero *but they*, quum *since* non advertissent *they hadn't noticed (it)*,

Hi vero, quum non advertissent, abiere confestim.

419

abiere they went away confestim immediately.

Ut when, igitur therefore, vidit she saw eos them vulpes the fox praeterisse to have passed by (i.e. when the fox saw they'd passed by), exivit she went out nihil (with) nothing allocuta being spoken.

Accusante accusing autem but ipsam her illo him (i.e. but the man, accusing her), quod because, servata being preserved (i.e. saved) a se by him, gratias thanks sibi to him non ageret she didn't make (i.e. because she didn't thank him for saving her), vulpes the fox, conversa having turned, inquit said, Heus tu he you, ego I, vero indeed, egissem would have given tibi you gratias thanks, si id verbis to (your) words

Ut igitur vidit eos vulpes praeterisse, exivit nihil allocuta.

Accusante autem ipsam illo, quod, servata a se, gratias sibi non ageret, vulpes conversa inquit, Heus tu, ego vero egissem tibi gratias, si verbis similes manuum gestus et mores habuisses.

similes *similar* manuum *(your) hands'* gestus *gestures* et mores *and manners* habuisses *you'd kept* (i.e. I'd have thank you if you'd kept the gestures and manners of your hands to/in line with your words).

Fabula a fable *in eos* against those, *qui* who *utilia* useful things *quidem* indeed *promittunt* promise *verbis* with (their) words, *sed* but *contra* the opposite *faciunt* they do *rebus* in (their) things (i.e. their deeds).

Fabula in eos, qui utilia quidem promittunt verbis, sed contra faciunt rebus.

HOMO THE MAN, PERFRACTOR THE DESTROYER STATUAE OF THE STATUE

HOMO PERFRACTOR STATUAE

Homo quidam *a certain man*, ligneum *a wooden* habens *having* deum *god* (i.e. having a wooden god), quum *since* pauper

Homo quidam, ligneum habens deum, quum pauper esset, supplicabat, ut sibi benefaceret.

421

poor **esset** he was (i.e. he was poor), **supplicabat** he prayed (to the god), **ut** that **sibi** to himself **benefaceret** he would benefit.

Quum when, **igitur** therefore, **haec** these things **faceret** he did, **et** and **nihilominus** nevertheless **in paupertate** in poverty **degeret** he (still) lived, **iratus** being angry, **elevatum** having lifted **ipsum** it **cruribus** by its legs **projecit** he threw (it) **in pavimentum** against the pavement.

Illiso being dashed **igitur** therefore **capite** its head (i.e. its head having been shattered), **ac** and **statim** immediately **diffracto** being broken, **auri** of gold **effluxit** flowed out **quamplurimum** a very large amount (i.e. a large

Quum igitur haec faceret, et nihilominus in paupertate degeret, iratus elevatum ipsum cruribus projecit in pavimentum.

Illiso igitur capite, ac statim diffracto, auri effluxit quamplurimum;

422

amount of gold flowed out);

quod which, ille he jam now colligens collecting, exclamabat cried out, Peversus es you are perverse, ut puto as (i.e. so) I think, et ingratus and ungrateful:

colenti enim for me worshipping te you mihi to me nequaquam by no means profusi you profited (i.e. for you didn't benefit me at all when I worshipped you), verberantem autem but, beating te you, multis with many bonis goods remuneravisti you've remunerated (me).

Fabula significat the fable signifies, non profuturum not about to profit te you tibi to yourself (i.e. you won't benefit yourself), honorantem honouring

quod ille jam colligens exclamabat, Peversus es, ut puto, et ingratus:

colenti enim te mihi nequaquam profusi, verberantem autem te multis bonis remuneravisti.

Fabula significat, non profuturum te tibi, honorantem pravum hominem, sed verberantem ipsum magis profuturum.

423

pravum a corrupt hominem *person,* sed *but* verberantem *beating* ipsum *him* magis *more* profuturum *about to profit (i.e. will you benefit).*

HOMO THE MAN ET CANIS AND THE DOG

HOMO ET CANIS

Homo quidam *a certain man* parabat *prepared* coenam *dinner,* accepturus *about to receive* quendam *a certain* amicorum *of friends* suorum *his own (i.e. going to receive in his house one of his friends),* et familiarium *and of his acquaintances.*

Homo quidam parabat coenam, accepturus quendam amicorum suorum, et familiarium.

Canis vero *but the dog* ipsius *of him (i.e. his dog)* alium *another* canem *dog* invitavit *invited,* dicens *saying,* O amice *O friend,* veni *come,* coena *dine* una

Canis vero ipsius alium canem invitavit, dicens, O amice, veni, coena una mecum.

424

as one (i.e. together) mecum with me.

Is vero but he, quum when accessisset he'd approached, laetus happy adstabat he stood by, spectans looking at magnam the great coenam dinner, clamans crying out in in corde suo his heart, Papae strange, quanta how much mihi to me laetitiae gladness nuper lately derepente suddenly oblata est has been gifted (i.e. it's strange how much gladness has lately been given to me)! nam for et nutria I'm both nourished, et and ad satietatem to (the point of) satiety (i.e. being full) coenabo I'll dine, adeo ut so that cras tomorrow nullo in no modo way esuriero will I hunger.

Haec these things secum to himself dicente saying

Is vero, quum accessisset, laetus adstabat, spectans magnam coenam, clamans in corde suo, Papae, quanta mihi laetitiae nuper derepente oblata est! nam et nutriar, et ad satietatem coenabo, adeo ut cras nullo modo esuriero.

Haec secum dicente cane, simulque movente

425

cane the dog (i.e. the dog, saying these things to himself), simulque and at the same time movente moving (wagging) caudam (his) tail, ut as qui one who jam now amico (his) friend fideret might trust, coquus the cook, ut when vidit he saw ipsum him huc et illuc here and there caudam (his) tail circumagentem shaking about, arreptis having seized (him) ipsius his cruribus by the legs (i.e. having seized him by his legs), ejecit threw (him) out de fenestris from the windows.

caudam, ut qui jam amico fideret, coquus, ut vidit ipsum huc et illuc caudam circumagentem, arreptis ipsius cruribus, ejecit de fenestris.

At is but he, quum when decidisset he'd fallen down, abibat went away vehementer vehemently exclamans crying out.

At is, quum decidisset, abibat vehementer exclamans.

Sed but quidam a certain one canum of the dogs, illi to him in via on the way

Sed quidam canum, illi in via occurrentium,

426

occurrentium meeting (i.e. but one of the dogs who ran into him on the way), percontabatur questioned (him), Ut how belle beautifully coenatus es have you dined, amice (my) friend?

Ille vero but he, respondens answering, ei to him dixit said, Multo with much potu drink inebriatus being inebriated supra beyond satietatem fullness (i.e. being drunk with a lot of drink beyond my fill), ne not ipsam itself quidem indeed viam the way (i.e. not even the way itself), qua from which egressus sum I came out, novi do I know.

Fabula significat the fable signifies, non oportere one oughtn't confidere to trust iis those, qui who ex alienis from strangers benefacere to benefit pollicentur

percontabatur, Ut belle coenatus es, amice?

Ille vero respondens ei dixit, Multo potu inebriatus supra satietatem, ne ipsam quidem viam, qua egressus sum, novi.

Fabula significat, non oportere confidere iis, qui ex alienis benefacere pollicentur.

427

promise (i.e. we shouldn't trust those who claim to benefit from strangers).

PISCATOR THE FISHERMAN

Piscator a fisherman, piscendi of fishing rudis unskilled (i.e. unskilled in fishing), acceptis having received tibiis the pipes ac retibus and the nets, perrexit proceeded ad mare to the sea, et and, stans standing super upon quandam a certain petram rock, primum first, quidem indeed, sonabat he sounded (i.e. played) tibiis with his pipes, existimans thinking, ad to vocis (his) voice's suavitatem sweetness pisces the fish assilire to leap up (i..e thinking the fish would leap up to the sweetness of his playing).

PISCATOR

Piscator, piscendi rudis, acceptis tibiis ac retibus, perrexit ad mare, et stans super quandam petram, primium quidem sonabat tibiis, existimans, ad vocis suavitatem pisces assilire.

Ut vero *but indeed*, multum *much* contendens *striving (i.e. working hard)*, proficeret *he profited* nihil *nothing*, depositis *(and) putting aside* tibiis *his pipes*, assumit *he took up* rete *a net*, ac *and,* jacto *having thrown (it)* in aquam *into the water*, multum *much (i.e. a lot)* piscium *of fish* cepit *he took*.

Cum vero *but when* ejecisset *he'd thrown out* illos *them* e reti *from the net (i.e. when he'd thrown the fish out of the net)*, ut *when,* salientes *leaping about* vidit *he saw (i.e. when he saw the fish leaping about)*, ait *he said*, O pessimae *O worst* animantes *creatures*, quum *when* sonebam *I played* tibia *with a pipe*, non saltabatis *you didn't jump*;

Ut vero, multum contendens, proficeret nihil, depositis tibiis, assumit rete, ac jacto in aquam, multum piscium cepit.

Cum vero ejecisset illos e reti, ut salientes vidit, ait, O pessimae animantes, quum sonebam tibia, non saltabatis;

429

quum vero but when cessavi I stopped, id agitis you do it.

Fabula a fable in eos against those, qui who praeter beyond rationem reason, et inopportune and at a bad time, aliquid something agunt do (i.e. against those who do something unreasonably and unseasonably).

BUBULCUS THE HERDSMAN

Bubulcus a herdsman armentum a herd taurorum of bulls pascens feeding amisit lost vitulum a calf.

Cum vero but when lustrasset he'd viewed omnem all solitudinem the desert, moram a delay traxit he drew quaerens looking for it (i.e. but when, looking for it, he'd

quum vero cessavi, id agitis.

Fabula in eos, qui praeter rationem, et inopportune, aliquid agunt.

BUBULCUS

Bubulcus armentum taurorum pascens amisit vitulum.

Cum vero lustrasset omnem solitudinem, moram traxit quaerens.

checked all the desert, he delayed).

Ubi autem but when nihil nothing invenire to find potuit he was able (i.e. but when he couldn't find anything), votum a vow fecit he made Jovi to Jupiter, si (that) if, qui who cepisset had taken vitulum the calf, furem the thief ostenderet he (Jupiter) would show (i.e. that if Jupiter would show the thief who had taken the calf), hoedum a kid (i.e. a young goat) in sacrificium in sacrifice se oblaturum he'd offer.

Ubi autem nihil invenire potuit, votum fecit Jovi, si, qui cepisset vitulum, furem ostenderet, hoedum in sacrificium se oblaturum.

Ceterum but proficiscens having set out in quoddam into a certain quercetum oak-grove, invenit he found leonem a lion devorantem devouring vitulum the calf.

Ceterum proficiscens in quoddam quercetum, invenit leonem devorantem vitulum.

Trepidus *afraid,* igitur *therefore,* factus *being made (i.e. being made afraid, therefore),* et *and* valde *greatly* territus *terrified,* elevatis *with raised* manibus *hands* suis *his own (i.e. with his hands raised)* in coelom *into the sky,* ait *he said,* O Domine Jupiter *O Lord Jupiter,* promiseram *I'd promised* tibi *to you* hoedum *a kid* me *myself* daturum *about to give* esse *to be (i.e. I'd promised I'd give you a kid),* si *if* furem *the thief* invenirem *I'd find*;

nunc autem *but now* taurum *a bull* tibi *to you* polliceor *I promise* sacrificaturum *to sacrifice,* si *if* hujus *of him (i.e. of the thief, the lion)* manus *the hands* effugero *I flee (i.e. if I escape his hands).*

Trepidus igitur factus, et valde territus, elevatis manibus suis in coelum, ait, O Domine Jupiter, promisuram tibi hoedum me daturum esse, si furem invenirem;

nunc autem taurum tibi polliceor sacrificaturum, so hujus manus effugero.

432

Fabula a fable *in homines* against people *infortunatos* unfortunate, *qui* who, *dum* while *carent* they lack, *ut inveniant* that they may find, *precantur* pray *(i.e. against those unfortunate people who, when they lack something, pray that they may have it)*;

quum vero but when *invenerint* they've found (it), *quaerunt* they seek *effugere* to escape (it).

Fabula in homines infortunatos, qui, dum carent, ut inveniant, precantur;

quum vero invenerint, quaerunt effugere.

Decoding Latin – Day 38

Don't forget the rules:

1. Don't try to memorise anything
2. Focus on the story, not the language – don't try to analyse!
3. Read one section from the left column and then the same from the right.
4. Always read for speed and general gist, not for accuracy and perfection.

CORVUS THE RAVEN	**CORVUS**
Corvus a raven, aegrotans becoming sick ait says matri to (his) mother, Mater mother, precare pray (to) deum god, nec nor lamentare lament.	Corvus aegrotans ait matri, Mater, precare deum, nec lamentare.
Ea vero but she respondens answering, ait said, Quis who tui of you, O fili O (my) son, deorum of the gods miserebitur will pity (i.e. who/which of the gods will take pity on you, my son)?	Ea vero respondens, ait, Quis tui, O fili, deorum miserebitur?

cujus enim *for whose* carnes *meats (i.e. sacrificial meats offered to the gods)* non *not* a te *by you* surreptae fuerunt *have been stolen (i.e. for which of the gods have you not stolen the offerings from)*?

Fabula significat the fable signifies, *qui* (those) who *multos* many *inimicos* enemies *in vita* in life *habent* have, *eos* those *neminem* no *amicum* friend *in necessitate* in need *inventuros* will find (i.e. those who have many enemies in life will find no friends in need).

AQUILA THE EAGLE

Super *upon* petram *a rock* Aquila *an eagle* sedebat *sat*, leporem *a hare* capere *to seize* quaerens *looking (i.e. looking to snatch a hare/rabbit).*

cujus enim carnes non a te surreptae fuerunt?

Fabula significat, qui multos inimicos in vita habent, eos neminem amicum in necessitate inventuros.

AQUILA

Super petram Aquila sedebat, leporem capere quaerens.

435

Hanc autem *but this (bird)* quidam *a certain* percussit *struck* sagitta *an arrow* (i.e. but a certain arrow struck this bird), et *and* sagitta *the arrow* quidem *indeed* ipsam *her (the eagle)* ingressa est *entered* (i.e. it pierced her).	Hanc autem quidam percussit sagitta, et sagitta quidem ipsam ingressa est.
Sed *but* crena *the notch (on the arrow)* cum pennis *with the feathers* ante oculos *before (her) eyes* stabat *stood* (i.e. the feathers were right in front of her eyes):	Sed crena cum pennis ante oculos stabat:
illa vero *but she* conspicata *having caught sight of (it)* inquit *said*, Et haec *and this (is)* mihi *to me* altera *another* moestitia *sorrow*, quod *because* propriis *by my own* pennis *feathers* interam *will I perish*[13].	illa vero conspicata inquit, Et haec mihi altera moestitia, quod propriis pennis interam.

---

[13] The arrow was notched with eagle feathers.

Fabula significat the fable signifies, *durum* hard *esse* to be *(i.e. the fable signifies it's hard)*, *quum* when *quis* anyone *a suis* by his own *periculum* danger *patitur* suffers *(i.e. when anyone suffers danger from his own things).*

CICADA THE CICADA ET FORMICAE AND THE ANTS

Hyemis of winter *tempore* in the time *(i.e. in the time of winter)*, *tritico* with the wheat *madente* being wet, *formicae* the ants *ventilabant* fanned *(it, i.e. they dried it).*

Cicada autem but a cicada *esuriens* being hungry *rogabat* asked *eas* them *cibum* (for) food.

Fabula significat, durum esse, quum quis a suis periculum patitur.

CICADA ET FORMICAE

Hyemis tempore, tritico madente, formicae ventilabant.

Cicada autem esuriens rogabat eas cibum.

Formicae vero *but the ants* dixerunt *said* ei *to her* Cur *why* aestate *in the summer* non colligebas *did you not collect* alimentum *nourishment?*

Haec vero *but she* ait *said*, Non eram *I wasn't* otiose *lazy*, sed *but* canebam *I sang* musice *musically*.

Tum *then* hae *these (ants)* ridentes *laughing* dixerunt *said*, Si *if* aestatis *of summer* tempore *in the time (i.e. in the time of summer)* modulabaris *you tuned*, hyeme *in winter* salta *dance*.

Fabula significat the fable signifies, non oportere *it doesn't behove* quenquam *anyone (i.e. no one ought)* esse *to be* negligentem *negligent* in aliqua re *in anything*, ne *lest* moereat *he*

Formicae vero dixerunt ei Cur aestate non colligebas alimentum?

Formicae vero dixerunt ei Cur aestate non colligebas alimentum?

Tum hae ridentes dixerunt, Si aestatis tempore modulabaris, hyeme salta.

Fabula significat, non oportere quenquam esse negligentem in aliqua re, ne moereat ac periclitetur.

438

may grieve ac periclitetur *and be in danger*.

VERMIS THE WORM ET VULPES AND THE FOX

Qui *which* sub coeno *under the mud* celabatur *was hidden* vermis *a worm (i.e. a worm, which was hidden under the mud)*, super terram *upon the earth* egressus *came out*, dicebat *(and) said* omnibus *to all* animalibus *the animals*, Medicus *a doctor* sum *I am (i.e. I'm a doctor)*, medicaminum *of medicines* doctus *learned (i.e. skilled in medicines)*, qualis *such as* est *is* Paeon *Paeon*, deorum *the gods'* medicus *physician*.

Et *and*, quomodo *how*, ait *said* vulpes *a fox*, alios *others* curans *curing*, teipsum *yourself* claudum *lame* non curavisti *you*

VERMIS ET VULPES

Qui sub coeno celabatur vermis, super terram egressus, dicebat omnibus animalibus, Medicus sum, medicaminum doctus, qualis est Paeon, deorum medicus.

Et, quomodo, ait vulpes, alios currans, teipsum claudum non curavisti?

439

haven't cured (i.e. and how, in curing others, you haven't cured yourself of being lame)?

Fabula significat the fable signifies, *nisi* unless *praesto* at hand *experientia* experience *fuerit* may be, *omne* every *verbum* word *inane esse* be (i.e. is) inane (i.e. unless experience/evidence is at hand, all words are useless).

GALLINA THE HEN AURIPARA GOLD-PRODUCING

Gallinam a hen *quidam* a certain (person) *habebat* had (i.e. a certain person had a hen), *ova* eggs *aurea* golden *parientem* producing, *et* and *ratus* having thought *intra* within *ipsam* her, *massam* a mass *auri* of gold *esse* to be (i.e. and having thought there was a mass of gold

Fabula significat, nisi praesto experientia fuerit, omne verbum inane esse.

GALLINA AURIPARA

Gallinam quidam habebat, ova aurea parientem, et ratus intra ipsam, massam auri esse, occisam reperit similem aliis gallinis.

440

inside her), **occisam** having killed (her) **reperit** he found (her) **similem** like **aliis** to other **gallinis** hens (i.e. and, having killed her, he looked inside and found she was like all other hens).

Hic vero but he, **multum a** lot **divitiarum** of riches **sperans** hoping **se** himself **inventurum** about to find (i.e. hoping he'd find a lot of riches), **etiam** even **exiguis** the little **privatus est** he was deprived (of) **illis** from them.

Fabula significat the fable signifies, *oportere* to behove (i.e. one ought) *praesentibus* with present (things) *contentum* content *esse* to be (i.e. one ought to be content with present things), *et* and *insatiabilitatem* insatiableness *fugere* to flee.

Hic vero, multum divitiarum sperans se inventurum, etiam exiguis privatus est illis.

Fabula significat, oportere praesentibus contentum esse, et insatiabilitatem fugere.

Decoding Latin – Day 39

Don't forget the rules:

1. Don't try to memorise anything
2. Focus on the story, not the language – don't try to analyse!
3. Read one section from the left column and then the same from the right.
4. *Always read for speed and general gist, not for accuracy and perfection.*

LEO THE LION ET VULPES AND THE FOX	**LEO ET VULPES**
Leo a lion senio with old age confectus being spent (i.e. worn out with age), et and non valens not being able suppeditare to supply sibi for himself cibum food (i.e. not being able to get himself food), decrevit resolved astu by cunning aliquid something facere to do.	Leo senio confectus, et non valens suppeditare sibi cibum, decrevit astu aliquid facere.
Itaque and so, profectus having gone in antrum into a cave quoddam a	Itaque profectus in antrum quoddam, et inclusus, simulabat se aegrotare.

443

certain (i.e. into a certain cave), **et** and **inclusus** being shut in, **simulabat** he pretended **se** himself **aegrotare** to be sick (i.e. he pretended he was sick).

Advenientia soming to (him) **igitur** therefore **animalia** the animales, **visitationis** of visiting (him) **gratia** for the sake (i.e. for the sake of visiting him), **comprehendens** seizing, **devoravit** he devoured (i.e. seizing the animals coming to him for the sake of visiting him, he ate them).

Multis many **igitur** therefore **animalibus** animals **absumptis** being consumed (i.e. therefore, many animals being eaten), **vulpes** a fox, **ea** that **arte** art (i.e. that trick) **cognita** being known (i.e. having figured out the trick),

Advenientia igitur animalia, visitationis gratia, comprehendens, devoravit.

Multis igitur animalibus absumptis, vulpes, ea arte cognita, accessit ad ipsum, et, stans extra speluncam, rogabat, quomodo se haberet.

444

accessit approached ad ipsum to him (the lion), et and, stans standing extra beyond speluncam the cave, rogabat he asked, quomodo how se himself (the lion) haberet he had (i.e. he asked the lion how he was keeping himself/how he was doing).

Quum autem but when is he (the lion) dixisset said, Male 'Badly';

causamque and the reason rogaret he'd asked, quamobrem for which non ingrederetur he (the fox) didn't enter;

vulpes ait the fox said, Quia because video I see vestigia the footprints multorum of meny introeuntium going in, paucorum vero but of few exeuntium going out.

Quum autem is dixisset, Male;

causamque rogaret, quamobrem non ingrederetur;

vulpes ait, Quia video vestigia multorum introeuntium, paucorum vero exeuntium.

Fabula significat *the fable signifies*, prudentes *prudent* homines *people*, ex conjecturis *from conjectures* praevidentes *foreseeing* pericula *dangers (i.e. predicting dangers from reasoning)*, evitare *avoid (them)*.

LUPUS **THE WOLF** ET VETULA **AND THE OLD WOMAN**

Lupus *a wolf,* esuriens *being hungry,* circumibat *went around,* quaerens *seeking* cibum *food* .

Profectus autem *but having set out* ad locum *to a place* quendam *a certain (i.e. to a certain place),* audivit *he heard* puerulum *a boy* lugentem *crying,* et *and* anum *an old woman* dicentem *saying* ei *to him,* Desine *cease* plorare *to weep (i.e. stop crying)*:

Fabula significat, prudentes homines, ex conjecturis praevidentes pericula, evitare.

LUPUS ET VETULA

Lupus esuriens circumibat, quaerens cibum.

Profectus autem ad locum quendam, audivit puerulum lugentem, et anum dicentem ei, Desine plorare:

446

sin minus *if not*, hac *in this* hora *hour* tradam *I'll hand over* te *you* lupo *to a wolf*.	sin minus, hac hora tradam te lupo.
Ratus *having thought,* igitur *therefore,* Lupus *the wolf,* quod *thar* serio *seriously* loquitur *spoke* anicula *the little old woman (i.e. thinking that the little old woman spoke seriously),* stetit *stood* multam *much* expectans *waiting* horam *the hour (i.e. stood waiting for most of the hour).*	Ratus igitur Lupus, quod serio loquitur anicula, stetit multam expectans horam.
Sed quum *but when* oppressisset *had pressed on* vespera *the evening (i.e. when evening came up),* audit *he heard* rursus *again* anum *the old woman* blandientem *coaxing* puerulo *to the little boy (i.e. coaxing the little boy),* ac *and* dicentem *saying* ei *to him,*	Sed quum oppressisset vespera, audit rursus anum blandientem puerulo, ac dicentem ei, Si venerit lupus huc, interficimus, O fili, eum.

Si *if* venerit *there came* lupus *a wolf* huc *here*, interficimus *we'll kill*, O fili *O (my) son*, eum *him (i.e. if a wolf came, we'd kill him, my son)*.

His *this* auditis *being heard (i.e. hearing this)*, lupus *the wolf* abivit *went away*, dicens *saying*, In hoc *in this* tugurio *cottage*, aliud *another (i.e. one thing)* dicunt *they say*, aliud vero *but another* faciunt *they do*.

Fabula *a fable* in homines *against people*, qui *who* facta *deeds* verbis *to (their) words* non habent *they don't have* similia *alike (i.e. people who don't have actions similar to/matching their words)*.

HOEDUS *THE KID* ET LUPUS *AND THE WOLF*

His auditis, lupus abivit, dicens, In hoc tugurio, aliud dicunt, aliud vero faciunt.

Fabula in homines, qui facta verbis non habent similia.

HOEDUS ET LUPUS

Hoedus *a kid (i.e. a young goat)* super *upon* quodam *a certain* tecto *roof* stans standing *(i.e. standing on a certain roof)*, cum *when* lupum *a wolf* praetereuntem *passing by* videret *he saw*, conviciabatur *abused* et mordebat *and bit (i.e. sniped)* ipsum *(at) him*.

Sed lupus *but the wolf* ait *said*, Heus tu *Ho, (look at) you*, non tu *not you* mihi *to me* conviciaris *abuses*, sed *but* locus *the place (i.e. it's not you who mocks me, it's the location/the fact that you're on a roof)*.

Fabula significat the fable signifies, quod *that* plerumque *generally* et locus *both the place*, et tempus *and the time*, praebet *afford (i.e. provide)* audaciam *boldness* adversus *against*

Hoedus super quodam tecto stans, cum lupum praetereuntem videret, conviciabatur et mordebat ipsum.

Sed lupus ait, Heus tu, non tu mihi conviciaris, sed locus.

Fabula significat, quod plerumque et locus, et tempus, praebet audaciam adversus praestantiores.

449

praestantiores (one's) betters.

MULUS THE MULE

Mulus *a mule* hordeo *with barley* pinguefactus *fattened (i.e. grown large from eating barley)*, lasciviebat *ran riot* clamans *crying out*, ac dicens *and saying*, Pater *father* meus *my (i.e. my father)* est *is* equus *a horse* cursor *racer (i.e. a racing horse)*, et ego *and I* ei *to him* totus *completely* sum *am* similis *the same*.

Atque *and* aliquando *sometime (later)*, quum *when* necesse esset *it was necessary* ei *for him* currere *to run*, ut *when* a curso *from the race* cessaverat *he'd stopped*, patris *of his father* asini *the ass* statim *immediately* recordatus est *he recalled (i.e. he said he was a*

MULUS

Mulus hordeo pinguefactus, lasciviebat clamans, ac dicens, Pater meus est equus cursor, et ego ei totus sum similis.

Atque aliquando, quum necesse esset ei currere, ut a curso cessaverat, patris asini statim recordatus est.

450

racehorse; when he had to run, he was reminded he was an ass).

Fabula significat the fable signifies, *etsi* although *tempus* time *ad gloriam* for glort *promoveat* promotes *aliquem* someone *(i.e. although time may promote someone to glory),* non suae *not of his own,* tamen *however,* ipsius *his* fortunae *fortune* obliviscatur *should he forget (i.e. yet he shouldn't forget his own fortune/good luck):*

instabilis enim for unstable *est* is *vita* life *haec* this *(i.e. this life).*

SERPENS THE SERPENT ET AGRICOLA AND THE FARMER

Serpens a serpent *in agricolae* in a farmer's *vestibulis* entrances

Fabula significat, etsi tempus ad gloriam promoveat aliquem, non suae tamen ipsius fortunae obliviscatur:

instabilis enim est vita haec.

SERPENS ET AGRICOLA

Serpens in agricolae vestibulis antrum habens,

451

antrum a cave habens having (i.e. having a cave at the entrances of a farmer), sustulit took away (i.e. killed) ejus his infantem baby puerulum boy.

Luctus autem but grief parentibus to the parents fuit was magnus great (i.e. the parents' grief was great).

At pater and the father, prae for moerore grief, securi with an axe accepta being taken up egressum (and) having come out serpentem the serpent (i.e. and, with the serpent having come out of his cave) occisurus erat he (the farmer) was about to kill (him).

Ut vero but when inclinavit he he bent se himself parumper a little festinans hurrying,

sustulit ejus infantem puerulum.

Luctus autem parentibus fuit magnus.

At pater, prae moerore securi accepta egressum serpentem occisurus erat.

Ut vero inclinavit se parumper festinans agricola, ut ipsum percuteret, erravit,

Agricola the farmer, ut so that ipsum him (the serpent) percuteret he could strike (i.e. the farmer, quickly bending so he could strike the snake), erravit missed, tantum only percusso being struck foraminis the hole's orificio opening.	tantum percusso foraminis orificio.
Digresso autem but having departed serpente the serpent (i.e. bu, the serpent having left), agricola the farmer ratus thought serpentem the serpent non amplius no more injuriae of the injury meminisse mindful (i.e. thinking the serpent had forgotten the attack), accepit took panem bread et salem and salt, apposuitque and placed (them) in foramine in the hole.	Digresso autem serpente, agricola ratus serpentem non amplius injuriae meminisse, accepit panem et salem, apposuitque in foramine.
Sed serpens but the serpent, tenui with a slight	Sed serpens, tenui sibilo, ait, Non erit nobis post

sibilo *hiss*, ait *said*, Non erit *there will not be* nobis *to us* post hac *after this* fides *trust*, vel amicitia *or friendship*, quamdiu *as long as* ego *I* lapidem *a stone* video *see*, tu vero *but (i.e. and) you* tumulum *a tomb* filii tui *of your son (i.e. there can be no friendship with us, because the reminder of past injury remains).*

Fabula significat the fable signifies, *nullum* no one *odii* of hatred, *aut vindicate* or revenge, *oblivisci* forgets *(i.e nobody forgets hatred or revenge), quamdiu* as long as *videt* he sees *monimentum* the monument, *quo* (of that) by which *trustatus est* he was grieved (i.e. hurt).

TUBICEN THE TRUMPETER

hac fides, vel amicitia, quamdiu ego lapidem video, tu vero tumulum filii tui.

Fabula significat, nullum odii, qut vindictae, oblivisci, quamdiu videt monimentum, quo trustatus est.

TUBICEN

454

Tubicen a trumpeter, exercitu with the army congregato brought together, ac and superatus being overcome ab hostibus by (their) enemies, clamabat cried out, Ne occidite me don't kill me, viri men, temere rashly et frustra and in vain:

non enim for not vestrum of you quemquam anyone occidi have I killed (i.e. for I haven't killed anyone of you); nam for, praeter besides aes brass hoc this (i.e. this brass, the trumpet), nihil nothing aliud else possideo do I possess.

Hi vero but they illi to him dixere said, Ob on account of hac this magis (all the) more morieris will you die, qui (you) who, quum when nequeas you're unable, ipse you

Tubicen, exercitu congregato, ac superatus ab hostibus, clamabat, Ne occidite me, viri, temere et frustra:

non enim vestrum quemquam occidi nam, praeter aes hoc, nihil aliud possideo.

Hi vero illi dixere, Ob hac magis morieris, qui, quum nequeas, ipse pugnare, omnes ad pugnam excitas.

455

yourself **pugnare** *to fight,* **omnes** *all (i.e. everyone else)* **ad pugnam** *to battle* **excites** *you rouse up.*

Fabula significat **the fable signifies***,* **eos** *those* **plus more** **peccare** *sin (i.e. those sin more),* **qui** *who* **malos** *bad* **ac graves** *and severe* **principes** *princes* **concitant** *they rouse up* **ad** *to* **male** *badly* **agendum** *agcting (i.e. those sin the most who rouse bad and harsh kings to do bad things).*

Fabula significat, eos plus peccare, qui malos ac graves principes concitant ad male agendum.

456

Decoding Latin – Day 40

Don't forget the rules:

1. Don't try to memorise anything
2. Focus on the story, not the language – don't try to analyse!
3. Read one section from the left column and then the same from the right.
4. *Always read for speed and general gist, not for accuracy and perfection.*

ARUNDO THE REED ET OLIVA AND THE OLIVE (TREE)	**ARUNDO ET OLIVA**
De tolerantia about (their) endurance, et viribus and (their) strengths, et quiete and (their) quietness, arundo a reed et oliva and an olive (tree) contendebant contended (i.e. argued).	De tolerantia, et viribus, et quiete, arundo et oliva contendebant.
Arundine vero but with the reed conviciis with criticisms affecta being affected ab olive by the olive (i.e. with the reed being criticised by the	Arundine vero conviciis affecta ab oliva, utpote imbecilia, ac facile cedente ventis omnibus, arundo tacens nihil locutus est.

457

olive), utpote as imbecilia weak (i.e. criticised as being weak), ac facile and easily cedente falling ventis to the winds omnibus all (i.e. bending to all the winds), arundo the reed tacens being silent, nihil nothing locutus est said (i.e. the reed said nothing).

Ac and parumper a little while praestolata having waited, ubi when acer a sharp afflavit blew ventus a wind (i.e. a sharp wind blew), arundo the reed succussa being shaken, et declinata and having bent down ventis to the winds, facile easily evasit escaped.

Ac parumper praestolata, ubi acer afflavit ventus, arundo succussa et declinata ventis, facile evasit.

Oliva autem but the olive (tree), quum when ventis to the winds restisset it had resisted, diffracta est was broken vi by (iits) force.

Oliva autem, quum ventis restisset, diffracta est vi.

458

Fabula significat the fable signifies *eos* those, *qui* who *tempori* to time, *ac prasetantioribus* or to (their) betters *non resistunt* don't resist, *meliores* better *esse* be (i.e. they're better) *iis* (than) those, *qui* who *cum potentioribus* with (those) more powerful *contendunt* contend.

LUPUS THE WOLF ET GRUS AND THE CRANE

Lupi of a wolf *gutturi* in the throat *os* a bone *infixam erat* was fastened (i.e. a bone was stuck in a wolf's throat).

Ille vero but he *Grui* to a crane *mercedem* a reward *se* himself *praebiturum* about to afford *dixit* said (i.e. he said he'd afford/give a reward to the crane), *si* if, *capite* with his head *injecto* being

Fabula significat eos, qui tempori, ac prasetantioribus non resistunt, meliores esse iis, qui cum potentioribus contendunt.

LUPUS ET GRUS

Lupi gutturi os infixam erat.

Ille vero Grui mercedem se praebiturum dixit, si, capite injecto, os ex gutture sibi extraxerit:

459

cast in(to the throat), os the bone ex gutture from the throat sibi for him extraxerit she (the crane) would extract (i.e. if she'd extract it from his throat, having put her head in):

Haec autem but she, eo with it extracto extracted, quippe quae for the reason which (i.e. because) procero with a tall/long esset she was collo neck (i.e. because she/the crane had a long neck), mercedem the reward efflagitabat she demanded:

qui who, subridendo in smiling, dentesque and (his) teeth exacuendo whetting, Sufficit it suffices tibi for you, ait he (the wolf) said, hoc this solum only, quod that ex lupi from a wolf's ore mouth, et dentibus and teeth, exemeris you've taken out

Haec autem, eo extracto, quippe quae procero esset collo, mercedem efflagitabat:

qui subridendo, dentesque exacuendo, Sufficit tibi, ait, hoc solum, quod ex lupi ore, et dentibus, exemeris caput salvum, nihil mali passum.

460

caput (your) head salvum safe(ly), nihil nothing mali of evil passum having suffered.

Fabula *a fable* in viros *against men*, qui *who*, a periculo *from danger* servati *being preserved*, bene *well* de se *of themselves* meritis *deserved* eam *that* referent *they return* gratiam *favour* (i.e. a fable against those who, having been saved from danger, return such favour to those deserving of themselves)[14].

SENEX THE OLD MAN ET MORS AND DEATH

Senex *an old man* olim *once*, sectis *having cut* lignis *logs*, et *and* ea *them* ferens *carrying*, multam *much* ibat *he went* viam *way* (i.e. he went a long

Fabula in viros, qui, a periculo servati, bene de se meritis eam referent gratiam.

SENEX ET MORS

Senex olim, sectis lignis, et ea ferens, multam ibat viam, ac ob multum laborem, deposito in loco

---

[14] This moral is oblique and obscure. The idea is that one should be careful to whom one gives help.

way), ac and and ob on account of multum much laborem effort, deposito having put down in loco in a place quodam a certain (i.e. in a certain pplace) onere (his) burden, Mortem Death invocabat he invoked (i.e. he called on Death).

Sed but, Morte with Death praesente being present, et rogante and asking causam the reason, propter quam on account of which se he vocaret he (the old man) had called, perterrefactus being terrified Senex the old man ait said, Ut so that meum my onus burden attollas you may lift up[15].

Fabula significat the fable signifies, omnem every hominem person esse be (i.e. is) vitae of life

quodam onere, Mortem invocabat.

Sed, Morte praesente, et rogante causam, propter quam se vocaret, perterrefactus Senex ait, Ut meum onus attollas.

Fabula significat, omnem hominem esse vitae

---

[15] I.e. Death's arrival scared the man into picking up his burden again and continuing on.

462

studiosum *zealous*, licet *although* infortunatus *unfortunate* sit *he might be*, et *and* mendicus *a beggar* (i.e. everyone is protective of his life, however unfortunate he might be, and even if he's a beggar).

RANAE THE FROGS

Ranae *frogs* duae *two* (i.e. two frogs), siccata *being dried up* palude *the marsh* ubi *where* habitabant *they lived* (i.e. with the marsh in which they lived being dried up), circumibant *they went about* quaerentes *weeking* ubi *(a place) where* manerent *they could remain*;

ac *and* profectae *having set out* ad profundum *to a deep* puteum *well*, et *and* acclinatae *having bent* deorsum *downwards* (i.e. looking over the edge of the well), conspicatae *and*

---

studiosum, licet infortunatus sit, et mendicus.

RANAE

Ranae duae, siccata palude ubi habitabant, circumibant quaerentes ubi manerent;

ac profectae ad profundum puteum, et acclinatae deorsum, conspicatae aquam, altera monebat, ut saltarent continuo deorsum:

463

having caught sight of aquam *water,* altera *the other (i.e. one)* monebat *advised (i.e. suggested),* ut *that* saltarent *they should jump* continuo *immediately* deorsum *down:*

altera vero *but the other* ait *said,* Si *if* et *also* hic *this* aruerit *has dried,* quomodo *how* poterimus *will we* ascendere *ascend (i.e. get back up)?*

Fabula significat the fable signifies, sine *without* consilio *a plan* ut *that* ne *not* quid *anything* agas *should you do (i.e. the fable signifies that you shouldn't do anything without a plan).*

AGNUS **THE LAMB** ET LUPUS **AND THE WOLF**

Agnus *a lamb* in alto *in a high* loco *place* stans

altera vero ait, Si et hic aruerit, quomodo poterimus ascendere?

Fabula significat, sine consilio ut ne quid agas.

AGNUS ET LUPUS

Agnus in alto loco stans lupum inferius

standing (i.e. standing in a high place) **lupum** a wolf **inferius** lower **praetereuntem** passing by **viam** the way **maledictis** with insults/curses **insectabatur** cut (i.e. a lamb, standing in a high place, and seeing a wolf passing by below, started shouting at him), **et feram** and a beast **malam** evil **appellabat** called (him, i.e. called him an evil beast), **et** and **crudivoram** raw-flesh-eating.

Sed lupus but the wolf, **conversus** having turned, **ait** said **illi** to him, **Non tu** not you **conviciaris** you reproach **mihi** me (i.e. *you* don't reproach me), **sed** but **turris** the tower, **in qua** in which **stas** you stand.

Fabula a fable **in eos** against those, **qui** who **ferunt** carry **injurias** injuries **ab indignis**

praetereuntem viam maledictis insectabatur, et feram malam appellabat, et crudivoram.

Sed lupus conversus ait illi, Non tu conviciaris mihi, sed turris, in qua stas.

Fabula in eos, qui ferunt injurias ab indignis

465

from unworthy hominibus *people*, metu *from fear* sublimiorum *of higher (people)*.

CULEX **THE GNAT** ET LEO **AND THE LION**

Culex *a gnat* ad leonem *to a lion* profectus *having gone (i.e. having gone to a lion)* ait *said*, Neque *neither* timeo *do I fear* te *you*, neque *nor* fortior *braver* me *than me* es *are you*.

Sin minus *but if not*, quid *what* tibi *to you* est *is there* robur *strength (i.e. what's more, what strength do you have)*?

quod *because* laceras *you tear apart* unguibus *with (your) claws*, et *and* mordes *you bite* dentibus *with your teeth*?

---

hominibus, metu sublimiorum.

CULEX ET LEO

Culex ad leonem profectus ait, Neque timeo te, neque fortior me es.

Sin minus, quid tibi est robur?

quod laceras unguibus, et mordes dentibus?

hoc this et also foemina a woman, cum with viro a man pugnans fighting, facit does (i.e. a woman also does this).

Ego vero but I longe by far sum am te (than) you fortiori braver.

Si vero but if vis you want, veniamus let us come ad pugnam to battle (i.e. let's fight).

Et quum and when tuba the trumpet cecinisset had sung (i.e. had sounded, to indicate the battle had begun), culex the gnat inhaesit cleaved (him), mordens biting circa around nares nostrils ipsius of him (i.e. his nostrils) nudas the naked genas cheeks (i.e. biting his bare cheeks around his nose).

hoc et foemina, cum viro pugnans, facit.

Ego vero longe sum te fortior.

Si vero vis, veniamus ad pugnam.

Et quum tuba cecinisset, culex inhaesit, mordens circa nares ipsius nudas genas.

Leo autem *but the lion* propriis *with his own* unguibus *claws* dilaniavit *tore apart* seipsum *himself*, donec *until* indignatus est *he was enraged*.	Leo autem propriis unguibus dilaniavit seipsum, donec indignatus est.
Culex autem *but the gnat*, victo *having defeated* leone *the lion*, quum *when* sonuisset *had sounded* tuba *the trumpet* (i.e. when the trumpet had sounded to indicate the end of battle), et *and* carmen *a poem* triumphale *triumphant* cecinisset *he'd sung* (i.e. and when he'd sung a triumphant poem/song), avolavit *flew away*.	Culex autem, victo leone, quum sonuisset tuba, et carmen triumphale cecinisset, avolavit.
Araneae vero *but of a spider* vinculo *in the chain* (i.e. web) implicitus *being entangled*, quum *when* devoraretur *he was devoured*, lamentabatur *he lamented*, quod *that*	Araneae vero vinculo implicitus, quum devoraretur, lamentabatur, quod cum maximis pugnans, a vili animali, aranea, occideretur.

cum maximis *while with the greatest* pugnans *fighting*, a vili *by a vile* animali *animal*, aranea *the spider*, occideretur *he was killed*.

Fabula a fable in eos *against those*, qui *who* prosternunt *overthrow* magnos *the great*, et *and* a pravis *by the corrupt* prosternuntur *are overthrown*.

Fabula in eos, qui prosternunt magnos, et a pravis prosternuntur.

Congratulations!

Congratulations!

You've made it through 47 days of reading (or more, depending on how you chose to go through the book), and read more Latin than most people read in a whole semester - and you've built a solid foundation to turn your language learning into a habit.

If you've stuck with it this far, and not tried to memorise, you'll have found you've made a lot of progress in the language, and are able to understand way more Latin than when you began, and improved your vocabulary enormously.

So enjoy yourself, and maybe give yourself a congratulatory gift - I'm a chocolate man, myself...

On my mailing list I share my favourite tips on learning Latin, resource recommendations, and more, all for free! I'll be publishing more books in this series in the future, so my list is the best place to stay up to date on those! Here's the link again to sign up and get the masterclass and a weekly Latin fable for free:

decodinglatin.org

I really hope you've enjoyed this book, and if you have – or if you have any questions or comments at all – please shoot me an email at alexander@decodinglatin.org. I'd love to hear from you.

Officially you're done. Congratulations again - you've graduated! They grow up so fast... *sniff*.

I hope this has helped you on your way to Latin fluency, and I'd love to hear how you went, so send me an email and let me know!

- Alexander Westenberg, PhD